the lowdown on the biggest manga group going down

written during lockdown

Ian Wolf

CLAMP down

the lowdown on the biggest manga group going down

written during lockdown

Ian Wolf

Published in paperback in 2022 by Sixth Element Publishing
on behalf of Ian Wolf

Sixth Element Publishing
Arthur Robinson House
13-14 The Green
Billingham TS23 1EU
www.6epublishing.net

ISBN 978-1-914170-31-7

British Library Cataloguing in Publication Data. A catalogue record for this book is available from the British Library.

Cover illustration by Robin Kaplan.
Cover text design by A.L. Kaplan.

Printed in Great Britain.

"Normal? What's normal? To only do what the masses do? And what is the benefit in that? Where is the problem in adopting a custom that is 'abnormal' if it has no negative effect on the world at large?"

Yuko Ichihara in xxxHOLiC, Vol. 4, p. 5, by CLAMP

CONTENTS

READING LIST

This book starts with a warning: there will be spoilers. CLAMP are famous for their works being interconnected and they have written sequels to several of their previous works. Thus I am often forced to give away the ending of one series in order for the next one to make sense.

But if you are already interested in reading their work, and want to do some advance reading before pursuing this book, I happily encourage it. In fact, getting more people to read CLAMP's work, and indeed manga in general, is part of the reason I wrote this and why I became a manga critic in the first place.

The following list displays the titles in the order in which they are covered in this book. While it is mostly in chronological order, this is not entirely so due to their sequels. For example, *Cardcaptor Sakura: Clear Card* debuted in 2016, but for ease I write about it in the *Cardcaptor Sakura* chapter, the original series running from 1996-2000, and there were many more CLAMP releases between the two manga.

There are also series, such as *Chobits* and again *Cardcaptor Sakura*, which are currently being reissued in English. Some CLAMP titles like *Magic Knight Rayearth* have been given English-language releases by three different publishers. In order to allow you the reader to be given the chance to read as many titles as possible in full, the main publisher listed for each book is the company that has most recently released the series in English. However, in cases where it is currently being re-released by a new firm, I will mention them too. I will also mention the total number of volumes and whether the release is currently in print, is available as an e-book, both or neither.

This list will also mention where possible the English-language translators, letterers and editors. In recent months and years, there has been an increased effort to show their contribution, including movements to try and give translators credit on the front covers of manga, alongside the original creators.

Please also note that as far as I know, there are no manga available in any of the British Isle's minority languages (i.e. Welsh, Gaelic, Cornish, Manx etc.), which might spark some interest in publishers in those languages.

•

RG Veda – Ten volumes. Japanese publisher: Shinshokan. English publisher: Dark Horse (released in three omnibuses). Translation – Haruko Furukawa and Christine Schilling. Lettering – IHL. Editor – Carl Gustav Horn. Print and e-book.

Man of Many Faces – Two volumes. Japanese publisher: Kadokawa Shoten. English publisher: Viz Media. Translation – Ikoi Hiroe. Lettering – Tomas Montalvo-Lagos. Editor – Jake Forbes. E-book.

Duklyon: CLAMP School Defenders – Two volumes. Japanese publisher: Kadokawa Shoten. English publisher: Viz Media. Translation – Ray Yoshimoto. Lettering – Brian Bossin. Editor – Jake Forbes. E-book.

CLAMP School Detectives – Three volumes. Japanese publisher: Kadokawa Shoten. English publisher: Viz Media. Translation – Ray Yoshimoto. Lettering – Rob Steen. Editor – Jake Forbes. E-book.

Tokyo Babylon – Seven volumes. Japanese publisher: Shinsokan, later by Kadokawa Shoten. English publisher – Dark Horse (released in two omnibuses). Translation – Ray Yoshimoto, Alexis Kirsch and Carol Fox. Lettering – IHL. Editor – Carl Gustav Horn. Print.

X – 18 volumes. Japanese publisher: Kadokawa Shoten. English publisher: Viz Media (released in six omnibuses). Translation – Lillian Olsen. Lettering – Annaliese Christman. Editor – Leyla Aker. Print and e-book.

Shirahime-Syo: Snow Goddess Tales – One volume. Japanese publisher: Kadokawa Shoten. English publisher: Viz Media. Translation – Ray Yoshimoto. Lettering – James Lee. Editor – Jake Forbes. E-book.

Legend of Chun Hyang – One volume. Japanese publisher: Hakusensha. English publisher: Viz Media. Translation – Ray Yoshimoto. Lettering – Jose Macasocol Jr. Editor – Jake Forbes. E-book.

Miyuki-chan in Wonderland – One volume. Japanese publisher: Kadokawa Shoten. English publisher: Viz Media. Translation – Ray Yoshimoto. Lettering – James Lee. Editor – Jake Forbes. E-book.

The One I Love – One volume. Japanese publisher: Kadokawa Shoten. English publisher: Viz Media. Translation – Ray Yoshimoto. Lettering – Abelardo Bigting. Editor – Nicole Monastirsky. E-book.

Magic Knight Rayearth – Six volumes across two series, three volumes per series. Japanese publisher: Kodansha. English publisher: Kodansha Comics (released in two collector's edition boxsets). Translation – Melissa Tanaka. Lettering – Abigail Blackman. Editor – Paul Starr. Print and e-book.

Wish – Four volumes. Japanese publisher: Kadokawa Shoten. English publisher: Dark Horse (as a single omnibus). Translation – Ray Yoshimoto and Jamie S. Rich. Lettering – Deron Bennett. Editor – Jemiah Jefferson. Print.

Cardcaptor Sakura – 12 volumes. Japanese publisher: Kodansha. English publisher: Dark Horse (complete, in four omnibuses) & Kodansha Comics (currently as a series of collector's editions). Translation – Mika Onishi and Anita Sengupta (Dark Horse & Kodansha). Lettering – IHL (Dark Horse) / Aaron Alexovich (Kodansha). Editor – Carl Gustav Horn (Dark Horse) / Paul Starr (Kodansha). Print and e-book.

Cardcaptor Sakura: Clear Card – 12 volumes and counting. Japanese publisher: Kodansha. English publisher: Kodansha Comics. Translation – Devon Corwin. Lettering – Erika Terriquez. Editor – Not credited. Print and e-book.

Clover – Four volumes. Japanese publisher: Kodansha. English publisher: Kodansha Comics (in a single collector's edition). Translation – Ray Yoshimoto. Lettering – Scott O. Brown. Editor – Vanessa Tenazas. Print and e-book.

Angelic Layer – Five volumes. Japanese publisher: Kadokawa Shoten. English publisher: Dark Horse (as two omnibus editions). Translation – Anita Sengupta. Lettering – John Clark. Editor – Carl Gustav Horn. Print.

Suki: A Like Story – Three volumes. Japanese publisher: Kadokawa Shoten. English publisher: Viz Media. Translation – Ray Yoshimoto. Lettering – Fae Kuen. Editor – Jake Forbes. E-book.

Legal Drug – Three volumes. Japanese publisher: Kadokawa Shoten. English publisher: Dark Horse (as a single omnibus). Translation – Ray Yoshimoto, Jamie S. Rich, Lillian Diaz-Przybyl, Jake Forbes and Luis Reyes. Lettering – John Clark. Editor – Carl Gustav Horn. Print and e-book.

Drug & Drop – two volumes. Japanese publisher: Kadokawa Shoten. English publisher: Dark Horse. Translation – William Flanagan. Lettering – John Clark. Editor – Carl Gustav Horn. Print and e-book.

Chobits – Eight volumes. Japanese publisher: Kodansha. English publisher: Dark Horse (complete, in two omnibuses) & Kodansha Comics (currently as a series of collector's editions). Translation – Shirley Kubo. Lettering – John Clark (Dark Horse) / Michael Martin (Kodansha). Editor – Carl Gustav Horn (Dark Horse) / Tiff Ferentini (Kodansha). Print and e-book.

Murikuri – One short volume. Japanese publisher: Kodansha. Not available in English.

xxxHOLiC – 19 volumes. Japanese publisher: Kodansha. English publisher: Kodansha Comics (released as seven omnibuses). Translator – William Flanagan. Lettering – Dana Hayward. Editor uncredited. Print and e-book.

xxxHOLiC: Rei – Four volumes. Japanese publisher: Kodansha. English publisher: Kodansha Comics. Translator – Stephen Paul. Lettering – Paige Pumphrey. Editor uncredited. Print and e-book.

Tsubasa: RESERVoir CHRoNiCLE – 28 volumes. Japanese publisher: Kodansha. English publisher: Kodansha Comics (released as ten omnibuses). Translator – Anthony Gerard (up to Vol. 22) and William Flanagan. Lettering – Dana Hayward. Editor uncredited. Print and e-book.

Tsubasa: WoRLD CHRoNiCLE – Three volumes. Japanese publisher: Kodansha. English publisher: Kodansha Comics. Translator – Stephen Paul. Lettering – James Dashiell. Editor uncredited. Print and e-book.

Kobato – Six volumes. Japanese publisher: Shogakukan and Kadokawa Shoten. English publisher: Yen Press. Translator – William Flanagan. Lettering – Alexis Eckerman. Editor uncredited. Print and e-book.

Gate 7 – Four volumes. Japanese publisher: Shueisha. English publisher: Dark Horse. Translator – William Flanagan. Lettering – Steve Dutro. Editor – Philip Simon. Out of print.

PREFACE

In Britain, there appears to be two kinds of people: people who like Japanese animation (anime) and comics (manga), and people who think that any adult who likes cartoons is secretly a paedophile.

This lamentable view is partly due to the video nasty scares of the 1980s and 1990s, with Japanese animation's biggest 'contribution' to this being *Urotsukidoji: Legend of the Overfiend*, originally a manga comic that was later adapted into a series of straight-to-video anime or 'Original Video Animations' (OVA). The series is most noted for including 'tentacle porn/rape'. Not surprisingly, when it was released in the UK it attracted derision from the press. The impact of this is best described in a speech given by the anime critic and co-author of *The Anime Encyclopedia,* Jonathan Clements, a speech later transcribed in the book that inspired me to take up anime criticism, *Schoolgirl Milky Crisis: Adventures in the Anime and Manga Trade*:[1]

"The thing is that at the height of the video nasty scare, in 1997 – when the Daily Mail *and the* Daily Telegraph *and* The Guardian *were going on and on about how these awful animated erotica were taking over the minds of our children – at the height of all that, the average British anime convention was attracting 500 attendees. Meanwhile,* Urotsukidoji: Legend of the Overfiend, *which was the most notorious of the anime 'nasties', sold 40,000 copies in Britain in that year alone. So anime 'fans' weren't buying it, it was selling to somebody else, in quantities far larger than the average sales for 'normal' anime. Believe me, the people who sell anime in this country would love it if every tale of magical girlfriends and silly princesses and talking animals sold as well as* Urotsukidoji.*"*

It has to be said however that it does feel that the British criticising another country for having pornographic cartoons feels hypocritical, when you consider the fact that perhaps the most influential British TV show of all time, *Monty Python's Flying Circus*, contained so many cartoon drawings of nude women.[2]

In Britain, anime's reputation has been improving since the video nasty days. While little is shown on TV and many series released on DVD only make it to the USA, streaming means we can now watch most of the latest shows. As well as anime and manga conventions expanding, increasing sales, more books translated and available to download, and more chances to watch anime as they are broadcast in Japan, 2019 witnessed perhaps the biggest acceptance yet of manga as a proper art form, when the British Museum held a special exhibition devoted to the subject. Before writing this book, I would have said the chances of the BBC showing any anime was almost zero, but then in August 2021, it got the rights to show *Pokemon*, streaming it on iPlayer and broadcasting it on children's channel CBBC. Of course, not everyone at the BBC is up on the anime knowledge. In the same week they started showing *Pokemon*, which was during the delayed Tokyo 2020 Summer Olympics, the BBC Sport Twitter feed posted a picture from the speed climbing which showed a type of 'Gundam'. *Gundam* is one of the longest-running sci-fi anime, beginning in 1979 and part of the 'mecha' genre which features robotic tanks. This is something no one at BBC Sport knew because they said it was a Transformer. You know when nerds get annoyed when people confuse *Star Trek* and *Star Wars*? This is the anime equivalent.[3]

This is not to say that there are still issues concerning the more extreme pornographic elements of the medium. In Japan, anime and manga pornographic works featuring underage children are legal, known as 'shotacon' when it features boys and 'lolicon' when it features girls.[4] This has been the subject of long debate in Japan, with those against it saying it promotes child abuse, and those for it saying that getting rid of it is censorship, which Article 21 of the country's constitution forbids, although Article 175 of the Criminal Code of Japan prohibits obscene material. Not surprisingly, this has been the subject of documentaries in the UK, including some on the BBC. This is totally understandable, although personally speaking I do think that if the BBC is presenting a documentary about the dangers of paedophilia, it ought to introduce it with the words: "From the broadcaster that gave you Jimmy Savile, Rolf Harris, Stuart Hall and Dave Lee Travis..." The other side of the debate is suspect as well of course. People say that no conclusive evidence has been shown as to what effect this kind of adult material has, but that also tends to be the argument used by tobacco companies when they say that there is no conclusive evidence to suggest that smoking causes cancer, when everything points to the fact that it does.

However, it is still wrong for people to think that 'all anime is porn' and 'cartoons are only for kids'. Saying that all Japanese animation is porn is like saying that all British comedy is like *Confessions of a Window Cleaner*. It is not just the British who have issues regarding attitudes to manga. In Australia, there is a blanket ban on all pornographic manga (ecchi/hentai) imports because of worries over paedophilia. The BBC may have had paedophiles presenting some episodes of their music shows, but they never went as far as to never repeat *Top of the Pops* ever again. Sorry Aussies, but it's a bit overkill. While the USA has more of an understanding attitude, oddities crop up. In 2020, the academic book *Anime from Akira to Howl's Moving Castle: Experiencing Contemporary Japanese Animation* by Susan Napier (2005, originally published in 2001 as *Anime from Akira to Princess Mononoke*) entered the news when Ohio lawmakers tried to get the book removed from the shelves of Kent State

University, even threatening to withdraw the college's funds, over claims of adult content.[5]

Of course, plain and simple ignorance of the subject by journalists is also a problem. This is perhaps best demonstrated by a review in *The Guardian* of the 2020 film *Demon Slayer: Mugen Train*, the first picture to top the worldwide box office for a particular year outside Hollywood. The reviewer, Leslie Felperin, begins the article with: "If, like me, you have not watched the hit 2019 Japanese TV series *Demon Slayer: Kimetsu no Yaiba*, let alone read the manga series it was based on…", then you might as well not bother finish reading that sentence, let alone read the entire review and why Felperin gave it three out of five stars.

One of the great joys of anime and manga is the sheer diversity of the art form, covering every genre. Yes, there is adult material and it is wrong to ignore it entirely as this book will demonstrate, as just about every subject that you can think of has been covered by manga.

This is why my favourite manga artists are a group which has this range. CLAMP, a group of women that united in the 1980s and are still working today, have produced a series of dazzlingly beautiful works covering so many genres. This includes fantasy, science fiction, crime, horror, historical, comedy, children's stories, gay fiction and erotica. In this book, I will be taking a sometimes subjective look at all of the manga CLAMP have so far both written and drawn – that is over 20 series created over a period of more than 30 years.

This subjectivity mainly comes down to some of the influences behind the book: not just CLAMP themselves and other anime critics, but also due to my work in the world of British comedy. One of my favourite styles of comedy is where you learn things. Examples include the TV panel show *QI* and its spin-offs *The*

Museum of Curiosity and *No Such Thing as a Fish*, Andrew O'Neill's *A History of Heavy Metal*, Bill Bailey's *Remarkable Guide to the Orchestra*, the Radio 4 comedies of Paul Sinha, Helen Keen, Mark Steel and Natalie Haynes, the comic PowerPoint presentations of Dave Gorman and podcasts like Angela Barnes and John O'Farrell's *We Are History* and Greg Jenner's *You're Dead to Me*. There are also funny educational manga too, such as the biological *Cells at Work!*[6], the not-as-rude-as-you-think-it-is *Sex Ed 120%* and possibly the most politically correct politically incorrect manga around *Hetalia: Axis Powers* – a comedy about World War II, made by a country that lost World War II, in which all the characters are the stereotypical personifications of the nations of the world. The subjectivity is also due to some personal aspects, with a full acknowledgement that there are better critics out there. Put it this way: I don't speak Japanese, or indeed any languages other than English. People who speak Japanese will be able to provide you with more information than I can.

There are various reasons for writing this book. One is that CLAMP are one of the most popular creators of manga around. To quote Cristal Marie from the YouTube series Beyond The Bot in her February 2021 video *A History of CLAMP (and The Future of Netflix)*: "CLAMP is one of the few creative groups that somehow appeal to both male and female readerships, crossing both gender and genre lines with many, many series. They've somehow hit on a narrative formula where whatever they create, regardless of the medium, will be consumed by anyone, so they don't favour one audience over the other." Despite this, not much has been written about them in English outside of more academic works or dedicated fan projects. There have been some past attempts. In 2008, the publisher Del Rey Manga announced at Comic-Con a book called *CLAMP in America* by Shaenon K. Garrity, which would include 300 pieces of art and document their worldwide success, but Del Rey were taken over by Kodansha and in 2011 the project was sadly cancelled due to copyright issues.

This book is for people who perhaps are only just learning about manga or are completely new to it. Having said that, I am aware that a man explaining about what a group of women have done might come across as mansplaining, and if so, I apologise in advance of any issues that might arise. If you are interested in a more in-depth look at CLAMP, I would recommend the American podcast *CLAMPcast in Wonderland* presented by Lucy Softich and Robin Kaplan, who have certain advantages over me when it comes to explaining CLAMP's work, given that a) the hosts are both women and I do worry that I will be guilty of mansplaining,[7] and b) they have a much better grasp of the Japanese language than I do. The only problem with the podcast is that they only do two episodes per month, and as it only began in 2019 they have only covered the early works so far. It has taken them all of 2020 to discuss just one series, *X*, but at least they go into the true detail of what is my favourite CLAMP title.

Another reason for writing this was a moment of inspiration on the radio. I remember listening to an episode of *The Museum of Curiosity* in which one guest, future *QI* host Sandi Toksvig, donated the alphabet, commenting that while literacy gave the world much that is great, it also harmed women because before the written word, societies were mainly women-dominated with goddess cultures, but with literacy, society became more male-dominated and sexist. For me, graphic novels and manga are a great unifier, combining the written word with the visual. The women who make up CLAMP are not only great storytellers, but the thing that often makes them stand out from the crowd in the manga world is the quality of the artwork. It should be pointed out that women in manga are not the minority. According to a poll of 723 manga creators by the ManNavi Manga Award, 77% of them were women.

CLAMP's art is a joy to see. You can just look at their pictures without the words and still be captivated by it. Their character illustrations and outfit designs especially are glorious, which has seen them doing several side projects as character designers for other people's series. Whether it is children in their school uniforms, warriors fighting in battle, witches and priests practising rituals, or just someone in a strange, avant-garde get-up, their characters are a major draw for much of their fan base. This is helped by the fact that CLAMP's works constantly cross reference each other, with characters from one series appearing in another, creating a complete fictional world or 'CLAMPverse' as it shall be referred to in this book.

There is also a third reason for this book being written: the UK's multiple COVID-19 lockdowns. People said when it started that this would be an ideal time to write a book, when you are stuck in the house with nothing else to do. The difference is that I actually have written a book. This is what I did with my time during lockdown.[8] However, it should be pointed out that I was already working from home before lockdown, namely for Anime UK News, the British Comedy Guide, and I had just finished some TV jobs too. I worked for Remarkable as a question writer for the quiz shows *Richard Osman's House of Games* and *The Wall*, and before that I briefly worked as a *Countdown* conundrum setter. These TV jobs involved making conference calls on Zoom over a month before most of the population had heard of the conference calling software programme.

The point of this book, and indeed all of my anime criticism, is a simple one: if I can get at least one person to start reading some of these works and enjoy this art form, it will be worth it. I hope I can make a difference in some way, in expanding people's taste in entertainment, beyond the more established media like Hollywood films.[9]

If you already know the basic history of manga, feel free to go straight into the first chapter and read about CLAMP's earliest works. If however, you are new to the whole thing, the introduction will give you the basic info you need to know about anime and manga in general. Hope you enjoy my book, and I hope that it will inspire you to read the manga of CLAMP.

Ian Wolf
Stockton-on-Tees

---

1 – The odd title of the book is reference to a bit of code created by Clements. Whenever he has talked to someone in one of his articles, but doesn't want to give away the name of person or the series that person is working on, he says they are working on a made-up show called *Schoolgirl Milky Crisis*. The title references genuine anime with odd titles in English, mainly the cyberpunk series *Bubblegum Crisis*. By the way, the speech in question was called 'Five Girls Named Moe: The Anime Erotic', a talk about animated porn Clements gave at Swansea Metropolitan University on 1st December 2007. 'Moe' here is pronounced 'mo-A', and a term meaning an attraction towards someone, especially a cute character. Another anime term is 'moe anthropomorphism', which is to cutely anthropomorphise something. *Cells at Work!* is such an example, anthropomorphising the cells of the human body.

2 – For a sign of the influence of *Monty Python* in Japan, look up the alternative history anime *Girls und Panzer*, set in a world where after World War II, all the tanks were kept and were re-used for the all-women sport of 'tankery'. The series follows a

school tankery team. In one scene the girls are camping and talk about army rations. This leads to a discussion about Spam and thus the girls end up quoting and singing from the Spam sketch. However, due to strict Japanese product placement laws, every time the word 'Spam' is mentioned, it gets bleeped over, thus resulting in a chorus of girls dressed as Vikings singing: "S***, S***, S***, S***, S***, S***, S***, S***", while another girl screams at them to: "Shut up! Shut up!"

3 – It should be stated that the BBC was not the only broadcaster to make this error. Spain's Teledeporte sports channel did the same thing during the triathlon.

4 – Please note, it's pronounced 'LOW-lee-con' not 'LOL-lee-con', as it is a portmanteau of the English words 'Lolita complex'. Confusingly, 'Lolita' is also the name of a popular form of Japanese street fashion, based on Victorian costumes and themes, so be careful when searching for this sort of thing online.

5 – Regarding my book, firstly as is made clear by material so far written in this preface, we do cover adult works; secondly, it includes swearing including both the f-word and the c-word, so if this does offend you then feel free to stop reading now; thirdly, this book is comedic rather than academic and thus not one to use if you are researching a degree.

6 – Serious, you've never seen more adorable platelets.

7 – Not to be confused with *Mangasplaining*, a podcast designed to introduce manga to those new to it, and which I would also recommend to those new to the medium.

8 – Not helped by the fact that the last series I needed to read before writing this book, *Gate 7*, was not available digitally to read, and with the books out-of-print in English I had to search eBay for them. Due to delays in the post, the books took a month to arrive.

9 – By the way, here's a general rule-of-thumb for anyone starting to look into anime and manga… avoid any Hollywood adaptations. Hardcore anime fans, AKA 'otaku' (although in Japan the word refers to an obsessive fan of anything, not just anime and manga), generally hate these, due to a mixture of whitewashed casting and lack of faithfulness to the original works. We still haven't forgiven Hollywood for the 2009 film *Dragon Ball Evolution.*

INTRODUCTION

A (Very) Brief History of Anime and Manga

There are several points which could be discussed regarding the question of when anime and manga started. Did it start with the first comics? The first amusing drawings? The first ever written stories?

I go with the last of these, and thus argue the whole thing began with the first ever novel, which appropriately for a book covering the work of Japanese women, began with a Japanese woman. Murasaki Shikibu, a lady-in-waiting in Japan's imperial court in the early 11th century, wrote what many consider to be the first novel in the world, *The Tale of Genji*.[1] The story follows the title character, the son of an ancient emperor, who is removed from the line of succession for political reasons.

The novel is noted for the way it portrays the Imperial court at the time. It is also, from personal experience, incredibly difficult to read. There are some spoilers coming up so feel free to skip to the next paragraph if you wish to avoid them, but the Penguin Classics edition is over 1,200 pages long. Not only that, Genji is the only named character in the entire book with everyone else referred to by their title, and the entire book ends mid-sentence. It is so difficult to read that when I tried to do so many years ago, my mind became such a confused mush that I totally failed to spot that I had read an entire gay sex scene. I must confess that I gave up. If that makes you believe I'm not qualified to review anything, including manga comics, I wouldn't blame you for putting this book down now.

In terms of amusing drawings, things get more troublesome when trying to pin-point a date. Referring to *A Brief History of Manga* by Helen McCarthy – the other author of *The Anime Encyclopedia* with Jonathan Clements – some argue that the first manga were caricatures from the Horyu-ji temple in Nara from c. 700 CE. Others argue in favour of the art of Buddhist priest Toba Sojo from the 12th century. One scholar, Adam L. Kern from the University of Wisconsin-Madison, claims that the first person to use the term 'manga' as we would use it today comes from the writer and artist Santo Kyoden in 1798.

By the early 19th century, Japan's most famous artist appears on the manga scene. Several manga drawings were created by Katsushika Hokusai, but these were mainly funny drawings rather than something with a proper story. Before moving on however, one important thing about reading manga is best illustrated by looking at Hokusai's most famous work, *The Great Wave off Kanagawa* (1831). One thing that you will notice when buying most manga is that the vast majority of them will be published 'backwards' to us English readers. That is because Japanese reads right-to-left. To be exact, it reads up-to-down, then right-to-left, hence the speech bubbles are often more column-like in shape. This can be intimidating to those who are new to manga, and indeed all of CLAMP's manga that have been published in English read right-to-left. The fact that almost all manga are published in black-and-white also puts off readers more used to colourful Western comics. However, other titles have been published for English readers in a 'flipped' style, with images mirrored the other way around which new readers might prefer. If you want to get an idea of what is like to read right-to-left, you can use *The Great Wave* as a quick guide. This woodblock print features a giant wave on the left, three fishing boats on the right, and Mount Fuji in the distance. To us English-readers, reading it to left-to-right makes us think: "Oh no, there's a huge wave! Hang on, are those boats down there?" To Japanese-readers, going right-to-left the story becomes more dramatic as the tension builds up, as you go: "Oh, look at those fishermen working in the boats. Oh hang on, there's a huge wave coming! They're in danger! Get out of the way!" Another of Hokusai's works, *The Dream of the Fisherman's Wife* (1814), features a woman entwined with octopuses, arguably an early example of tentacle porn, although others had done similar pieces before him.

As mentioned in the preface, many British people have a hostile attitude to manga and anime. It may come as a shock to these people that arguably modern manga as we know it today actually has British origins. In 1861, a few years after Japan finally re-opened its borders to the world after a period of over 200 years in self-isolation, a new magazine was launched in Yokohama. *Japan Punch*, published by journalist Charles Wirgman, was modelled after the British *Punch* magazine, and like the original it featured satirical cartoons. This was followed in 1874 by the first cartoon magazine published by the Japanese themselves, *Eshibun Nipponchi*, by Robun Kanagaki and Kyosuke Kawanabe. More magazines, some for children, were published during this period. Then in 1902, artist and political cartoonist Rakuten Kitazawa, the 'father of manga', published *Tagosaku & Mokube's Tokyo Trip*, the story of two people from the country visiting the capital. Kitazawa was the first person to use the term manga as we know it today.

1907 marks the start of what is considered to be the first ever Japanese animation. The short known today as *Katsudo Shashin* is the oldest known anime to survive and can be seen in its entirety on Wikipedia. The film features a boy in a sailor suit who writes on the wall behind him the phrase 'Katsudo Shashin', meaning 'Moving picture'. He then turns to face the camera, takes his hat off and bows: the end. It is just three seconds long, but this short marks the earliest known origins of an entire industry. Despite its importance, it was lost for a long time, not being discovered until it was found in a film and projector collection in Kyoto in 2005.

We would have to wait nearly 40 years to get the first full-length anime feature film. At 74 minutes long, *Momotaro, Sacred Sailors* is a sequel to an earlier short two years earlier named *Momotaro's Sea Eagles*, and is based on a classic children's story. In the original, Momotaro is a boy born in a giant peach. He then goes on a journey to fight a band of demons/ogres called 'oni', during which he becomes friends with a dog, a monkey and a pheasant. Momotaro succeeds in his task, taking home the oni's treasure and capturing their chief. In *Sea Eagles*, Momotaro and the animals are depicted as sailors attacking a harbour controlled by the demons. In *Sacred Sailors*, the animals are trained to be parachutists as they invade 'Devil's Island'.

As you may have gathered by the fact it was made nearly 40 years after 1907, and the more naval tone the stories take from the original tale, these anime were made during World War II. *Sea Eagles* was released in 1943 and *Sacred Sailors* in 1945. Sadly, the first ever anime feature film was wartime propaganda aimed at children, commissioned by the Japanese Naval Ministry. The harbour in *Sea Eagles* is Pearl Harbour, while *Sacred Sailors* appears to be based on the Japanese invasion of Singapore. The oni in *Sacred Sailors* are demonic versions of Popeye and Bluto (the oni Bluto also appears in *Sea Eagles*). When the commanders of Devil's Island surrender in *Sacred Sailors*, they all have clear-cut posh English accents. Whether or not actual British POWs were used to voice the commanders remains a mystery. You can buy *Sacred Sailors* in the UK if you are interested in the origins of anime, but it is hard to watch.[2]

However, it cannot be denied that these films did have an influence on the post-war generation of animators and comic book artists. In 1946, the comedy manga *Sazae-san* debuted. Created by one of the first women manga artists, Machiko

Hasegawa, it focuses on the title character, a liberated feminist young woman whose mother is worried that she will never find a husband. *Sazae-san* was later adapted into an anime in 1969, and the series is still running today. It is in the Guinness Book of Records as the world's longest-running animated TV series.

But also in 1946, New Year's Day to be exact, someone even more influential made his debut. While Rakuten Kitazawa might be considered the 'father of manga', it is the man often dubbed 'the god of comics' in Japan, and the 'godfather of manga' in the US, who is much more well-known, respected and loved. The work was called *Ma-chan's Diary*, and it was written by a man named Osamu Tezuka.[3]

Born in 1928, it is hard to underestimate the impact Tezuka would have on the entire manga industry. Fortunately, there are plenty of English language works that you can read which examine his life and career in great detail. Often referred to as the Japanese Walt Disney, Tezuka, like the later CLAMP, was famous for his versatility. His most famous works were his children's stories, the most famous of all being *Astro Boy* (1952-1968) a sci-fi story about a robot who uses his seven powers to right the world's wrongs. These powers include strength equal to 100,000 horsepower, flight, the ability to tell if someone is good or evil, and retractable machine guns – in his arse. Some people say they are in his hips, but looking at them I would definitely argue that it is the bottom. *Astro Boy* was the first manga series to be adapted for television, airing in both Japan and the US in 1963.

Another of his children's stories was published in Japan with a title that translates as *Jungle Emperor Leo* (1950-54). The story begins with a white lion, the leader of the animals in the local jungle, who is killed by a human hunter and whose pregnant mate is captured. She is put on a ship where she is to be transported to a zoo. During the trip, she gives birth to the cub Leo, but a storm breaks her cage and wrecks the ship. She drowns, but the fish in the sea teach Leo to swim. Stars in the night's sky depicting his mother and swarms of butterflies lead Leo back to the jungle, where he needs to learn to become a responsible king, as well as seeking peace between animals and humankind. At the same time, Leo must do battle with some evil humans, as well as Bubu, a rival one-eyed lion with a scar across his face who wants to dethrone Leo, and who is assisted by a pair of comic hyenas.

If this seems rather familiar, you are not alone. If not, things should become more clear when I tell you that when the series debuted in the USA it was given a new title: *Kimba the White Lion*. Many have commented on the similarities, and some have argued down-right plagiarism, when you compare Leo, now named Kimba, to Simba and *The Lion King*. It's hard to imagine Disney thinking about creating a story about a lion cub whose father is killed, in a power rivalry with an older scarred lion who is helped by a funny band of hyenas, completely separately. Quick online searches will show stills of both that look incredibly similar. Even *The Simpsons* made reference to it. In the episode 'Round Springfield', which features the death of Bleeding Gums Murphy, the episode ends with Lisa Simpson seeing a vision of Bleeding Gums in the clouds, who gets interrupted by other cloud-like depictions of other characters, real and fictional. The first of these is *The Lion King*'s Mufasa saying: "You must avenge my death Kimba – I mean Simba." In the index of Clement's *Schoolgirl Milky Crisis*, if you turn to the entry for 'Kimba' it says: 'See Simba'. Under 'Simba' it says: 'See Kimba'. You may be wondering why no one has take legal action over this. Well, do you want to try and sue Disney?

Aside from these children's stories, Tezuka created many adult titles as well. These include the biography *Buddha* and the suspense series *Black Jack*, which featured Tezuka's medical knowledge, having studied medicine at university. Tezuka died in 1989, the same year in which CLAMP would release their debut manga, at the untimely age of 60 from stomach cancer. He was still creating manga until his dying days, working on a biography of Ludwig van Beethoven called *Ludwig B*, and still working on the title considered his magnum opus, *Phoenix*, a series about the search for immortality which he began in 1954 and was still writing over 30 years later.

Tezuka was not the only big name at the time. Another key figure was Shotaro Ishinomori, 'The King of Manga', who worked as an assistant to Tezuka. His most famous contribution to manga was *Cyborg 009*, what we might consider to be manga's first example of a superhero team, although as the title clearly infers they are, strictly speaking, cyborgs with various different powers. Ishinomori holds the Guinness World Record for 'most comics published by one author', with 770 titles. He is also one of the central figures in 'tokusatsu', live-action shows that rely on the heavy use of special effects. Ishinomori's other works also include the motorbike-riding superhero *Kamen Rider*; and *Super Sentai*, the series which served as the source material for the US series *Power Rangers*.

During the 1950s and 60s more manga magazines started to get published. Some weekly, some fortnightly, some monthly. Of all of these magazines, the most famous and best-selling began in 1968 and is still going today. *Weekly Shōnen Jump*, or *Jump* for short, is a magazine aimed at a young male audience, but their series often have a broad appeal. Among the titles that it has produced include *KochiKame*, a comedy about the police which spanned a then record-breaking 200 collected volumes (tankobon);[4] *Dragon Ball*, a martial arts comedy adventure that began in the 1980s and whose spin-offs have made it one of the most popular and influential of all manga series globally;

One Piece, an adventure series about pirates entirely created by Eiichiro Oda, that at the time of writing has over 1,000 chapters, sold half-a-billion copies, and holds the Guinness World Record for 'most copies published for the same comic book series by a single author'; *My Hero Academia*, arguably manga's biggest recent contribution to superheroes, it being set in a world where 80% of the world's population have some kind of superpower;[5] and its most recent hit *Demon Slayer: Kimetsu no Yaiba*, a period supernatural drama about a boy who kills demonic beings but is also protecting his sister, who has been transformed into a demon. The 2020 anime film version, *Mugen Train*, smashed box office records. The manga of *Demon Slayer* was the best-selling manga of 2020, selling over 82 million copies as of November, outselling the entire top 10 best-selling manga of 2019 combined, which totalled just under 65 million copies.

In terms of problems, *Jump* do have a history of continuing to employ people even after major scandals. For example, Mitsutoshi Shimabukuro, creator of the manga *Seikimatsu Leader den Takeshi!*, had its run stopped in 2002 after Shimabukuro was arrested for violating child prostitution laws, including paying a 16-year-old girl to have sex with him. He was given a two year suspended prison sentence, but would later return to *Jump*, with his later series *Toriko* being released in English. In November 2020, another new series by him, *Build King*, started in *Shonen Jump*, and was released digitally in English. Oda happily defends Shimabukuro.

Another troublesome *Jump* author is Nobuhiro Watsuki, creator of the period martial arts series *Rurouni Kenshin*, also known in some English-language versions as *Samurai X*. In 2017, Watsuki was raided by the police, who found that he possessed DVDs of naked girls in their early teens – and I don't mean anime drawings; I mean images of real-life girls. He was charged with possessing child pornography and was found guilty. He was thus treated as severely as you can imagine any paedophile would be. He was… fined. To be exact, he was fined ¥200,000.[6] Despite this, Watsuki is still writing *Rurouni Kenshin* for *Jump* and his work is still being translated into English. For a more detailed overview on this subject, I would recommend the article 'Shonen Jump and the Cycle of Letting it Slide' from the website *Anime Feminist*.

More recently was the case of Tatsuya Matsuki, the writer of the *Shonen Jump* manga *Act-Age*, which is about an aspiring actress. In August 2020, Matsuki was arrested for inappropriately touching two schoolgirls in June 2020. When the news broke, it seemed things would be different: *Jump* immediately cancelled the manga and stopped putting it on sale. Matsuki was found guilty and was given a prison sentence. Unfortunately, the sentence was just three years, and even then it was suspended for 18 months. You just dread that after the sentence is over, *Jump* will invite him back.[7] Even then, people on other publications have also been in similar scandals. In March 2022, Kenya Suzuki, creator of comedy manga *Please Tell Me! Galko-chan*, published by *ComicWalker*, was found guilty of importing child porn from Germany. He was sentenced to 14 months in jail, suspended for three years.

While magazines like *Jump* were aimed at the boys, there were also plenty of women who were getting creative too. In the 1970s, the most famous of these women artists were known collectively as the 'Year 24 Group', so called because most were born the 24th year of Japan's Showa period, 1949.[8] Often writing on the themes of gender, sexuality and coming-of-age, the most famous of these artists was Moto Hagio. Her most famous works include *The Poe Clan* which follows a family of vampires, and *The Heart of Thomas*, a tale of death and adolescent gay love in a German all-boys school. Another artist often considered part of the Year 24

Group is Riyoko Ikeda, most famous for her historical romance *The Rose of Versailles*. Set in 18th century France, this manga follows a girl who is raised a boy and is thus named Oscar François de Jayjayes. She is employed as a guard to the palace and her story is intertwined with that of Marie Antoinette and the French Revolution. The manga is partly remembered for containing the art form's first 'bed scene' to be written by a woman. In 1979, the series was adapted into an English-language, French-Japanese live action film called *Lady Oscar*, in which a young Oscar was portrayed on screen by Patsy Kensit.

Outside of the Year 24 Group arguably the most famous woman, to us in the West anyway, to have arrived on the manga scene in the 1970s was Rumiko Takahashi. She is mainly famous for her romantic titles, her first being the sci-fi romcom *Urusei Yatsura* (literally 'obnoxious people'). Later she created *Ranma ½*, a martial arts romcom whose main character is a boy who changes gender when splashed with water. Her more recent titles became increasingly dramatic, like the time travel fantasy *Inuyasha*.

The 1970s witnessed the birth of a genre of manga known as 'mecha'. Mecha is a branch of science fiction featuring bipedal tank machines, the most famous Western example being the film *Pacific Rim*. It is something we will later touch upon in the book when we cover CLAMP's series *Magic Knight Rayearth*, but probably the first mecha proper would be *Mazinger Z* – the 'Z' being pronounced 'zetto' in Japanese so it would appear Japan prefers the British pronunciation over the American. I have come across arguments that the genre really starts with Mitsuteru Yokoyama's 1956 manga *Tetsunjin 28-go*, but this machine was controlled via a remote control rather than a pilot inside and thus I would argue is not a true mecha, but it helped to inspire it.

Mazinger Z's creator Go Nagai was involved in other genres such as horror (*Devilman*) and erotica (*Harenchi Gakuen*), but one of his strangest lasting legacies is one of manga's key recurring tropes: characters shouting out the name of their attacks. The reason for this is that because most manga are drawn in black-and-white, you need the characters to make clear who is doing what attack. Another figure to highlight in the world of sci-fi manga is Leiji Matsumoto, famous for his space operas such as *Space Pirate Captain Harlock* and *Space Battleship Yamato*.

At the end of the decade came one of anime's biggest franchises. If the British have *Doctor Who* and the Americans have *Star Trek*, then the closest to a Japanese equivalent would almost certainly be the mecha series *Gundam*. The original series in the franchise, 1979's *Mobile Suit Gundam*, would go on to spawn a franchise that has produced dozens of spin-offs and is still going today. *Mobile Suit Gundam* is a space opera, with the lead character Amuro Ray becoming the unwilling pilot of the 'Gundam', a gigantic, robotic, bipedal tank. As the series progresses, Ray starts to develop psychic abilities, making him what is dubbed in the series a 'Newtype', a new evolution of human being. The term 'Newtype' lives on today in the title of one of Japan's best selling magazines about anime. Although it was not the first, *Gundam* is certainly the most famous mecha pioneer.

A few years later, a manga would come about which would have a bigger impact on the art form, on a global scale. In 1982, Katsuhiro Otomo launched the dystopian cyberpunk series *Akira*, the same year which witnessed the release of the classic cyberpunk film *Blade Runner*. Set in the city of Neo-Tokyo, with the old Tokyo being destroyed in a nuclear explosion which starts World War III, it is a complex tale following a motorcycle gang who find themselves caught up with terrorists and a government scheme involving children with psychic abilities. The manga was adapted into an even more confusing but influential anime film released in 1988. Confusing because the manga was still being written and thus only adapted the first half of the story, but influential because it strongly influenced not just anime, but science fiction and in particular cyberpunk, especially films like *The Matrix*. Today, the film is massively critically acclaimed, and often referenced in works from both the West and the East. One particular scene, in which the hero Kaneda comes from the bottom of the frame and slides his motorbike to a halt in the middle of the frame, has been referenced in many series, montages of which can be seen online. *Akira* is also noted for accurately predicting that Japan would win the right to stage the 2020 Olympics. One notable scene sees a sign at the construction site for the new stadium saying: '147 days until the Games', with some graffiti below reading: 'Just cancel it!' This image ended up trending when the Games were 147 days away in February 2020, during the height of the Coronavirus pandemic, with some people wanting the entire thing cancelled. The Olympics instead got postponed until 2021.[9]

1986 was an important year. I was born then for starters, but more important than that was the debut of another anime film, *Laputa: Castle in the Sky*. Partly inspired by the film's director holidaying in Wales during the time of the 1984 Miners' Strike, this steampunk fantasy film follows a boy and girl trying to prevent a magic crystal falling into the wrong hands, while also searching for a floating castle. Notable features of this film include the fact that it is responsible for the busiest single second on Twitter. In the film, our two heroes say a key magical word, 'balse' (pronounced with a silent e, as one syllable), at a pivotal moment. It has since become custom that when the film is shown on Japanese TV, for viewers to tweet the word 'balse' at the exact moment it is said in the film. At 11:21:50pm Japan Standard

Time (3:21:50pm BST) on 2nd August 2013, this resulted in 143,199 tweets being sent at the exact same second.

Laputa is noted for another reason. That director who visited Wales was named Hayao Miyazaki, and that film was the first released by Studio Ghibli, Japan's most famous anime film studio. Now it should be stated that this was not Miyazaki's first film. That was the 1979 comedy *The Castle of Cagliostro*, a film based on the long-running manga *Lupin III*, a series about a master thief and an homage to the Maurice Leblanc's gentleman thief character, Arsene Lupin. Also before *Laputa* was *Nausicaä of the Valley of the Wind* in 1982, a science fantasy epic with a deep environmental message, that Miyazaki would later expand upon in manga form.

However, since these films Miyazaki and Studio Ghibli have gone on to create the biggest Japanese anime films. These include the children's fantasy *My Neighbour Totoro*, which is one of the greatest kids' films ever, and *Spirited Away*, which to this day remains the only anime feature film to have won the Oscar for Best Animated Feature. Miyazaki remains the most famous anime director, and almost certainly the one who has come out of retirement the most times. It is hard to keep count of the number of times Miyazaki has quit the industry only to return again. He is currently working on a new film, *How Do You Live?*, which is awaiting release.[10]

The 1980s witnessed the release of both the aforementioned *Dragon Ball* and *Urotsukidoji*. Also from that decade came Junji Ito, the most famous exponent of horror manga. Series such as *Tomie*, about a demonic woman with the power to make men fall in love with her; *Uzumaki*, about a town cursed by spirals; and *Gyo*, which sees people battling against an army of stinking, metal-leg-walking, undead fish, helped to cement his reputation especially in body horror. Elsewhere was Naoki Urasawa, a great exponent of action and suspense. Brits may be interested in his series *Master Keaton*, which follows the adventures of an Anglo-Japanese ex-SAS soldier and Falklands veteran, who would rather be indulging in his passion for archaeology than having to work as an insurance investigator. Other titles by Urasawa include *Pluto*, a reworking of Tezuka's *Astro Boy*; the sci-fi thrillers *20th Century Boys* and *21st Century Boys*; and the utterly superb psychological thriller *Monster*. Aside from manga, Urasawa is also a talented folk musician.

By 1989, the year of Tezuka's death and CLAMP's debut, cyberpunk returned to manga with the release of *Ghost in the Shell* by Masamune Shirow, a series perhaps now best known for its 1995 anime feature film adaptation, and also for being adapted into a live-action Hollywood remake in 2017. The live-action film attracted complaints of racism following their decision to cast Scarlet Johansson in the lead role of Major Motoko Kusanagi, a cyborg cop who has undergone complete 'full-body prosthesis'. For those interested in reading the manga, you are best advised to search for older second-hand copies from former publisher Dark Horse rather than the more recent re-releases from Kodansha, which have cut out scenes in which the Major is seen having sex on a boat with other women, thus showing the Major to be bisexual.

Tragically, 1989 also witnessed the case of what became known as 'The Otaku Murderer'. Anime and manga fan Tsutomu Miyazaki abducted and murdered four young girls between the ages of four and seven, in Tokyo and Saitama, and committed necrophilia with the bodies, among other horrific activities. His arrest resulted in a moral panic against otaku and other anime fans. Miyazaki was eventually executed in 2008. In 1991, otaku culture itself was parodied in the brilliant spoof OVA *Otaku no Video*, which mixed animation displaying the joys of otaku culture with a spoof live-action documentary called *A Portrait of an Otaku* showing the downsides of the culture.

As well as the Otaku Murderer, another problem was on the horizon. The mid-to-late 80s had been a period of economic growth in Japan, but by the time of the 1990s the bubble had burst and the country entered into a period of economic stagnation dubbed the 'Lost Decade', although many argue that the effects were longer and perhaps never fully solved at all. We will see this being commented on in CLAMP's series *Tokyo Babylon.*

It was around the late 1980s and early 1990s that the infamous *Urotsukidoji: Legend of the Overfiend* came out. In the UK, the anime distributors at the time wanted to be seen as edgy and alternative. There was the practice of 'fifteening' for example. If a release would have been given a 12 age-rating certificate, often the English dub would have extra swearing in it just so it would be given an edgier 15 rating instead. It is partly because of this that in the UK anime has its unfair reputation for being material that is unsuitable for children. Series like the 1990 cyberpunk OVA *Cyber City Oedo 808* fit this mould. The UK dub starred American *Jonathan Creek* actor Stuart Milligan (under the pseudonym Bruce Martin) performing a dub script that at times had swearing so over the top it is laughable compared to the Japanese, but now people like the series because of the UK dub. Both the UK and Japanese versions have their own merit, with the UK version even having its own separate soundtrack. The UK released *Cyber City Oedo 808* on Blu-Ray before Japan did.

Key titles created in the 1990s include *Sailor Moon*, the most famous example of what is known as the 'magical girl' genre: fantasies featuring girls (and sometimes boys) who have magical powers and fight evil. As for rivals to it in terms of fame, one of the few that challenge *Sailor Moon* is CLAMP's most popular work, *Cardcaptor Sakura*, but we will get to that later.

Aside from anime and manga, the art form was spreading to other places too. One example is the 'light novel', story series consisting of on average about 50,000 words per volume, with many series running into multiple volumes. In the early 1990s, one series of light novels perhaps became a cornerstone of another anime-centric genre. *Ai no Kusabi* is one of the most famous examples of 'yaoi' or 'boy's love' (BL) – a branch of homoerotic fiction that is often created and marketed at women. This eight-volume long sci-fi yaoi series is set in a dystopian world with a caste system based on hair colour with the dominant figure, blond-haired Iason Mink, turning a black-haired low cast guy called Riki into his 'pet', setting up a kind of BDSM scenario.

Personally however, I believe this series is more interesting for its setting. Set on a planet called Amoï, Riki originally comes from an area called Ceres, which years before the story began decides to break off from the rest of society and seek greater freedom. The attitude of everyone else was one of: "Okay, but if you want to break away from us, that's it. You will get nothing from us in return. You are on your own." Ceres goes ahead, breaks off, and because it receives nothing, becomes a massive slum. It's a fantastical scenario, and obviously one that could never happen in real-life. Could you imagine somewhere, a country for example, breaking away from a body of other countries under the guise of 'seeking freedom', only to end up so much worse off because of it?[11]

Aside from novels, the other medium anime struck into was video games. This was happening long before the 1990s of course. Today, you can argue that most British people's first experience with manga-style art was in games. This was certainly true for me. My first experience of any manga-style was in my parents' video game collection. They are not in any way particularly nerdy or geeky people, but they had some games that displayed this art, namely the first two *Phantasy Star* games. *Phantasy Star II*, released on the Sega Mega Drive in Japan in 1989 and in Europe the following year, in particular features manga art and is a game I still remember fondly.

However, in terms of games, the most impactful came about in the mid-to-late 1990s. First released in 1996, but not arriving in Europe until 1999, we experienced the arrival of *Pokemon*, and soon afterwards the anime adaptation, which followed the electric mouse Pikachu and his trainer, called Satoshi in Japan but better known in the West as Ash Ketchum. As more games have been released, more episodes of the anime have been made, now totalling over 1,100 since it debuted on April Fools' Day 1997. There have also been several films, including the recent CGI/live-action film *Detective Pikachu*.[12]

The franchise has spawned eight generations, based on different regions of the world, with a ninth due in late 2022. The location for Generation VIII's games *Sword* and *Shield*, Galar, is based on Britain. Look at a picture of Galar and it looks like Britain upside-down with Scotland in the south. The game starts in the south and the main female playable character, Gloria, wears a tam o'shanter, leading to lots of memes depicting the character as having a broad Scottish accent. To the disappointment of many however, Gloria's hometown of Wedgehurst is based on the English region of Cumbria and she has an English accent to match.

A year before *Pokemon*'s debut, mecha was on the rise again with the apocalyptic and controversial series *Neon Genesis Evangelion*.[13] The 1995 series set in 2015, which mixed sci-fi with elements of religion, and followed Shinji Ikari, the unwilling pilot of the 'Evangelion' mecha. He is forced to battle creatures called 'Angels', seemingly on his unloving father's bidding. The series has been the subject of much debate over the years, with a new four-part anime film version known as the *Rebuild of Evangelion* being released over a period of a decade. The last of these four films was scheduled to be released in 2020, eight years after the third film, but the Coronavirus resulted in further delays. Problems regarding *Evangelion* are nothing new. When the original TV series ended, the conclusion was so controversial that the studio, Gainax, was attacked. Soon afterwards, a two-part film series *Revival of Evangelion* was released in 1997, and used images of the studio attacks in montages.

1997 also witnessed the release of *One Piece* in *Weekly Shonen Jump*, a series so popular across the world that it is surprising that it took so long to reach British audiences. The anime version, consisting of over 900 episodes since it began in 1999, didn't get a British DVD release until May 2013. Later years resulted in the release of two more hugely popular *Jump* titles: *Naruto*, about ninjas; and *Bleach*, about 'shinigami' – death gods in Japanese folklore – although the English release referred to the characters as 'Soul Reapers'.

But entering into the new millennium, perhaps the best new title from *Jump* around that time was one of the darkest. Created by duo Tsugumi Ohba and Takeshi Obata in 2003, *Death Note* also features a shinigami. His name is Ryuk, and he records the deaths of humans in a note book called a 'Death Note'. When he gets hold of a second book, he decides to drop it into the human world to see what will happen. It gets picked up by a genius student called Light Yagami, who, when he discovers its powers, decides to use it to make the world a better place. However, his idea of making the world better is to kill everyone in the world he even remotely suspects of committing any crime. Being dubbed 'Kira' (a Japanese pronunciation of the English 'killer') by the press, he rapidly develops a god complex as he fights the law, including his own cop father, as well as a strange foreign detective known only as 'L', in his mission to create what he sees as a utopian society.

The main reason for suggesting that *Death Note* is one of the best manga from that time is the character of Light, because despite the fact he is clearly a horrific, genocidal, dictatorial, draconian monster, he is also strangely appealing. There is that tiny bit in all of us who would wish that certain people were wiped off the face of the planet: racists, sexists, homophobes, transphobes etc. If you had that book and you could kill the people you hated the most just by writing their names in it while thinking of their faces, you would probably do it. For me, Light is not just one of the best manga characters ever written, but is one of the best fictional characters full stop. The fact his creators can make someone so horrific also so charismatic is a triumph to them. Of course, the series had its problems, and, my word, they were big. Perhaps inevitably, there was eventually a series of murders inspired by *Death Note.* In Belgium in 2007, a case known as the 'Manga Murder' witnessed a person being killed with a message at the scene which was a mistranslation of the phrase: 'I am Kira'. This event would later be referenced by Ohba and Obata in their next series, *Bakuman*, the story about two friends who create their own manga. One of their series is about students who try to commit 'perfect crimes', which results in what is seen as a real-life copycat crime.

The early-to-mid 2000s witnessed a 'manga boom' in the USA, with publishers bringing out popular and strange titles, and prices falling. More popular series released at around this time included:

Black Butler, a fantasy thriller which has since become the most famous manga set in Britain, taking place in Victorian England.

The online webcomic *Hetalia: Axis Powers*, a comedy telling the story of historical events including World War II, where the main characters are the anthropomorphic personifications of the nations of the world including Japan itself – making it possibly the most PC non-PC anime ever made.[14]

The massively over-the-top mecha anime series *Gurren Lagann*, which is also unashamedly my favourite anime ever.

The horror series *Attack on Titan*, which sees humanity doing battle with a race of man-eating giants.

Steampunk fantasy *Fullmetal Alchemist* by female author Hiromu Arakawa, which answers the question: 'What costs an arm and a leg?' with 'Trying to bring your mother back from the dead' for the leg, and 'Rescuing your brother's soul and transposing it into a massive suit of armour' for the arm.

And in the 2010s possibly the first big anime series to make waves was *Puella Magi Madoka Magica*, a magical girl series that turned things around by being a tragedy rather than light-hearted fun.

The late 2000s and the 2010s have seen two very different types of anime and manga achieve much attention. One of these is 'isekai', literally 'different world', a genre of speculative fiction in which someone finds themselves transported into an entirely new world, whether it be a fantasy world, a parallel universe or a man-made virtual world. This genre is nothing new: CLAMP's *Magic Knight Rayearth* and Miyazaki's *Spirited Away* are both early examples, but the genre rapidly grew during this time.

Key series in this genre include works like *Sword Art Online* (*SAO*), in which the hero Kirito finds himself and 10,000 other players of a new virtual reality video game (released 6th November 2022) trapped in the game by its creator. If they die in the game, they are killed in real-life by their headsets releasing microwaves and frying their brains. While the series is popular with many fans, it is also frequently derided by others for lazy and sometimes sexist storytelling. Remarkably however, the author of the original light novels, Reki Kawahara, has since taken these complaints on board and vowed to write with more care, especially for Western audiences.

Another isekai title is *Log Horizon* by Mamare Touno, which again is set in a virtual world, but unlike *SAO* the players are not killed in real-life if they die in the game, but are reincarnated, meaning there is seemingly no escape. The main story follows the efforts of the trapped players to improve their virtual world while trying to find a way out, mainly lead by master player Shiroe, who sets up his own guild in the game, the titular 'Log Horizon'. This series is more respected among fans than *SAO*, but like the former its author has had problems. In the case of Touno however, it was not the quality of his writing that was under question, but his tax arrangements. In 2015, he was charged with tax evasion, reportedly owing the government ¥30million (approximately $250,000). Touno has since paid this money.

Isekai continue to be popular. In fact, the genre has gotten popular to the point of saturation. Several Japanese story contests have issued rules banning isekai entries because they are so numerous. You could argue that isekai is now to anime what superhero movies are to Hollywood.

Aside from isekai, the other genre that rapidly gained attention in the 2010s was sports anime. Again, sports series are nothing new. There have been dozens of sports anime over the decades. But the reason for the sudden rise dates back to a live-action programme from 2000. *Kamen Rider*, created by Shotaro Ishinomori of *Cyborg 009*-fame, is a long-running superhero series aimed at children about a motorbike-riding hero. However, the 2000 series *Kamen Rider Kuuga* attracted the attention of the producers when they noticed that the series was not only popular with kids, but with women around the age of 30. They later discovered that the reason for this was because the women found lead actor Joe Odagiri attractive, and watched the show because he was in it. This has since sparked the 'Odagiri effect' – the phenomenon that TV shows will attract higher audience figures if they star attractive male performers and characters.[15]

The Odagiri effect has been used on various anime, with sports series mainly featuring schoolboy teams being one of the primary focuses of attention. Series considered to have been affected include *Kuroko's Basketball*, the swimming-based *Free!*, the surprisingly popular volleyball series *Haikyu!*, and the road cycling series *Yowamushi Pedal*. Even series about fictional sports like *Prince of Stride*, about a sport which is akin to a relay parkour, seem to have fallen under the influence. You can argue that the effect happens in the West too. See for example the media attention attracted by the topless Aidan Turner in *Poldark*, or the rise in popularity of shows starring Benedict Cumberbatch after he appeared in *Sherlock*. Before taking the role, he had been starring in the BBC Radio 4 sitcom *Cabin Pressure*, which features a live studio audience. After *Sherlock*, ticket requests for recordings of *Cabin Pressure* reached record figures.

It should be mentioned that aside from the Odagiri effect, another issue also highlighted is the sexualisation of female characters for male audiences. Part of the problem with manga, even in Japan, is that people often see it as niche and much of the content being unsuitable for some people, despite there being manga for just about all groups of people.

One other side-effect the Odagiri effect had was the kind of people these shows now attracted. Among the women who started watching these shows were 'fujoshi' – BL fans. This also attracted some gay male fans, including BL fans known as 'fudanshi', to these shows. As a result, these anime characters kind of became gay icons. Some of the shows seemed to play on this. One such show was *Cheer Boys!!*, about an all-male cheerleading squad. It got to the point where you think to yourself: "Look, just admit you're fucking gay, alright! Stop teasing us!"

By 2016 however, a sports anime came about that gripped its target audience, including those looking for something more loving. France's most popular dictionary, *Petit Robert*, took a surprisingly long time to include a term for 'French kissing'. The word that came to define the phrase: 'to kiss with tongues' was:

'Galocher'. Also in the dictionary is: 'La galoche', which means: 'an ice-skating boot'. Both terms go well together and are fitting with the figure-skating anime *Yuri!!! on Ice*, the series whose title song includes the line: 'We were born to make history.'

The anime follows the relationships between Japanese skater Yuri Katsuki, his Russian idol, figure-skating champion Victor Nikiforov, and rising Russian star Yuri 'Yurio' Plisetsky. When a video of Yuri performing one of Victor's routines goes viral, Victor flies to Japan and demands to be Yuri's coach, much to the annoyance of Yurio, who he was meant to be working with. Following a contest between the two Yuris, Victor does indeed become Yuri's coach and the two start working together.

The series quickly attracted praise from real-life figure skaters to the point where skaters in the 2018 Winter Olympics skated to music from the show, but the biggest event occurred in the seventh episode. Yuri performs a brilliant routine, and Victor in celebration runs onto the ice to celebrate with him. As they do, Victor dives into Yuri's arms. While his arm covers the main action in the mid-shot, we do see a close up of Victor and Yuri's lips getting close. As Victor lands, we see the faces on everyone watching, as we witness them seeing our two leads having a gay kiss. Later episodes see the relationship flourish. After so much teasing from other shows, we finally had a proper gay couple in a sports anime. It became the big hit at the time and a feature film, *Ice Adolescence*, is in production.

In more recent years, things have become darker again. While the Coronavirus has given the industry a fair number of problems, with many series having to be delayed as production was forced to stop, the most shocking event of all occurred earlier, on 18th July 2019 in Kyoto. The city is home to the appropriately named Kyoto Animation studio (KyoAni). The studio has produced many hit series, normally focusing on school life. These include the sci-fi comedy *The Melancholy of Haruhi Suzumiya*; the gut-wrenchingly tragic and brilliant *Clannad*; *K-On!*, a music-based comedy whose lead characters became the first ever anime characters to be credited with their own number one single, and the already mentioned swimming anime *Free!*.

On 18th July 2019, someone entered the studio via the front door, doused the area, many employees and himself with petrol, and set fire to it. The Kyoto Animation arson attack was responsible for the deaths of at least 36 people, injuring another 33, including the chief suspect. It is the single deadliest disaster in the entire history of animation. The chief suspect was so badly burned that the police had to wait 10 months before they were able to question them. It was a tragic event, but one that also united the entire anime community, from creators to fans, in rallying support for those who were victim to this horrific attack.

I know it is a shame to end this introduction on such a sad note, but with this and the Coronavirus pandemic, much has hit the industry. How long it will take to recover remains to be seen. What people can do is buy the books, buy the DVDs, buy the Blu-Rays, and stream and legally download the latest offerings.

Among the stuff that I believe you should pick up is the work of a group of women whose collective body of work covers so much, in such a beautiful way. Let's turn the clock back to the 1980s, and begin looking in depth at the CLAMPverse.

1 – A title which, due to me playing a lot of the video game *Overwatch* back in the day, I cannot read without thinking of someone continuously repeating the sentence: "I require healing."

2 – It is also hard to review, as I found out myself in a piece I did for *Anime UK News*. As I wrote at the time: "Reviewing *Momotaro* is akin to reviewing something like Leni Riefenstahl's Nazi propaganda film *Triumph of the Will* or D. W. Griffith's *The Birth of a Nation* which features the Ku Klux Klan as the heroes." The entire review is available online.

3 – Helen McCarthy wrote on Twitter on 12th August 2021 that she was annoyed by the 'godfather of manga' title given to Tezuka. She wrote that this title was given by Americans because they thought it was offensive to call someone as a god. She wrote: "Osamu Tezuka is the god of comics. An America godfather is a criminal mastermind leading a demonised minority cultural nexus that preys on mainstream society to survive. That term should not be applied to a great creative artist who detested violence and loved all of life."

4 – *Kochikame* lost the record to *Golgo 13* by Takao Saito, a series about a hitman which began in 1968 in *Big Comic* magazine (published by Shogakukan). It published its 201st volume in July 2021. Saito said he wanted the series to continue even after he died. Saito died on 24th September 2021 and indeed the series is still going on.

5 – The superpowers in *My Hero Academia* are referred to as 'quirks', with those without powers, i.e. people who are perfectly normal, referred to as being 'quirkless'. Given my Asperger's and the fact that 'quirkless' is an insult to describe people in this fictional world who are normal, I for one am quite keen on we

disabled people using the word 'quirkless' as our insult towards the able bodied. Also, if you are interested in Asperger's and the autistic spectrum, I would recommend the manga *With the Light: Raising an Autistic Child* by the late Keiko Tobe, published in English by Yen Press.

6 – Although it is hard to give exact translation, the rough guide is that one Japanese yen is worth about one US cent, so ¥100 equals $1. Thus ¥200,000 is normally given as $2,000, although when the fine was issued the figure was closer to $1,900.

7 – Looking back at a review I wrote for Volume 1 on *Act-Age* for Anime UK News, it is disturbing that some of the things I commented on may have been early signs of the crime that was to come. Writing in July 2020, by which time the crime had been committed but not reported, I wrote, "*Act-Age* does have some issues. The scene in which [film director] Sumiji grabs [wannabe actress] Kei off the street and into his car is one. It does all feel non-consensual. It feels even more troublesome when you realise that Kei is 16 and Sumiji is 35. At one point Kei even asks Sumiji out straight if he has a Lolita complex, which he denies."

8 – The Showa period refers to the reign of Emperor Hirohito, 1926-89.

9 – In 2019, I was going to give a talk about cyberpunk anime as part of the Teesside Cyberpunk Convention, an event held mainly to mark the fact that *Blade Runner*, like *Akira*, is set in that year, and that industrial Teesside, the part of Britain where I live, inspired the look of *Blade Runner*. Smoggies are proud of this, making Teesside one of the few places in the world proud to have influenced a dystopia. Annoyingly, not enough tickets

were sold by the convention and my talk got cancelled, a fact that was made more annoying by the fact I had a special cyberpunk outfit made for me by my local comic book shop, Geek Corner of Stockton-on-Tees. In the end I decided to do a stand-up gig wearing the outfit. It went down okay. We will cover cyberpunk more in the chapter on *Clover*. Also, a bit of advice: if you are planning to buy the 4K UHD version of *Akira*, avoid the UK release from Manga Entertainment as it does not feature the top of the range 4K HDR presentation format, unlike versions released in other countries.

10 – Another personal favourite Ghibli film is 1994's *Pom Poko* directed by Isao Takahata, probably the only film given a Parental Guidance rating by the British Board of Film Classification to feature male tanuki (Japanese raccoon dogs) crushing police officers to death with their shape-shifting testicles. At least that's what you hear in the original Japanese dub and read in the English subtitles. If you listen to it in the English dub, the actors refer instead to shape-shifting 'pouches'.

11 – Insert your own Brexit jokes.

12 – My personal highlight of the *Pokemon* craze was reading a listing in *TV Quick* when there was a *Pokemon* marathon in the days when the series was shown on Sky One. The listing ended with the line: 'Parents are advised to take the dog out for a very long walk.'

13 – Which is, coincidentally, the first anime I ever purchased. The first manga I ever purchased, for those interested, was *Hyper Police*, a now out-of-print sci-fi comedy about a half-human, half-cat bounty hunter.

14 – In case you are wondering, England/the United Kingdom (Scotland, Wales, Northern Ireland and Eire never appeared as separate characters, although the never-recognised micronation of Sealand did) is depicted as cynical, terrible at cooking, and has the ability to see mythical creatures as the country is home to so many legends.

15 – There is I believe an equivalent where men are more likely to watch something if it contains attractive women in it. It's called 'porn'.

CHAPTER 1

From Gay Guys to Genderless Gods – CLAMP's early years (1967-1992) and *RG Veda* (1989-1996)

CLAMP's members and early works

Let's begin by getting to the issue of CLAMP's name. Where does it come from? Clearly it comes from the English language rather than Japanese, but it has nothing to do with actual clamps that you use to hold things to stop them from moving. According to various sources, the name 'CLAMP' actually comes from a typo. It is a misspelling of 'clump', as in 'a bunch of potatoes'. Why a group of women manga artists would want to name themselves after a pile of spuds is mystery, but this idea appears to be confirmed in *Duklyon: CLAMP School Defenders* (see Chapter 2) where a character is quoted as saying on p. 44 of Volume 1: "The name 'CLAMP' incorporates the words 'hinge,' as well as 'potato mountain,' within its definition." A very peculiar origin concerning a group who are themselves a mystery.

If you are interested in knowing the personal stories of all the women in CLAMP, that is a problem. The group rarely give interviews, which are obviously in Japanese in the first place and therefore have to be translated, and they keep themselves private.[1] Fortunately many interviews have been archived, with one English-language Brazilian website, Chibi Yuuto's Chronicles, collecting just about all interviews the group have given in the past. As mentioned in the preface, the podcast *CLAMPcast in Wonderland* has also been a very useful source of information and I must give a lot of credit to both of them.

But let's start at the beginning. CLAMP first formed in the mid-1980s. Today, the group consists of four members: Nanase Ohkawa, Mokona Apapa, Mick Nekoi and Satsuki Igarashi. However, when the group celebrated their 15th anniversary, the four women all decided to adopt new names, respectively becoming Ageha Ohkawa (although Ohkawa changed her name back in 2008), Mokona (one single name), Tsubaki Nekoi and, err, Satsuki Igarashi, but now written using different Japanese characters. All were born in the late 1960s (Ohkawa in 1967, Mokona in 1968, Nekoi in January 1969, and Igarashi in February 1969) and all were born in Kyoto, except for Ohkawa who came from Osaka.

But this is the group today. The original 'Clamp Cluster' consisted of at least 11 members, most of whom are now forgotten. These women included O-Kyon, Sei Nanao, Leeze Sei, Soshi Hishika, Kazue Nakamori, Shinya Omi, and most famously Tamayo Akiyama, who would become a successful manga artist on her own, with fantasy series *Mouryou Kiden* and *Zyword*, sci-fi comedy *Hyper Rune*, and horror *Secret Chaser* being released in English. CLAMP would still have seven members by the time their first serialised manga, *RG Veda*, began.

The three Kyoto members – Mokona, Nekoi and Igarashi – all took up drawing manga at school and were members of their school's astronomy club. Ohkawa became part of the group after a school friend showed her some drawings by Mokona, and asked to be introduced to her. The four were constantly travelling between Osaka and Kyoto, and so would frequently meet. Eventually they formed CLAMP. According to Ohkawa in an interview published in the *CLAMP North Side art book* (August 2002): "In the end more people joined, but since the group was too large we ended up not doing anything. *laughs*" Roles among the group also became more established. Ohkawa became the main writer, storyboarder and director, while the other three were mainly artists. Mokona is normally the lead artist on most works, although sometimes Nekoi will be the main artist on other series, while Igarashi mainly works as the designer and art assistant. All four members however are considered equals.

While on the surface CLAMP would appear to have an advantage in numbers compared to most manga artists, titles normally being credited to a single person or a pair of creators, this is wrong. Most manga are credited to one or two people, but creators in turn are helped by many assistants, often between four and six people, doing minor tasks like shading or particularly detailed work. Thus the foursome of CLAMP working on their own are at a disadvantage in terms of the number of people working on them, but on the other hand have more control over their creations. CLAMP do everything themselves, with no outside interference. Igarashi said in the *North Side* interview that, "…if we added anyone else we wouldn't be able to work in the same speed as we do."

Regarding their writing progress, in a 2006 interview CLAMP gave at the Anime Expo convention in Anaheim, California, their first time in the USA, they revealed that each story is written with the ending predetermined. Thus, the women know how each story is going to start and finish before they put it down on paper. This is particularly interesting given that there are quite a few series that CLAMP have never got round to finishing.

The first works that CLAMP published were 'doujinshi'. These are self-published stories, mostly by amateurs, but also by some professionals. They are mainly sold at conventions, the most famous of these being Comiket (Comic Market). While many of these doujinshi are original works, a lot are based on already popular titles. While this clearly breaches copyright law, something Japan normally takes very seriously,[2] the vast majority of doujinshi is not prosecuted against, including pornographic versions of normally non-pornographic titles. The belief is that these fan-works have an overall positive effect on the entire commercial manga market and that it inspires amateur artists to go professional. As these are small, independent works, most are never released outside of Japan and thus are not released in English.

This is true with CLAMP's doujinshi. The first of a total of 22 volumes of *CLAMP Book* was released on 19th July 1987, although each book was also referred to as a 'mook'. These volumes varied in terms of content. These include early versions of their early characters including those from their first traditionally published series *RG Veda*, a gay romcom called *Shoten*, and various other fan works. The fan works include stories based on series such as the space opera light novels *Legend of the Galactic Heroes*, sports manga like the football series *Captain Tsubasa* and pool/billiards manga *Break Shot*, and *Weekly Shonen Jump* hits like the fantasy *Saint Seiya* and *JoJo's Bizarre Adventure*, the last of which of these featured a male pregnancy story. CLAMP continued to make doujinshi until 1992. For more information on these works, I would recommend Chibi Yuuto's YouTube channel, where he has been covering all of the releases.

It was these works that gave CLAMP their break. The editor of the magazine *Wings* contacted the group about their story *RG Veda*. CLAMP first created a 60-page work for the magazine, but to quote Ohkawa in the same *North Side* interview: "The truth is that you could recycle very little of that work… *laughs* We had never worked as a group so it consisted of an unfinished work in every aspect. Of course that wasn't worth anything, but they told us to take that as a base to create something from scratch. The result of that rework became our debut."

The first chapter however was still a risk. Like most manga magazines, the publishers relied on surveys of their readers to see which of the stories they were publishing were popular. They also had to surpass the sales of the first print run in order to continue their work. Luckily, the readers liked it, and so *RG Veda* became a full series, despite the fact that not many people appeared to understand the actual plot. After the first print run sold out, there were no more conditions given. By 1989, the year *RG Veda* officially began, all of CLAMP had now moved to Tokyo except Akiyama, which may be part of the reason why she left the group. At first the move was troublesome, as they were in a small flat with no privacy, but obviously things improved from there.

The original *Rigveda* (with an 'i')

Before writing about the manga *RG Veda*, I thought it best to at least try and familiarise myself with the work it is based on.

The original *Rigveda* or *Rig Veda* (with an 'i')[3] is one of the four sacred texts of Hinduism, and the oldest, with some parts dating to c. 1,500 BCE. It contains a collection of 1,028 poems or hymns, collected in ten books or mandalas. For my research purposes, I was lucky in that a reading of the entire unabridged and modernised version of the *Rigveda* was released on Audible on 18th April 2020, during the lockdown. I thus downloaded it and listened to it. All 41 hours and 22 minutes of it. It is safe to say that this research took longer than I was expecting.

Now, a book of ancient Hindu texts might seem odd for a comic book adaptation, but as mentioned in the introduction, Osamu Tezuka had created a manga biography of Buddha, and CLAMP constantly return to religion, the supernatural and the occult in their work.

It should be noted however that CLAMP's adaptation is a very loose one. For example, in the original *Rigveda*, the chief of the gods is Indra, the thunder god who destroys great evils. In the manga *RG Veda*, Indra becomes Taishakuten, the villain of the story. There are also some characters in the original work that don't appear in the manga. For example, one character in the *Rigveda* was Vishpala, a female warrior with an artificial iron leg, argued to be one of the earliest depictions of a person with a disability. As someone with a disability myself, I am annoyed that she never got depicted by CLAMP.

Another key difference is something called 'soma'. In the original *Rigveda*, this is a drink used in rituals, but is of unknown origin. It appears in many rituals, and the ninth book in the text is entirely devoted to it. In *RG Veda* the manga, it is not mentioned once.[4] This is even more confusing when you consider that both the ancient text and the manga include characters called Soma, or Souma. (We'll discuss the issue of the spelling later).

There are some other things I was not expecting to hear when listening to the audiobook. One such part is in Hymn 58 of the third book, where it says: "Destroy in us the counsel of the niggard come hitherward, for we have shown you favour." I did a double-take when listening to that sentence, as soon as what I thought was the 'n-word' being mentioned. Turns out 'niggard' and 'niggardly' are old Middle English terms for 'miserly', and are completely unrelated to the racist 'n-word' which comes from languages on the European continent. There is an entire Wikipedia article about 'Controversies about the word *niggardly*' if you want to learn more.

Interestingly, parts of the story that do not appear in the manga also fail to appear in the original *Rigveda* too. Many of the translated versions of the text censor some rather adult references. For example, Verses 16-17 from Hymn 86 in Book 10 talk quite a bit about Indra's penis. The audiobook version I listened to kept this in, but if you try to look it up online you'll find that many websites have removed these verses entirely, and at no point do you see Taishakuten's penis in *RG Veda*.

As the manga is clearly very different to the original source material, I will only refer to the religious text when needs be, normally in brackets. CLAMP's manga is the main focus in this book.

RG Veda (without the 'i', 1989-1996)

The manga *RG Veda* first began in the monthly magazine *South*, published by the company Shinshokan, in 1989, but after the series was given a proper go-ahead, it moved to sister magazine *Wings*. The series would go on to span ten completed paperback books (tankobon) by the time the story ended in 1996. The series was not released in English until 2005.

The manga, like most of CLAMP's early works, was first published in English by the company Tokyopop. However, in the late 2000s the company lost a significant number of titles, and in 2011 the North American, English-speaking part of the company closed down. Tokyopop have since returned and have started releasing manga translated into English again, but all the CLAMP licences have now gone, being split among various publishers.

In the case of *RG Veda*, it went to the publisher Dark Horse. They own several CLAMP titles, but have been publishing them in a different way to Tokyopop. Namely, rather than selling the series in the original ten volumes, they have compiled the entire story into just three editions, meaning that each book includes a rather odd three-and-a-third volumes. However, they do include some special colour illustrations with each one. They also released their versions as e-books.

One thing to mention regarding Dark Horse's versions of the story is the spelling of certain words, especially the character names. When written out in English text, one common form of character used is 'ō', but in these manga Dark Horse do not use the accent and instead write the letter as 'ou' as a way of showing how to pronounce the letter. For the benefit of English readers, I will stick to the spellings given by each publisher and will avoid accents in this book. Thus, 'Sōma' will henceforth be spelled 'Souma'.

Anyway, let's dive into the actual story.

•

RG Veda takes place 300 years after a rebellion in the land of Tenkai. Previously, the land was ruled by the king of the gods, Tentei. However, the warrior Taishakuten (Indra in the original *Rigveda*) raised a rebel army, killed Tentei, and became the new 'God-King', bearing among other things a third eye in the middle of his forehead, a sign of sin.

Now, while it is bad form to break off from the plot this early, it is worth commenting that before we go any further something should be mentioned before we get to the present day plot. Just reading a few of the opening pages you might notice a peculiarity about the way *RG Veda* is presented. Namely, that for a story based on a Hindu text, a text that comes from the Indian subcontinent, most of the characters in this story appear to be white.

Whether CLAMP drew them as ethnically Japanese, Caucasian or something else is unknown, but it has to be said that it is problematic that the story doesn't have that many people of colour in it despite the source material. The only person of colour who appears regularly in the manga is Souma. I have heard the women on the *CLAMPcast in Wonderland* podcast describe it as cultural appropriation. To me it feels a bit like whitewashing, although obviously that's the wrong term. I'm not entire sure what the right term would be. Nipponwashing, perhaps? When having my book fact checked, Chibi Yuuto brought up the possibility that this may be an editorial decision to appeal to Japanese readers, given that CLAMP were still rookies. Anyway, the story…

A woman named Kuyou, the blind 'Royal Stargazer' (a kind

of priestess) has fled from Taishakuten's court, Zenmi Palace. Taishakuten thus summons one of his strongest warriors, Yasha (Yaksha – a form of spirit in various Eastern faiths, sometimes benevolent, sometimes malevolent), to track Kuyou down and kill her. Yasha finds her in some ruins and Kuyou gives him the following prophecy:

"Six Stars will fall to this plane. The dark stars that will defy the heavens. And you shall undertake a journey that begins when you find the child of a vanished race. I cannot discern the child's alignment, but I know that the child alone can turn the wheels of Tenkai's destiny. For it is by Heavenly Mandate that through this child, the Six Stars shall begin to gather. And then someone shall appear from the shadows. Even my powers cannot clearly discern him… but he knows the future… and can turn the path of those Stars whether evil or heavenly. A roaring flame will raze the wicked. Six Stars will overpower all others… And inevitably… they will form the schism that splits the Heavens."

Kuyou also tells Yasha that it will be the child's fate to kill Yasha. After learning this, rather than kill Kuyou, Yasha goes off and tries to find the child. Searching in a forest, he comes across a dead tree stump, out of which comes a baby. Suddenly, the baby transforms into an adult, and a most unusual one. The adult has pointed ears, golden eyes, and seemingly no gender. The adult demands to know why they have been awoken, and Yasha says it is to free this person from their deep slumber. The adult replies: "Free me? Thou fool. Ye have freed an evil onto this world that will turn it into a living hell. For I am… Ashura." (Asura – a form of Buddhist demigod) The Ashura clan were the mightiest of warriors under the previous God-King, Tentei, but they were all wiped out by Taishakuten, except for this one. Ashura then turns back into a baby, which Yasha takes with him.

Another break from the narrative here, but this time it is not a problem with the manga, but with the English language. The issue is how to refer to Ashura. As Ashura has no gender, it does not seem right to refer to Ashura as either 'he' or 'she'. This is where the Japanese language has one clear advantage, in the form of its honorifics, which tend to refer to one's rank and position rather than gender. These varied titles given to all kinds of people are virtually all gender neutral, making them very useful when referring to a person of either unknown gender or who is perhaps transgender.[5] The most famous of these honorifics is '-san' and can be used for just about anyone, and it is always wise to use honorifics as in Japan not doing so is seen as being very forward and rude in your attitude. You only ever drop the honorifics for very close people such as your partner. Anyway, the story…

Yasha plans to show Kuyou the baby Ashura, but before he can do so a member of Yasha's tribe tells him that the tribe is being attacked by monsters. Yasha puts Ashura into the care of the messenger as he successfully fights off the monsters, but when Yasha returns he sees a new tree has formed, with Ashura inside it, with his tribe unable to break it. However, when the hilt of Yasha's sword touches the tree, it opens up and out comes Ashura, this time as a child rather than a baby or adult. A village elder warns Yasha that if he keeps on guarding Ashura, then Taishakuten will take violent action. Yasha ignores him.

Soon, Ashura bumps into a man who falls out of a tree. Helping him, Ashura and Yasha learn that this man is called Kujaku, a strange traveller with purple eyes, another sign of sin. He appears to know of Kuyou's prophecy, but he refuses to explain how he knows. Kujaku does say however that Ashura will bring Yasha misfortune. Later, more monsters attack, with Yasha deciding to fight them while carrying Ashura on his horse, to make sure Ashura is safe. As one monster is about to attack Yasha, Ashura is able to save him by casting a magic spell that brings forth fire to destroy the monster.

After this, Yasha finally takes Ashura to see Kuyou, but when he arrives, he sees that Kuyou has already been killed, stabbed through the chest with her own staff, hanging from a wall. Kujaku then appears again, telling Yasha that he was right about the misfortune Ashura would bring. He also tells Yasha who killed Kuyou: one of Taishakuten's four most trusted generals. As Kujaku explains, this is proof that Yasha is now considered a traitor for not killing Kuyou and for hiding Ashura, and thus the prophecy is starting to be fulfilled. As Yasha and Kujaku talk, Ashura approaches Kuyou's body, touches it, and is covered in her blood – which Ashura starts to lick. This awakens Ashura's more destructive powers, the ones displayed in the adult version of Ashura. Ashura tells Yasha that this is part of the price for awakening Ashura in the first place. The full price is the entire slaughter of Yasha's tribe by Taishakuten's army.

There is nothing Yasha can do to stop this. Every single last member of his tribe in the area is killed, except for himself. As a result of this, Yasha vows to find the Six Stars and to finally put an end to Taishakuten's rule.

Who are these Six Stars? Well, you already know the first two: Yasha and Ashura. If you want to know the others, you can see them in a double-page spread at the beginning of the chapter: Storm of the Six Stars, Part One, which appears at the start of the second of the ten original volumes, which obviously appears in Book One of Dark Horse's release. We shall cover them in the chronological order of when they officially join the original duo.

The first of these is Souma (Soma), the only person of colour in the main story. In Hindu mythology, Soma was deity of the moon, and thus sees our Souma fighting with a pair of crescent moon-shaped boomerang blades that she throws at her enemies. Like Yasha, her tribe were all killed and she is the last survivor, her tribe being one made up of alchemists whose blood can grant immortality. In her youth she was taken by a woman named Kendappa (Gandharva – heavenly beings), a queen of an Eastern realm, reigning from a flying castle. As well as loving Souma, Kendappa is also the royal musician to Taishakuten, playing on a bow harp. Souma first meets Yasha and Ashura when Yasha is fighting off some of Taishakuten's soldiers. She invites the pair to Kendappa's castle. Soon after this, Souma asks to join Yasha as she too wants revenge against Taishakuten for killing her tribe. Kendappa reluctantly agrees to let her join them.

After this meeting, Kujaku appears once again, telling Yasha that if he wants to assemble the Six Stars, he needs to find the Shura Sword, a blade that only Ashura can use. This leads to Yasha encountering the fourth of the Six Stars, Ryuu. Ryuu is based on the creatures called Nāga, who are half-human and half-snake. This reptilian aspect is probably why Ryuu represents the Dragon Tribe. He is meant to be the tribe's king as his grandfather is too sick to rule. Ryuu rejects this at first, but when he sees Yasha entering the tribe's lands, he wants to fight him to prove his strength. After losing one fight, Ryuu decides to join Yasha so he can fight him again. Thus, Ryuu decides to become the Dragon King, mainly so he can get hold of the tribe's strongest weapon, the Dragon Fang Sword – a massive and blunt weapon, but one that can control water and destroy boulders.[6]

Together, these four stars, with a bit of help from Kujaku, find the Shura Sword, which was being kept by another tribe who hoped to use Ashura for their own purposes. This brings about both power and problems – namely another awakening of the more violent side of Ashura, as well as revealing to Ashura a vision of his mother Shashi, who is now Taishakuten's Empress, when she tried to kill the pointy-eared, golden eyed being as a baby. The same vision also reveals that Ashura had a twin brother. We come to learn that Shashi is the real villain of the story, wanting more power for herself. In comparison, Taishakuten appears to just want stability, albeit he goes to violent methods to achieve it, including some sex scenes which appear to be non-consensual. We also later discover Ashura's twin is Taishakuten's heir to the throne, the more kind-hearted Prince Tennou, a man who is also in love with Kendappa and who comes across as the nicest person in the whole of *RG Veda*. This is most clearly displayed when he confesses his love for Kendappa, but when she tells Tennou that she loves Souma, he takes the rejection well and is totally understanding.

The fifth star is Karura. She is based on Garuda, a bird-like creature from the mythology of several Eastern faiths, and Karura has a bird called Garuda at her side at all times. Karura also rides on larger birds to her own floating palace. Like Yasha and Souma, she too is motivated by revenge and her hatred of Taishakuten. However, rather than her whole tribe being killed, it was just one person: her sister Karyoubinga. Karyoubinga can only live within the grounds of her flying castle home, but her talent for singing made her a target for Taishakuten. Thus, he kidnapped her, took her to Zenmi Palace and forced her to perform, where the air outside of her home resulted in her death. Thus Karura vowed revenge. To prevent the rest of her tribe being killed, Karura fakes her own suicide before joining the main gang of heroes.

However, Karura does not join the others until much later in the story. In the Dark Horse collection, she doesn't appear to them until the end of Book Two (that's part-way through Volume 7 in the original collections). During this time, Yasha is kidnapped and rescued from a demon, Kujaku helps to awaken more of Ashura's destructive powers, and Yasha returns to his homeland to give his tribe a proper burial. When this happens, he encounters Rasetsu (Rakashasa – man-eating beings), his younger brother who had left the tribe some years before. At first Rasetsu fights Yasha and Ashura, blaming them for what has happened to the tribe, but eventually he changes his ways. However, he is soon killed by another of Taishakuten's generals. It is not until after all this, when Yasha and his friends are in another fight helping Rasetsu's widow Shara, that Karura finally joins and helps their cause.

After this, Ashura declares that now is the time to go to Zenmi Palace, for that is where they will find the Sixth Star and begin the final fight. As mentioned, all Sixth Stars are depicted early on in the series in a single image, and the Sixth Star is Kendappa, the court musician who rescued Souma. However, her attitude is different to the other five. She is not interested in overthrowing Taishakuten, believing the Six Stars will fail.

As the Six Stars all unite and the final showdown begins, Ashura's deadly powers become even stronger. Ashura finds Shashi and kills her, removing a gem from her forehead. Placing this gem in the Shura Sword, Ashura awakens into his full adult form, Ashura's true self. The true purpose of Ashura is finally explained: "My wish… is for total and absolute destruction." Ashura wants to completely destroy everything. Thus the story ends with Yasha not only trying to overthrow Taishakuten, but also trying to stop Ashura from obliterating the entire world.

•

As mentioned, *RG Veda* is a manga which has its issues. Aside from the already highlighted topics of the lack of people of colour, despite being based on Hindu mythology, and the fact it is a very loose reworking of the original work, the way the story is structured might put off some readers new to manga. Most manga have separate, clear chapters. *RG Veda* however does not do this, with most of the individual ten volumes being complete, stand-alone chapters themselves. This might be a bit daunting for some readers, but this is nothing new in terms of literature.

You can see it in Western fiction, with authors like Terry Pratchett often not writing in chapters.

The Dark Horse collection also has some odd translations by Haruko Furukawa and Christine Schilling that just don't feel right at times. One example in Book Two is a flashback scene between a young Ryuu and his late mother (who although she is a woman was also King of the Dragon Tribe, rather than Queen), in which Ryuu says: "Mama, you're the awesomest!!" It does feel appropriately childlike, but perhaps also a bit too American for such a work.

There are other areas however where *RG Veda* shines brightly. In fact, there is one area where all the works of CLAMP shine out. The way it looks.

CLAMP's titles are known for the high quality of their artwork. Some manga artists might be well known for the way they draw characters, others for action sequences or perhaps landscapes, but this four-strong unit are able to make all of these.

In *RG Veda*, the fantasy landscapes are always a joy to behold. Whenever a scene is set in a castle of some kind you know you are going to get a great view, and sometimes more than once. In the story about Yasha being kidnapped, he is taken to a castle made of ice. The rest of the gang, with help from Kujaku, are led to this castle which magically appears before their eyes. This results in several double-page spreads of the ice castle appearing before them. These can be found in the Dark Horse collections crossing between Books One and Two.

The character design is also a joy. Often you will come across a page or two where it is just the one character speaking or doing something, and you can get the full detail of the person. In Book Two of Dark Horse's release, on p164, there is a divine face-on drawing of Kendappa as she talks to Karura. Some people not used to manga art may at first be off-put by the largeness of Kendappa's eyes, but this kind of depiction is normal in manga and anime. Even so, as the eyes at first grab your attention, you are then led down to a shapely nose, wonderfully shaded so it casts a small shadow on her face. This nose leads to a small delicate mouth. It is a beautiful depiction of her face.

Also in Book Two, there is a double-page spread on p301-302 of Yasha weeping as he lays his tribe to rest, just before his encounter with Rasetsu. The sight of Yasha with tears rolling down his face as the wind blows through his long hair, his right hand clutching his hair in grief, catches the sadness of the moment dramatically.

Then you get to the action scenes. Many of the best involve Ashura. For example, in the fight against Rasetsu between p350-352, Ashura strikes the ground with the Shura Sword. This causes the ground to quake, swirling winds to form, and lightning bolts to crack as Rasetsu is brought to his knees by a young child.

However, the more violent scenes with the awakened adult Ashura also make for dramatic reading. The slaying of his mother and the ripping out of the jewel is a violent shock to the system, as are all the fights involving the Six Stars as the series reaches its climax. So much blood is spilled, and Ashura ends up adoring the violence he is committing. When it comes to violence, *RG Veda* has plenty of it. It is probably easier to draw up a list of characters who do NOT die in the story.

This ultimately leads to one of the recurring motifs in the work of CLAMP. Near the end of the story there is a fight between Yasha and the violence-craving adult Ashura. During this final battle, Yasha loses the sight in his right eye. The loss of the right eye, or at least the use of it, becomes a recurring element in many CLAMP works. This may be inspired by to the fact that Ohkawa herself has poor vision in this particular eye. As a result, several characters in CLAMP's works end up losing their right eye:

heroes, villains and people in the middle. Some recover, some lose just the vision, and others lose the eyeball completely. In the case of Yasha… well I'm not going to tell you the VERY end of the story here. This chapter has some spoilers but I'm not giving away the entire conclusion. All I will say is that for those who are worried about stereotyping of using disfigured characters as villains, remember this eye loss happens across many different characters, not just baddies, and Yasha is no baddie.

The issue of religion and myth is also one worth highlighting. Many of CLAMP's titles feature religious elements, but it would be wrong to say that their works are outright religious. It is certainly true to say that *RG Veda* has little to do with the stories actually told in the original work, and the fact that CLAMP used translated names makes things more confusing. As well as faith, the issue of fate and destiny is one that is a central focus, as Yasha is destined to raise Ashura, who according to the central prophecy is going to kill him. Characters in the story who are seen to subvert fate are considered sinful.

For CLAMP, many aspects of many different faiths are useful material. We will see this come up again in later series, whether it is to do with exorcisms (*Tokyo Babylon*), the apocalypse (*X*), or angels (*Wish*).

Meanwhile, the notion of fate is something that, while explored more in *Magic Knight Rayearth*, is also covered in *RG Veda*. The entire prophecy which encompasses the Six Stars dictates that Yasha will be killed by Ashura, but one of the recurring themes around CLAMP's work is a rejection of fate and the idea that you yourself can break away from such things no matter what. As to whether they do, you'll have to read the manga yourself.

•

While this book is mainly focused on the original manga versions of the story, it is only right to mention that *RG Veda* was also the subject of an anime adaptation.

This in turn leads me back, in an odd way, to my background in comedy. One of my favourite stand-up moments was by the satirist and political campaigner Mark Thomas in his show *Bravo Figaro*, about his late father and his love of opera. At one point in the show, Mark takes out an object and exclaims dramatically: "For the young people in the audience… this is vinyl," and holds a vinyl record aloft.

This connection with old technology is one I can also express, because in my job as a critic of anime as well as manga, I am interested in finding the more obscure releases. Many anime released in old formats do not make it to the next one. Many anime released on DVD don't make it to Blu-Ray. This is why, should I ever find myself talking about my book live on stage, at a book reading for example, I would hope to pay homage to Thomas, by dramatically taking out a copy of the *RG Veda* anime and exclaiming dramatically: "For the young people in the audience… this is a video cassette! There was a time when after watching any visual entertainment, it was followed by this sound…" and then I would play a recording of my video recorder rewinding.[7]

Regarding *RG Veda*, a two-part OVA was made between 1991-1992, which was released in the UK by Manga Entertainment. Now, you may remember that the *RG Veda* manga ended in 1996, so this clearly is an incomplete adaptation of the story. However, what is weirder is that these two episodes don't adapt the start of it. The anime is located in the middle of the manga, making no sense to anyone who hasn't read the original comic. The anime had other problems too. To quote *The Anime Encyclopedia*: "The production company pretentiously used Sanskrit orthography to write the title, not expecting the English distributors to mistake the opening two letters for initials – it's thus pronounced 'Rig

Veda', not 'Ah Gee Veda'." Thus, the *RG Veda* anime is not one to really worry about if you've not seen it.

In an article by Jonathan Clements, originally published in *SFX Total Anime* in 2007, later reprinted in his book *Schoolgirl Milky Crisis*, he writes that the *RG Veda* anime is one of a series of cheap anime video releases brought to the UK in the hope of finding something as successful as *Akira*, which ended up cheapening anime's reputation in the UK. He wrote: "When exported out of context to the UK, they made no sense. A glut of them gave anime a bad reputation in science fiction circles for boggling plotlines and thin characterisation, often marred still further for starting in the middle of a story and lacking a proper ending. Which is wrong, obviously."

•

By the time *RG Veda* had finished in 1996, CLAMP had firmly made a name for themselves. Perhaps one of the group's outstanding strengths is that they are able to make several different series simultaneously. This is best demonstrated much later on with their series *xxxHOLiC*[8] and *Tsubasa*, which cross-referenced each other constantly. Indeed, many of *RG Veda*'s characters would appear in other CLAMP titles, including *Tsubasa*.

Before that however, CLAMP created many other series, and had successfully built up not just their reputation, but a whole universe of characters and locations. In fact, they were soon able to trade off their name, as the next chapter will demonstrate.

---

1 – This level of anonymity is not too unusual in manga and anime. For example, *Demon Slayer* creator Koyoharu Gotouge only uses they/them pronouns in order to conceal their true

gender, and depicts themselves as a crocodile in their art. However, in a 2020 interview an employee at *Weekly Shonen Jump* disclosed some information and claimed that Gotouge was a woman.

2 – For example, when I review a manga, if I use a picture from inside the comic I would have to display the appropriate copyright information to avoid getting into trouble.

3 – However, the online *Encyclopaedia Britannica* gives the alternative spelling 'Ṛgveda'.

4 – Soma is referenced in another great work of fiction, Aldous Huxley's *Brave New World*, where 'Soma' is a drug used to control the population in his dystopian world. Huxley was also partly inspired by my native Teesside when writing the book, taking inspiration from a chemical works in Billingham. Thus, that's both *Blade Runner* and *Brave New World* we have inspired. Teesside really does a knack of helping people create horrific versions of the future. See also Ray Mallon, a policeman whose zero-tolerance approach to crime earned him the nickname 'RoboCop', who became mayor of Teesside's largest town, Middlesbrough (nicknamed 'Boro'), and installed *Nineteen Eighty-Four*-style talking security cameras in the town. I've also since learned there is a brief moment in the as-yet-released-in-the-UK anime *Dear Brother*, adapted from the never-translated-into-English manga by Riyoko Ikeda, where you see a poster advertising a film called *BoroCop*, which is not only an amazing coincidence, but is also a parody that needs to be made. It would be less of a case of: "Your move, creep," and more: "Owayy, doyle." I want to hear a cyborg cop exclaiming: "Please put down your parmo. You have 20 seconds to comply," and, if you refuse, him then saying: "I am now authorised to use béchamel sauce!"

5 – My personal favourite example of this is used in the horror manga *Attack on Titan*, which features a character called Hange whose gender is never revealed. As the character's first name is 'Zoë', English translations tend to always refer to Hange as female, but in the original manga Hange's gender is never fully disclosed. Indeed, in the comedy spin-off manga *Attack on Titan: Junior High*, which sets all of the characters from the original manga in a school, whenever someone says Hange's gender, black bars appear in the speech bubbles and censor the words that would give Hange's gender away.

6 – It is also one of many examples of anime and manga characters carrying weapons that in real-life would be impractical to use because they are so big.

7 – It is also worth highlighting at this point something called 'Galapagos syndrome'. This is a term used by the Japanese to explain how technology in the country has evolved differently to the rest of the world. For example, the Japanese still regularly use fax machines, while most of the world doesn't bother with them anymore. On the other hand, on mobile phones the Japanese don't use SMS texting, and instead just send emails, mainly because texts were so expensive when the technology came to the country that people didn't bother with it.

8 – Pronounced 'holic', despite the triple-x at the beginning, as we will later cover.

CHAPTER 2

The Pupils in the Pentagram – The CLAMP School Series (1989-1993)

The fact that CLAMP are a group rather than just one or two individuals means that they have the ability to work on multiple series at the same time. Their name has become associated with various different projects in various different styles. Eventually, the group's name would end up being in the titles of two of their manga. It is these two series, *Duklyon: CLAMP School Defenders* and *CLAMP School Detectives*, and an earlier work which established the CLAMP School or CLAMP Campus setting, *Man of Many Faces*, that is the focus of this chapter. The origins of it date back to their self-published works, and there was also a series of light novels set there, *CLAMP School Paranormal Investigators*, but as these were written by someone else with CLAMP mainly providing the art, it falls outside the remit of this book.

These three entertaining works help to show off CLAMP's differing styles. These series are much more family friendly than the violent *RG Veda*, and are more humorous in tone. Again, these were originally published in English by the label TokyoPop, but since the collapse of the company these have since been taken over and are now published (sadly as e-books only) by the giant of the English-language manga market: Viz Media.[1] Viz really are the kings of comic publishing. In 2017, it was revealed that in the USA, their share in the graphic novel and comic book market was 23%. To put that into context, DC Comics had 14% of the market, and Marvel had 10%.

In one of their *CLAMP no Kiseki* interviews, Ohkawa explained how the setting came about:

"Nowadays we all work together on creating a story, but back in our doujinshi days we would each come up with our own stories and characters. One day we created a common setting and had our characters live there, which let all our characters interact with one another's. For example, Igarashi's characters would show up in Nekoi's stories. That common setting was CLAMP Campus. The campus appeared in many of our first stories because we loved it so much, and also because it was easy to use."

The Japanese School System

Before we start talking about these three series, it is worth getting some background knowledge about Japan's education system, in order to familiarise ourselves with the setting.

There are some similarities to the British system: there are nursery schools/kindergartens (shougakkou), then you have the primary schools, which in Japan are elementary schools; and the secondary schools, which in Japan are called 'junior high schools' (chuugakkou). There is a difference in the ages covered however. At elementary level, the ages covered are 6-12, and at junior high 12-15. These are the compulsory years for education. Beyond this are Japan's equivalent of our colleges, the 'senior high schools', covering ages 15-18, and then university.

Like in Britain, Japanese schools have a long summer holiday, and there are two or three school terms. However, while Britain starts the school year in September, in Japan it starts in April. Most schools teach between Monday and Friday, but some also teach on Saturday mornings.

As for what school is actually like, one thing becomes very clear when you enter the school building. In fact, this becomes clear when you enter many buildings in Japan, including people's houses. That thing is this: the Japanese really hate people walking indoors with their shoes on. Shoes are considered incredibly unhygienic and while for many Brits the idea of being told to take off your shoes before coming inside is a prudish one, in Japan it's not just the norm, it's expected.

In most houses, the border between outside and inside is actually beyond the front door. The real boundary is an entrance area called the 'genkan' where you take your shoes off before going any further. The genkan is in a lower area compared to the main floor, and it is in the genkan where your shoes stay. The host of the house provides guests with slippers to walk around in. In schools, the main entrance will include a 'getabako' – cupboards for you to store your street shoes in during the day. Inside the school you wear a special type of slipper called a 'uwabaki'. As for getabako, they often come up in anime and manga stories. One common trope is the leaving of notes or even love letters of the owner of said locker by a mysterious person.

In terms of dress, Japanese school students have school uniform like those in the UK. In recent years these uniforms have become more Western in style, but for many years and still to this day more traditional uniforms are still worn. These are based on military uniforms, with the boys wearing a uniform based on the army, and the girls wearing navy-like sailor suits. It's these sailor uniforms that are referenced in series like *Sailor Moon*.

Most anime series set in schools tend to follow the high school years. For students at this age, the day normally starts at 8.30am with 'homeroom', the equivalent of our forms and tutor groups. The average lesson is around 40-45 minutes, but unlike British students, the vast majority of lessons all take place in the same classroom, which is normally the homeroom shared by the class. The teachers come to the students rather than the other way around, except in some specialist lessons such as home economics, P.E. or science lessons taking place in a lab.

As for lunch, this varies from school to school. Some have cafeterias, but in many schools the students eat in the homeroom. These lunches include the famous delicately-made 'bento' packed lunches, some of which are multi-tier packed lunch boxes full of stuff cooked in advance.

At the end of the school day, it is the custom for students to clean the building. Everything from sweeping the hallways to emptying the rubbish, wiping down blackboards to cleaning the toilets is carried out by the kids.[2]

After this, most schools have a variety of extracurricular activities. Many of these are sporting, which is the subject of many of the popular sports-based anime and manga that are currently available. There are also more scientific or artistic groups. We have previously mentioned that three members of CLAMP were part of their school's astronomical society, but there are societies for just about every kind of activity you can think of, covering art, music, science, or sometimes more unusual things. There are also plenty of manga about odd school clubs.[3] Students not in any of these societies are referred to as being in the 'Going-home Club'. For some of these students, they just have no interest in any of the clubs on offer. For others, they might have a part-time job instead. However, this differs between every school. Some make joining a club compulsory.

Something else that makes Japanese schools differ to those in Britain is the 'student council', which is more familiar to Brits from American schools, but the Japanese councils do more things than their American counterparts. This is partly down to the homeroom system. As every class is almost the same, each class tends to have a representative on the council, elected by the classmates, and the council has a chairperson, secretary, treasurer etc. The council tends to be involved in the running of special events. For example, most schools have a 'cultural festival' where classes and clubs perform activities and invite locals to visit. The council is often the body that keeps this in check. They also keep school clubs in check.

In anime and manga, school councils are often depicted unrealistically. Many comedic examples show councils having massive amounts of power, with some being even more powerful than the teachers themselves. In anime, the council can sometimes be the villain of the story, or the hero. In *CLAMP School Detectives*, the detectives are the council and thus fall into the heroic-but-unrealistic category, mostly. As we see in the first series, one member of the council does some things that are heroic, but also illegal.[4]

Man of Many Faces (1989-1991)

With *RG Veda* currently still going on, CLAMP were then given the chance to make another series in 1989 for the magazine *COMIC GENKi*, published by Kadokawa Shoten. This became the first of the major CLAMP School works, and was released in English as *Man of Many Faces*. The original Japanese title however, which can be seen on the front cover of the original TokyoPop release, was *20 Mensho Ni Onegai!!* This translates as *20 Faces, Please!!* This title is actually the better of the two, primarily because '20 Faces' is the main character's secret identity. However, we shall stick to the English title for the sake of clarity.

This two-volume series marked a very different style of storytelling in comparison to *RG Veda*, it originally being a crime caper but later morphing into a romcom. When asked in one of their *CLAMP no Kiseki* interviews if the mood of *RG Veda* crept into *Man of Many Faces*, Nekoi said: "No, we had a system. We created rules so that we could click!, switch from *RG Veda* to *20 Mensho* without dragging the mood of one series to the other. For example, there were screentones that were restricted to one series." Screentones is the applying of shade or texture to a drawing. Often this will involve creating different size and spacing of dots to make something lighter or darker.

The original Japanese title and indeed the pseudonym of the lead come from Japanese literature, namely from *The Fiend with Twenty Faces*, the title character of a novel by mystery writer Edogawa Rampo, who is an antagonist to his detective hero Kogoro Akechi. The character would reappear in several of Rampo's novels.

•

In *Man of Many Faces*, the original 20 Faces, Shigetoshi Ijyuin, was a master gentleman thief, but he has disappeared we know not where. Now 20 Faces is his son Akira – aged nine. Despite being so young he can seemingly steal things without any trouble whatsoever. He does have some surprising tools in his line of work however, such as escaping by jetpack – which is a bit risky given that he dresses in a full dinner suit with matching overcoat, which one imagines would be susceptible to catching fire from the jetpack's flames.

When it comes to what he steals, it's usually down to the whims of his parents. Akira's father may be absent, but he still lives with two parents. Namely, two mothers. Yes, in 1989 CLAMP made a strip about a 9-year-old boy living with LGBT parents. At least, that's what it looks like on the surface. It's never confirmed if they are lesbians or even if they are a couple (it should be said that polygamy is illegal in Japan), but readers will see what they want, and that's what I like to think is the case. If they are lesbians, then this would be forward thinking now, let alone back then, although the fact that neither of them is given a proper name and that we don't know which of the two is Akira's biological mother, lets it down a bit in terms of fleshing the characters out. In the opening of the first volume Akira says: "I have two mothers. My classmates and neighbours think it's kind of strange, but I don't think it's a big deal. They should be happy for me. I'm lucky enough to have two loving mothers instead of just one." As for the missing father, one recurring thing you will see in CLAMP's works is that there is often one, or sometimes both, parents missing if a child or teenager is the main character in the story.

Of course, what with them constantly forcing their 9-year-old son to steal all kinds of glamorous objects for them, Akira's mothers are not exactly model parents. They are pushy at times and seemingly make Akira do all the housework. The whole family is rather confusing. One of the other characters in the story is Shigetaka Akechi, a doctor at the CLAMP School who we later learn is Akira's uncle. We know this in one scene in the first volume which sees the mothers escape from the police while dressed as bunny girls (for some reason). Akechi meets them and provides them a means to escape: a hang glider shaped like a pterodactyl (for some reason). As they glide away, Akechi says to himself: "Be careful, my sisters-in-law."

Now, it has to be said that I found this remark very confusing when reading it. The first time I read it, I mistakenly thought that both of Akira's mothers were also sisters and some weird incest thing was going on. The fact that there are scenes in which Akira shares a bed with both his mothers made things seem worse. It wasn't until I plotted it all out on a family tree that things became clear.

Anyway, the story...

After one burglary and attempting to escape from the authorities, Akira decides to hide in the bedroom of a 5-year-old girl named Utako Okawa. Utako is very annoyed, not so much by the fact that a burglar has entered her bedroom, but from the fact she is still annoyed that the person she had recently confessed her love to turned her down. This is a good thing, as the person who rejected her was her kindergarten teacher 17 years her senior. The teacher in question turns out to be a character from CLAMP's *Shoten* series, who happens to be gay anyway. Akira and Utako chat and become increasingly close.

As the series progresses, Akira and Utako begin to fall in love with each other. At the same time, Akira continues to make daring thefts, leading to a running battle with a friend of his. Ryusuke Kobayashi is another student at his school who wants to be a police officer and thus is always trying to arrest 20 Faces, unaware of the fact that 20 Faces is Akira. We also see Akira having another job at the CLAMP School: treasurer for the school council, working alongside the chair Nokoru Imonoyama and secretary Suoh Takamura. All three would later become the main characters in *CLAMP School Detectives.*

•

Writing this section, it becomes clear that there are some things that surprise you when you look back at something you had not touched for a while. It had been a long time since I had read *Man of Many Faces*, and there was much I had forgotten about. One of these being the way it changed direction in terms of plot. While it started off being a comedy crime series, the relationship between Akira and Utako eventually became the main focus of the entire series. While it is only a short story, we still see love blossoming, tensions in the relationship, and then a fully fledged romance forming. The last two chapters of the story (there are eleven in total) see Akira and Utako as grown-ups and their love even stronger. The fact that we see an adult Akira also has implications for some later CLAMP titles, as we shall discuss in the chapter on *X*.

In terms of problems, other than ones in which I get confused about non-existent incest, there are some aspects of the translation I am unsure about. The TokyoPop translation by Ikoi Hiroe, which is also the version Viz Media used when they took over the rights to the series and released it digitally, has some dialogue that you suspect is a bit too American. The choice of rude words is obviously meant to avoid causing offense, especially as the series is aimed at children, but I suspect that in the original Japanese, on p79 of Volume 1, Ryusuke doesn't shout at a fleeing 20 Faces: "You dingus! You dirty pukestain!" Similarly, on p101 of Volume 2, when Akira and Utako have had a falling out, I suspect that in Japan Utako did not shout: "20 Faces is a *weenie*!"

The story itself does have some moments in it however that will be of interest to British readers. The final chapter in the first volume sees Akira having to kidnap a cook so that he can make a special cake for his mothers. The cook in question is one who works for the British royal family. The cook clearly enjoys his time with Akira, as he is seen on the final page serving a meal while dressed like 20 Faces, in Akira's trademark top hat, mask and coat. This scene is also one of the few examples of real-life people being depicted in a CLAMP manga, as the scene takes place in the 'royal dining room', where he is serving to a family. The family consist of two small boys, who are presumably Princes William and Harry, and a black-haired gentleman spilling his tea in shock, who just as presumably is Prince Charles. There is also a woman in the picture, but her face is away from us, so we cannot tell exactly who it is. However, given the other people in the picture and the time it was made, it seems most likely that it is Princess Diana rather than the Queen, but we cannot be sure.

As for fans of other manga, readers might be interested to note a similarity between *Man of Many Faces* and *Sailor Moon*. In *Man of Many Faces*, the outfit Akira wears as 20 Faces consists of a tuxedo, top hat and a white eye mask to protect his identity. In *Sailor Moon*, the title character's love interest is a guy who wears a tuxedo, top hat and a white eye mask to protect his identity, who is named Tuxedo Mask. Some non-anime and manga fans might actually recognise him from a famous meme where Tuxedo Mask proclaims: "My job here is done", to which Sailor Moon replies: "But you did nothing", before he vanishes. 20 Faces and Tuxedo Mask have almost identical costumes, but while Tuxedo Mask is the more famous character, 20 Faces had the look first.

Man of Many Faces also features the first example of what would become another trademark of CLAMP: their cross-referencing of other works they have made. On p134 in Volume 1, Utako is watching the news with her family, in the form of a show made for the kids in which the presenters appear to be puppet animals. As Utako watches with her parents and her older sister Mako, there is a report that 20 Faces has stolen a jewel encrusted sword. This sword is called 'RG Veda'. It would appear that the fantasy world created in their first work has some connection with what is meant to be our world.

Man of Many Faces is a fun, brisk read, and we will see more of Akira later in this chapter.

Duklyon: CLAMP School Defenders (1991-93)

Kadokawa Shoten's *COMIC GENKi* released the second CLAMP School title, *Gakuen Tokkei Dukylon*[5], although Western publishers would later make the most of the popularity of the creators by releasing it under the English title *Duklyon: CLAMP School Defenders.*

It is a manga that when they were asked at Anime Expo in 2006 which of their series they found the most enjoyable, the three artists in the group all said that this was the most fun (Ohkawa nominated *Cardcaptor Sakura* instead). Again, comedy is one of the main elements of this series, but in the two-volume long *Duklyon: CLAMP School Defenders* one of the main inspirations was 'tokusatsu'. Meaning 'special filming', this is a form of live-action TV show or film that mainly relies on special effects. The most famous of these is *Godzilla*, but the group's main inspirations were shows from the *Metal Hero* meta series about armour clad heroes protecting the Earth from invaders, which inspired Nekoi and Ohkawa; and the 'sentai' style shows featuring costumed teams of superheroes, the most famous to Westerners being *Power Rangers*, that inspired Mokona and Igarashi. As a result, while the series is almost entirely set in the school, it does have some otherworldly creatures in it, and as it progresses more alien elements appear.

This series is also the first to fully envision the CLAMP School. It features the first full map of the site. The school is shaped like a pentagram when seen from above, has classes covering kindergarten to post-graduates and also has plenty of other features including a hospital, bank, park, zoo, botanical gardens, and a subway.[6] The school's logo depicts a pufferfish.

•

Duklyon follows four main characters: Kentarou Higashikunimaru, Takeshi Shukaido, Kotobuki Sukiyabashi and Eri Chusonji. Kentarou, Takeshi and Kotobuki are all in the same homeroom in the high school branch of the CLAMP School, but for some reason the bespectacled Kotobuki will always disappear. Later, music will suddenly ring out at which point the athletic Kentarou and Takeshi have to make some excuse to their teachers and run to Duklyon, the name of the school's bakery. Inside one of the ovens is a chute that leads to the secret base of Duklyon's real operations.

It is the duty of Duklyon to protect the school from danger. For this, Kentarou and Takeshi wear special armoured suits and rush to the scene of the crime to help out. They do this under the supervision of Eri, the only girl out of the four leads, who spends most of the time hitting the boys with comically oversized mallets in frustration rather than actually helping out the armoured duo. All of Duklyon are told about what is going on and the dangers the school faces from the mysterious Director General, although CLAMP fans will immediately recognise the Director General as Nokoru Imonoyama, head of the CLAMP school elementary council and a relation to the school's chairwoman, but he has managed to cleverly disguise himself by wearing shades and a slightly different uniform. We'll learn more about Nokoru in *CLAMP School Detectives*.

It appears that is all part of the comedy in the series, particularly when you realise who the enemy is. As you might have already guessed, it is Kotobuki, who throughout the series causes several incidents, ranging from the serious, with the first chapter seeing him kidnapping Utako Okawa from *Man of Many Faces*; to the trivial, such as taking over the school cafeteria and eating all the food. Kotobuki wears a large, bulky costume which helps with the disguise, but given that the rest of his disguise consists of taking off his glasses and putting on a bit of face-paint, he seems to have adopted the Clark Kent/Superman school of doing sod all to hide his secret identity, yet somehow still gets away with it. Eri also does nothing to hide her face during the few times she does join the fight. At least Kentarou and Takeshi wear masks when fighting in their armoured suits. Kotobuki frequently summons 'evil beasts' to aid his battle, but Duklyon always come out on top.

There is another strange aspect about these fights that is never really highlighted in the story. Kotobuki says he is working for an evil secret society seeking world domination called: 'The Imonoyama Shopping District Association'. Imonoyama? As in Nokoru Imonoyama, the head of the CLAMP School's elementary council and Duklyon's Director General? We don't know. No connection between the association and Nokoru is ever explicitly stated. What we do know is that 'Imonoyama' is Japanese for, 'a mountain of sweet potatoes', and thus references CLAMP's potato-based typo etymology, while 'shopping district' in Japanese is 'shoten', referencing their early fan works. Anyway, the story…

As the manga progresses, Kotobuki, as his normal self, encounters Eri, and begins to fall in love with her, at first not realising that she is helping out our heroes. However, soon this relationship forms a major part of the story. In fact, it actually becomes the main story, with Kentarou and Takeshi making rather snide remarks about being sidelined and planning to write letters of complaint to CLAMP themselves. Given the shows that influenced the series, we eventually discover that Kotobuki is in fact an alien, and that he is not the only one, as we learn that his love for Eri has consequences for all concerned.

•

Out of the three CLAMP School series, in my personal opinion, this is probably the weakest. While the comedy is fine and the way they play up to some of the more ridiculous aspects of a series like this is entertaining, in particular the failure to recognise who people are despite the fact it's painfully obvious, the fact that the two main heroes get sidelined feels weird. It feels that it would have been better to make the romantic relationship between Kotobuki and Eri the main feature from the start, with Kentarou and Takeshi providing the comic relief.

That is not to say that the comedy is entirely wasted, and indeed the element of not spotting the secret identities is played nicely, in some extreme ways. It is best exemplified in a chapter where Nokoru, as his normal councillor self, decides to organise a school play. His play is a battle between Duklyon and 20 Faces, which he announces with Kentarou, Takeshi and Akira in the room. Not only that, he announces that Kentarou and Takeshi will be playing the Duklyon defenders, and Akira will play 20 Faces. This is particularly interesting because Nokoru knows that Kentarou and Takeshi are really Duklyon, but presumably he does not know that Akira is 20 Faces, and he still gets the casting exactly right. Not only that but when Akira tells his mothers about the play, his mothers immediately decide that they want Akira to steal Duklyon. It is thus in this scene where we see CLAMPs fondness for crossovers at their highest point so far, with all three CLAMP School series blending together in the same chapter.

However, this is not the only example of cross referencing. Again, *RG Veda* also crops up near the end of the second volume, with Kentarou and Takeshi being summoned once more and having to make an excuse to their teacher. A teacher who just happens to look rather like Yasha.

Of the three CLAMP School series, *Duklyon* is the one that is most referenced by CLAMP in later works, with 'Duklyon' becoming the name of a fast food chain with multiple branches, which is frequented by many characters across the CLAMPverse.

CLAMP School Detectives (1992-1993)

Again published by Kadokawa Shoten, but this time in various magazines, first in *Monthly Asuka* and then *Mystery DX*, the three-volume long *CLAMP School Detectives* is another series that references Edogawa Rampo and his crime novels, and would become the series where CLAMP became such a big name that they could intentionally mention themselves in their own titles, rather than English-language publishers crowbarring the name in. Rampo, the man who created the original 20 Faces also gave his heroic detective Kogoro Akechi some help in the form of the 'Boy Detectives Club', a kind of Japanese version of Sherlock Holmes' Baker Street Irregulars. This is one of the inspirations behind CLAMP's detectives, albeit 20 Faces turned out to be one of the detectives in the end. Each of the main age groups has their own school council, with this series following the elementary school council. Most of the other councils don't appear in the story, although we do see Utako Okawa working for the kindergarten school council.

•

The elementary council of the CLAMP School is made up of three members who we have already touched on. One is Akira Ijyuin, aka 20 Faces the gentleman thief, who is the treasurer. However, he is not seen getting up to any thieving in this series, and his persona of 20 Faces is only briefly mentioned, with only Akira knowing that this shady figure is himself. The other members are the secretary Suoh Takamura; and the chair of the council, as well as the leading character in this series, Nokoru Imonoyama.

Nokoru, as well as being *Duklyon*'s Director General, is incredibly intelligent and from a highly regarded 'zaibatsu' – a powerful conglomerate, and while he is rightly the brains of the entire council operation, there is also a lot of comedy from him due to his reluctance to get on with his council duties, causing paperwork to mount in gigantic piles. Suoh is the one who has to keep him on track. Suoh is also the muscle in the group, being brilliant at sports and martial arts, and descending from a family of ninjas. Akira meanwhile is the person that both Nokoru and

Suoh can act off from, as well as the guy who keeps the council's finances in order – perhaps not the best job to give him, seeing as how his sideline is stealing stuff.

The series begins with the council scouting for a place to host the school's Christmas party. They decide to travel via airship to one prime location: Tokyo Tower, the Japanese version of the Eiffel Tower, which is also a location of many other key scenes in CLAMP works as we shall later discover. While in their airship, Nokoru sees someone from the tower's main observation deck – an old woman crying. The boys thus decide to help her out, and upon visiting her, they realise just how much danger she is in, as they are attacked by a smartly-dressed gang. The boys fight them off and afterwards talk to the woman in her own home. They learn that her brother-in-law wants to kick her out of her house so that he can sell it and keep the money for himself. Nokoru decides that they must help this woman out, partly because he hates to see women being mistreated. To quote a caption from the manga: "They're feminists. Who'd have guessed?"[7]

The council are able to help the old woman, due to them managing to stop her brother-in-law's plans using a combination of Nokoru's massive wealth and a decent amount of disruption – i.e. buying the brother-in-law's office, filling it with every exotic animal you can think of, and then giving the brother-in-law his office back. How does it work? When the office is first sold, the brother-in-law signs a contract, and by getting the office back he breaks said contract, resulting in a hefty penalty. Part of this money goes to the old woman so that she can use it to secure the rights to her home.

Following this, Nokoru is then given a challenge by his mother, the chairwoman of the entire school whose face is never fully shown. She tasks him to find a stolen roster, which we later learn is on a specially designed 'microdisk' – a 1cm by 1cm floppy disk.[8] This, like most of the other cases in the series, follows a pattern of a mysterious incident which turns out to have a rather innocent explanation. While the first task involves a scurrilous individual, the thief in this story turns out to be a bird that took the disk as material to build a nest with. After recovering the disc, Nokoru decides to set up the CLAMP School Detective Agency, with all three of the boys coming to the aid of women who are in trouble.

As mentioned, most of the stories are fairly innocent. The cases the trio are involved with include helping someone find their missing pet peacock, solving a mysterious case of a ghost haunting the school, and unravelling a problem involving an odd smelling stocking.

•

Again, most of the strong points in this series are from the comedy. This primarily comes from Nokoru and his willingness to help any lady in trouble, which, while chivalrous, does also feel like a way for him to put off his massive backlog of paperwork. Suoh is frequently frustrated by this and is constantly having to force Nokoru to get his actual work done. Comedy also comes from the way that many of the girls in the school react when seeing the council. Nokoru, Suoh and Akira are all seen as heartthrobs by the girls. One scene sees the boys on Valentine's Day being given ridiculously enormous piles of chocolate from admirers.[9]

The mysteries that the group have to solve are also amusing, given that most of them are rather trivial in comparison to what happens in most crime stories. In a way, some of the bizarre nature of the tasks might ring bells to British readers. For example, rather than having these ladies coming to the boys to solve their problems, imagine if a 6 foot 2 inch bearded comedian, who is constantly described as 'little', presented the detectives to these ladies, then gave them a card sealed with wax that had the letters 'TM' on it, and upon opening the card they read aloud the phrase: "Find this lady's pet peacock. Fastest wins. Your time stars now." It looks like CLAMP invented *Taskmaster* about 20 years before Little Alex Horne did.

On the downside, there are once again issues to be highlighted with the English translation, this time done by Ray Yoshimoto. The most troublesome of which is a problem for us Brits, rather than for the Americans who translated it. In the third volume on p93, in a chapter which is a flashback telling the origins of Nokoru and Souh's relationship, some girls are talking about Souh. They say: "He's quiet and antisocial, but he's got a secret charm! Second graders are usually spastic, but he's cool and connected!"

Now, I obviously can't speak for everyone, as everyone takes the issue of language differently, but personally, as someone with Asperger's syndrome and thus is disabled, I wish to say this to any Americans who might be reading this: Please stop using the word 'spastic' to mean clumsy! Do you have any idea how offensive that word is over here? You wouldn't have someone going around saying: "Yeah, he's so cool. I mean, he's a bit of a mong, but still cute." Seriously, stop it!

CLAMP's art is also a joy to view in this collection, with the original TokyoPop releases having fold-out colour posters in each of three volumes. There are some more questionable drawings however. The title page of the third chapter in Volume 1 sees the trio dressed in very militaristic, almost Nazi-like uniforms. At the opening of Chapter 5 in Volume 2, the opening illustration is of the boys saluting a picture of a 'maneki-neko' – a beckoning cat with an upright paw. The boys salute this with their hands also upright. This is a problem because with their arms out upright, it does look like all three of them are actually doing a stiff-armed Nazi salute. Not only that, the way the beckoning cat is drawn has sunrays shining out of it, like the Rising Sun Flag used by the Japanese during World War II. The drawing in the manga is in black-and-white, which is a good thing because if you look at the colour covers, you can spot that the lead character, Nokoru, is blond with blue eyes. Somehow CLAMP created the most accidentally Aryan/fascist picture they possibly could. It is probably the most problematic thing CLAMP have drawn, although due to my disability, the use of 'spaz' is still what I find more offensive.

Out of the three CLAMP School series, *CLAMP School Detectives* is the most successful. This is most clearly demonstrated by the fact it is the only one of three to have been given an anime adaptation, first broadcast on TV Tokyo in 1997, which is notable for the fact that other manga by CLAMP that were released later got anime adaptations sooner, with the anime version of *Magic Knight Rayearth* debuting in 1994. The *CLAMP School Detectives* anime is actually longer than the original manga, consisting of 26 episodes in comparison to the manga's 12 chapters, and thus the anime contains its own original stories. They also feature Akira appearing as 20 Faces, the team from *Duklyon*, and an appearance from a character we have yet to come across in this book, Miyuki from *Miyuki-chan in Wonderland*, but more on her role in this anime later. The anime is fun and entertaining in its own right, and is worth a watch.

However, the series has never been given a DVD release in the UK, and thus you can only watch a Region 1 release on a hacked DVD player. Alternatively, you can do what I did, embrace old technology and scout it out on VHS. The entire series was released as eight-volume VHS box set, because it turns out box sets are older than most people would have you believe.

•

The CLAMP School titles are an intriguing collection of series. They share several elements aside from the same setting and the regular sharing of characters: they are child friendly, often comedic, and repeatedly deal with subjects like uniting to solve problems. Akira and Utako overcome various problems to unite in love. Duklyon unite to fight against threats to take over the world, and in the end of that series there is also another loving connection. Akira, Suoh and Nokoru team up to help any women who find themselves in trouble.

It is also in this collection we see CLAMP becoming more established as a force. The fact that they are able to include so many characters from their various series shows how much they are building their CLAMPverse. It is also not the last time we will see these characters, or indeed the CLAMP School, as that too appears in later works.

But what is also remarkable is the fact they could keep these series going while still working on other titles. Remember, all three CLAMP School series were still outlived by *RG Veda*, which did not finish until 1996. Not only that, but they were still working on more manga titles at the same times as these.

One of these series is the subject of the next chapter. Its darker tone stands in stark contrast to the fun, light-hearted tales told in the CLAMP School. It is a series that features romance, but of a different kind. It is also about family and tragedy. It features not only my favourite of all of CLAMP's characters, but I would argue the coolest-looking manga character of all. It is also a series that whenever I read the title, a tiny part of me has to constantly try to avoid saying it in a dodgy Rastafari accent.

---

1 – Viz Media being a company based in San Francisco that was established in July 1986, coincidentally the month in which I happened to be born in, is not to be confused with *Viz*, the adult

British comic book established in December 1979. Mind you, I'd be more than happy to see some crossover between the two. I can easily imagine Sid the Sexist getting into hentai, or Roger Mellie: The Man On The Telly giving a foul-mouthed live report of an attack on Tokyo by Godzilla. The March 2022 issue of *Viz* (No. 313) did feature 'nyotaimori', the practice of eating sushi off a naked woman, albeit here being practised by The Fat Slags, with San covering herself with items from their local fish and chip shop. To quote the strip: "I'm glad they've cooled down a bit… they were fresh out the fryer an' the first lot burnt me tits." It should be stated that Viz Media also published *Toriko*, *Rurouni Kenshin* and *Act-Age*, which you may remember from the introduction are series created by people who committed child sex offenses, so reading anything from Viz may be problematic for people (at least the BBC has stopped hiring paedophiles – so far as we know).

2 – Something that would never happen in the UK because a) you would never trust British students to do the cleaning at all, let alone properly, and b) you would most likely end up with a national strike of school caretakers.

3 – Personal favourite examples of odd school clubs in anime and manga include the following: from *The Melancholy of Haruhi Suzumiya* there is the 'Save the world by Overloading it with fun Haruhi Suzumiya Brigade' or 'SOS Brigade', which the title character sets up to investigate paranormal activity. An even odder club appears in the romcom *Love, Chunibyo & Other Delusions*. A 'chunibyo' ('middle school syndrome') is a disorder where a kid spends all their time creating their own fantasy world and even believing they have some kind of magical power. The 'chunibyo' character in the story and various other friends combine with other small groups in order to create their own new club, 'The

Far-East Magical Napping Society – Summer Thereof'. One of my favourite anime and manga series is the romcom *Ouran High School Host Club*, which features a club of boys who spend their time entertaining the girls at their school, and whose central figure is a girl who is dragged into it and has to pretend to be a boy.

4 – In terms of which system is better, all I will say is this: Any school would have been better to one I went to. The five years I spent at Our Lady and St. Bede's Roman Catholic Comprehensive in Stockton-on-Tees, now Our Lady and St. Bede's Catholic Academy, were the most miserable of my life so far. The thing I remember most vividly was the time some pro-life campaigners came to my R.E. class and presented us a slideshow full of pictures of aborted foetuses. The slideshow certainly had an effect on me, and it is mainly due to that slideshow that I am pro-choice. Seriously, fuck that place.

5 – Pronounced 'Duke-lee-ohn'.

6 – And you thought Eton was decadent.

7 – Well, you would hope they would be, what with them being the heroes of the story and written by women. If anything, you'd expect them to be feminists. Having said that, listening to the ladies behind *CLAMPcast in Wonderland*, the boys are much more akin to chivalrous than feminist, but simply describing the characters as feminist was a positive step forward.

8 – Which instantly dates the story. These days, nothing dates something more badly than technology, and a sight of a floppy disc does just that. In 2016, the manga artist Lynn Okamoto, most famous as the creator of the sci-fi horror series *Elfen Lied*, said he would stop adding mobile phones in his works, on the

grounds that phone technology progresses so quickly that they would also date a story badly. For more technological mishaps, see CLAMP's *Cardcaptor Sakura: Clear Card* and *Drug and Drop.*

9 – To explain, in Japan and South Korea the tradition on Valentine's Day is the girls give milk chocolates to the boys that they like. Most of the time this is shop bought stuff, but sometimes girls make their own chocolates if it is for someone special. This is followed up by White Day on 14th March, where the boys give white chocolates back to the girls. In South Korea, they go a stage further by holding Black Day on 14th April. If you haven't given or received any chocolates on Valentine's Day or White Day, then you have to go out in public and 'mourn' your loneliness by eating noodles in a black sauce.

CHAPTER 3

Dedicated Follower of My Sister's Fashion – *Tokyo Babylon* (1990-1993)

The fact that CLAMP were able to write *RG Veda* and *Man of Many Faces* at the same time is an achievement. The fact they were able to add a third series, *Tokyo Babylon* (subtitle: *A Save Tokyo City Story*), also at the same time, shows just how competent and talented they were.

Tokyo Babylon was published in Shinshokan's quarterly *South* magazine. The series showed that they were able to make another change in direction. While it primarily features the supernatural and fantasy elements that appear in *RG Veda*, the setting of modern-day Tokyo brings in new storylines. This came in the form of social commentary. In the *CLAMP no Kiseki* interviews Ohkawa said:

*"For a while I did consider writing a cute story but, because South is a quarterly magazine, one chapter gets a lot of pages, which led me to the decision to focus it on society-based issues. Also, I was young, so I had a lot of doubts and concerns aimed at society. *laughs* I decided that instead of having it all be occult, we would rather introduce a sense of realism to it."*

The quarterly nature of the magazine means that most of the chapters or 'Vol.' as they are styled, are stand-alone stories, written between the summer of 1990 and the winter of 1993. They spanned seven tankobon volumes published between 1991 and 1994. Again, they were eventually released in English by

TokyoPop, between 2004 and 2005, but when the company had their troubles, the series was picked up by Dark Horse. Like with *RG Veda*, they re-released the series in larger editions, this time in just two books, each one containing three-and-a-half of the standard tankobon. However, these are not available digitally. Also, the TokyoPop versions included things that the Dark Horse collections left out, like fold-out posters.

As for CLAMP themselves, they had now moved to Tokyo, namely to the busy district of Ikebukuro.[1] The fact that CLAMP decided to cover more real-life issues in this series was rather apt given what was going to happen to Japan. While the series started in 1990, the following year, which witnessed the first tankobon volume, marked the start of what some call the 'Lost Decade', and what others would even claim to be the 'Lost 20 Years' and even the 'Lost 30 Years', a long period of economic troubles for the entire country. With people feeling the effects at the time, and still feeling it today, perhaps it is no surprise that CLAMP decided to cover something that hit home. Actual news events became inspirations for stories.

However, on top of the discussion of topical events is an added layer of mysticism. As mentioned before, religion is never far away from CLAMP's works, and in the case of *Tokyo Babylon*, religious aspects form the background of the three main characters. The 'Babylon' in the manga's title is a reference to Babylon as depicted in the Bible, because to quote Ohkawa in the same interview mentioned earlier: "I feel that the Bible's Babylon suffered a similar fate to that of Tokyo now."[2] Tokyo Tower is meanwhile meant to symbolise the Tower of Babel in the Bible, and reference some of humanity's folly.

There is also the subject of fashion. While it does not form a major part of the plot, the look of the characters is one of the most striking things about *Tokyo Babylon*. Take for example the front cover of the first volume. If you go for either the original

Japanese cover, as displayed on TokyoPop release, or the re-edited version of the same drawing on the Dark Horse first book, what you see is the lead character: Subaru Sumeragi. He is seen in a red military-style uniform with a black cape, with brass plaques with the year 1991 inscribed on them adorning his peaked cap, his chest, and what we learn to be his trademark gloves. His left arm casually props up a globe, but the only country displayed on it is Japan. It is just so striking, as are so many of the clothes he and the other central characters appear in.[3]

Tokyo Babylon (1990-1993)

While one panel briefly mentions that 16-year-old Subaru Sumeragi is a high school student at the CLAMP School, he mainly works as an onmyoji. These people are specialists in magic, which in the West tend to get lumped in with exorcists, and the Sumeragi clan have served Japan's Emperors for centuries. Subaru is the (for us Westerners, unlucky) 13th head of the clan, and he finds himself having to deal with all kinds of spirits that haunt various places and other supernatural phenomena.

Subaru lives in the Shinjuku area of Tokyo.[4] He lives with his ever-so-slightly older twin sister Hokuto, the only person who outdoes Subaru in the over-the-top fashion stakes. The first time we see Subaru in the actual manga, he is wearing what is probably his most famous outfit, consisting of black shirt, black trousers, black shoes, a red jacket, a black boater with red trimming, and a black pair of his important gloves.[5] Subaru is under strict instructions to never expose his hands, even to Hokuto, and thus he is shown wearing gloves at all times. He even goes to bed wearing them (and polka dot pyjamas). Thus Hokuto, who makes all of Subaru's outfits, has to co-ordinate around the gloves. Hokuto meanwhile can be far more outlandish with her outfits. The first time we see her, she is dressed like a flower with large petals coming out from all over her top, and also her high-heeled shoes have petals. Only her legs, in dark tights, do not have these petals.

The other person in Subaru's life is 25-year-old Seishiro Sakurazuka. He works as a vet specialising in critical care, providing life-saving treatments for animals on the verge of death. All three hang around Seishiro's veterinary practice. However, like Seishiro, he too is an onmyoji, the heir of the Sakurazukamori clan, working in the shadows as an assassin as opposed to Subaru's more open work. However, Seishiro denies all this and says he is just a vet. As to why they are together, Subaru and Seishiro have another connection other than their occult backgrounds – they are a gay couple, with Subaru first encountering Seishiro at a train station.[6] Hokuto however has made it painfully clear to Seishiro that if he brings misery to her brother, she will kill him.

As to the mystery of Subaru's gloves, that dates back to an incident seven years earlier when Subaru was just nine, as told in various flashbacks throughout the story, which in manga are generally highlighted by the use of black pages rather than white. When we first see this flashback in Vol. 1.5, the young Subaru encounters a mysterious male figure under a cherry blossom tree. Cherry blossom trees are a big part of Japanese culture, with the blossoming of the trees marking the arrival of spring. It is the custom to enjoy the blossoming, known as 'hanami', every year, with people picnicking under the blossoms as they come into season. Whenever a cherry tree pops up in a CLAMP manga, something big normally happens, and indeed the word 'Sakura' as in Seishiro Sakurazuka and *Cardcaptor Sakura*, is the word for cherry blossoms.

As Subaru's memory is hazy, the figure's eyes are obscured by hair and shadow. The figure tells Subaru that the reason why the cherry blossoms are their beautiful pink colour is because under every tree is a corpse, and the trees drink the blood of those corpses.[7] The figure cuts a deal with Subaru, but a gust of wind makes it impossible for Subaru to hear what the deal is. The figure ends by saying that for now, he will let Subaru go. Although Subaru is unsure as to whom this figure is, it is heavily hinted throughout the story that the figure was a young Seishiro. As to what the meeting was about, we will come to that later.

Subaru's cases frequently deal with real world issues, albeit with him solving them using his supernatural abilities. Among the stories in *Tokyo Babylon*, we see Subaru and his friends dealing with subjects like rape, victim blaming, massively expensive phone party lines, a frustrated mother of a murdered child who is angered that the killer was not convicted due to him being ruled insane, bullying, religious cults/new religions, ageism, a foreigner working in Tokyo without a visa, extramarital affairs, organ donation, and disability.

In the opening chapter, Hokuto talks about the environment, saying that she knows that products she uses to make herself look good, like her can of hair mousse, contain Freon that damages the ozone layer. However, there is no point in her not using it because she knows someone else will use it. Subaru criticises his sister for her dangerous way of thinking, while Seishiro brings up the subject of the Chernobyl disaster, which had happened only four years earlier. This leads to one of Seishiro's darker comments. He says he loves Tokyo because: "Where else on Earth do so many people enjoy their descent into destruction?"

As the story moves along, we see more of the differences between Subaru and Seishiro's outlooks on life. Subaru is deeply involved with the well-being of his clients. He tends to care more about other people than himself. Seishiro meanwhile is more pragmatic, and he seems to have little care for anyone else. We begin to see Seishiro's powers as the manga develops, with him summoning the spirit of a bird of prey to use in his work in assassination.

The tension in the relationship builds up dramatically in the organ donation storyline. Subaru becomes friends with a boy, Yuya, who has renal failure and thus has to regularly use a dialysis machine. Yuya also had a sister who died from the same condition, despite their mother donating one of her kidneys to try and save her. Seishiro comments that organ donation (at the time the manga came out at least) is rare in Japan, hence why Yuya is on dialysis. This comment is made just after an incident where Yuya's mother has barged into the room of a man who has just been pronounced brain dead, with her demanding that one of his kidneys should be removed and given to her son (she obviously cannot donate her own last kidney).

Later, Subaru decides to donate one of his own kidneys, but soon after deciding this, Yuya's condition becomes much worse and he needs emergency treatment. Subaru meets the mother, where in a state of desperation she takes a knife and tries to take one of Subaru's kidneys by force. Before she can stab Subaru however, Hokuto and Seishiro arrive at the scene, and it is Seishiro who is instead stabbed… in his right eye. As a result of this, Seishiro, like Yasha in *RG Veda*, loses his eye.

This incident among others ultimately leads to the full revealing of Subaru's flashback. Now, I know this book has a fair amount of spoilers, and I try to avoid them as best as I can. However, due to Subaru and Seishiro also being major characters in CLAMP's next title, *X*, this needs to be revealed in order to make their relationship in *X* make sense. As a result of this, all spoilers will be written in mirror writing.

Anyway, the story…

Seishiro places a spell over Subaru and reveals that it was him that they first met when he was nine by the cherry blossom tree, and that Seishiro is the reason why parts of Subaru's recollection of the event are hazy as he wiped away part of Subaru's memory.

The reason is this: Subaru had witnessed Seishiro commit one of his assassinations. Normally, it is the rule of his clan, of which he is in fact the only member as it is the tradition that the new clan head must kill their master (in his case his own mother), to also kill any witnesses to an assassination, but Seishiro spared Subaru. He decided to mark Subaru so that they would meet again. The marks were a pair of five-pointed stars, symbols used by one particular 10th century onmyoji, Abe no Seimei. These marks are the reason why Subaru has to wear gloves, as when his grandmother, the previous master of Subaru's clan, discovered them she had to hide the mark from everyone else.

Seishiro also reveals the subject of the deal that Subaru could not hear or remember. When Seishiro met Subaru again at the station, they would live together for a year, and Seishiro would try his hardest to love him. If he considers Subaru to be different from everyone else he has encountered, he will spare him. If Seishiro considers Subaru not to be special, he will kill him. Seishiro feels nothing. He starts to torture Subaru and breaks one of his arms, but Subaru's grandmother breaks the spell. He is saved, but left in a state of shock, rendering Subaru immobile. In this state, Subaru has a dream in which he is shocked back into life. In this dream, one that is tragically true, Hokuto confronts Seishiro. Seishiro, in turn, murders Hokuto. Upon waking up and learning that his twin sister has really been killed, Subaru quits school and begins a mission to track down the man he loved and to get his revenge against his sister's killer.

•

There is much to unpack with *Tokyo Babylon*. Indeed, fans have been discussing what it is about for over 25 years. Let's start with the social aspect. The topics that CLAMP chose to cover are things that are still of concern today. There are certain topics highlighted that you can argue could give pause for thought about today's problems. For example, take the issue of the environment, where Hokuto says that she is happy to use polluting products because she knows that even if she doesn't someone else will. To me, writing this during the Coronavirus, it brings up memories of when, during the lockdown, Dominic Cummings drove all the way from London to Barnard Castle, a town that is around 30 miles from where I live in Stockton, at a time when my granddad could not travel about five miles to see me. At the time many people thought: 'If he can break the rules, why can't I?' It's the same mentality. If someone else is breaking the rules, you might as well. Why feel guilty about it even though it might cause the deaths of hundreds of people?

Similarly, the story of the woman being angered that the killer of her son could not be convicted due to him being ruled insane, raises the issue of the recent arson attack on Kyoto Animation. The chief suspect involved in the case has previously suffered from a mental illness, which may result in him avoiding the death penalty. Now, I personally am against the death penalty, but I can understand how the families of the victims or those who survived the disaster would be angered by this.

At the time of the manga's publication, CLAMP attracted plenty of attention for *Tokyo Babylon*, relating as it did to real people. The story about the kidney transplant came out at a time in Japan when there was a scandal about someone accepting an organ donation from a patient who was brain dead, which Ohkawa said in the *CLAMP no Kiseki* interviews, "…was a complicated matter," at the time.

CLAMP also received letters from readers during the time of *Tokyo Babylon*'s publication regarding one chapter that concerned a bullied schoolgirl who joins a cult, but the one chapter that got the most letters was about an elderly man who learns that his daughter considers him a burden on the family. Elderly readers wrote to CLAMP about the story, although Ohkawa also said: "People would write to us saying things like, 'your story says that, but isn't it actually like this...?' They would explore and share their opinions with us."

For me personally, the story that hits home the most is one in which after Seishiro loses his eye, Subaru encounters a blind man, who Subaru helps after some kids mess around with the man's guide dog. When they talk, the blind man says that: "Sadly, Japan is not the best place to be disabled." (Book Two, p415). As someone who has had their disability benefits stopped, part of me also thinks: 'Things are not exactly brilliant for us disabled Brits either.'

All of this brings up a point that is worth clarifying. Just because I like anime and manga, that doesn't mean that I like everything in Japan or want to import everything from there into Britain. I already mentioned that I am against their use of the death penalty.[8] I'm against their policy towards whaling. I strongly disapprove of Japanese nationalists who refuse to apologise for what the country did wrong during World War II. While in many ways their attitude towards gay people was more progressive than that of the UK for many years and is more progressive than most countries in the Far East, today it falls behind the UK as Japan does not recognise same-sex marriage. Neither country is exactly great when it comes to transgender rights, with the British media, including the BBC, happily giving better treatment to TERFs than it does to transpeople; while in Japan, if you want to be legally recognised under a new gender, then by law you have to be sterilised. Obviously, I imagine there are parts of British culture that the Japanese would not take kindly to either. You can't imagine a Japanese Anglophile saying: "I really wish our train system was more like that of the UK." It is hard to see a Japanese Anglophile admiring our football fans. If the England and Japan men's teams play each other, you would expect to see stereotypical images of England fans trashing the stadium and committing acts of racism, while the Japanese fans are politely tidying up the mess the English made. Anyway, by learning more about other cultures and attitudes perhaps we can all make more progress in creating fairer, more understanding societies.

These social stories relate to one of the key themes of *Tokyo Babylon*: the differing philosophies of Subaru and Seishiro. The main issues brought up by critics are those of individualism and empathy. Subaru comes across as the embodiment of selflessness, caring about everyone else more than himself, often to his own detriment. While it is good that he helps so many people, his actions often have unforeseen repercussions. His choice to help save Yuya ultimately results in Seishiro losing his eye. However, these tragedies ultimately help Subaru develop his own sense of self.

In a round-table discussion for the US website *Manga Bookshelf* in July 2012, editor Melinda J. Beasi writes in great detail about the nuance that CLAMP gave to Subaru. It is worth quoting an entire paragraph regarding this:

"*One personal philosophy that is stated over and over again in this series (expressed by both Subaru and Hokuto at various times) is that no person can ever truly understand another person's pain. Most often this idea is used to explain a lack of judgement made regarding other people's choices and decisions and a respect for their uniquely painful circumstances. But while this philosophy seems on the surface to be a grand acknowledgement of individuality, Subaru takes it so much to heart that he not only refuses to make his mark on anyone else, he also resists becoming a fully realized individual himself, as though even that might be an affront to others. He lets other people dictate his movements, his feelings, his personal appearance – he is deliberately a non-entity. And while someone else as spiritually powerful as he is might do these things deliberately to facilitate deception, Subaru does this to avoid being an influence on anyone else. Once I realized that this was what he was doing, I could see it everywhere – along with Hokuto's need to find a way to get him to rebel against it, even if it meant becoming involved with someone dangerous."*

Others have commented on the problems of Subaru being so empathic with others. In June 2019, Celeste Seifert wrote a feature entitled: 'Subaru Sumeragi and the dark side of total empathy in *Tokyo Babylon*' for the website *Anime Feminist*. She comments on both the positives and negatives on Subaru's empathy for others. The greatest sign of Subaru's misplaced empathy is displayed in his relationship with Seishiro, who ultimately brings Subaru the greatest harm. Seifert wrote: "Despite the many hints that Seishiro is not all he seems, I thought Subaru's empathy, selflessness, and capability to see good in people would win in the end. That might be how other stories end, but not Subaru's."

If Subaru is the ultimate in selflessness, then Seishiro is the ultimate in selfishness. Seishiro himself says he is selfish. He has no emotion when it comes to anyone else and is utterly cold-hearted to everyone around him. Some of the best scenes in *Tokyo Babylon* are moments of dramatic irony when we the reader learn more about his malevolent nature. When we witness the scenes in which he reveals all to Subaru, Seishiro is completely without feelings towards the man he claimed to have loved. There is a part of me that finds the character darkly appealing in his ruthlessness. When it comes to villains, for me the best ones are the silent, stealthy, unassuming types.[9]

While both characters are appealing in different ways, strangely, despite my Asperger's, a condition that is associated with people lacking empathy towards others, I still find Subaru the more appealing of the two. I am still more interested in the person who has some empathy rather than none at all. Who wouldn't be?

Anyone would want to associate themselves with the more caring person. At least that's what I want to say, when deep down I really do find the appalling Seishiro the more interesting person. Sorry, I like the villain more. Out of the two, I mostly like the one that Robin Kaplan at *CLAMPcast in Wonderland* describes as: "the murder pervert".

His lack of empathy is part of Seishiro's appeal. The fact that he is so cold and heartless makes him a more interesting villain, while also avoiding many of the stereotypical tropes, and CLAMP take care when writing about him. While Seishiro is only interested in killing, he is never described as psychopathic or sociopathic. He is selfish and mostly emotionless, but it is wrong to describe him as *completely* emotionless. He is often seen smiling when he is killing as it is the one thing he enjoys. This is the one thing that gives him purpose. To quote the *CLAMPcast in Wonderland* podcast: "…he can be the worst asshole in CLAMPverse and still have so many, like, specific personal fans."[10]

There is also the topic of the romantic, gay relationship between Subaru and Seishiro. There is the fact that Subaru slowly tries to come to terms with whether or not he loves Seishiro, with Hokuto toying with both guys. However, there are several bigger issues, one of which being the nine-year age gap between the two men, particularly as one of them is just sixteen. The other is the dramatic irony that we the reader know that Seishiro is a violent, horrific person, which Subaru doesn't. At first, you may object to the whole age gap, and rightly so, but I'd argue that the Seishiro murdering people is probably worse.

The sexuality in *Tokyo Babylon* is commented on by Kim Senior, lecturer at RMIT University, Melbourne, Australia, in her essay: 'Countless Intermediaries Between Reality and Symbols: Getting Fucked and Fucking Over', part of 'Queering the Quotation: Yaoi, Narrative Pleasures and Reader Response' by herself and Mark Vicars of Victoria University, Melbourne, as published in the book *Boys' Love Manga: Essays on the Sexual Ambiguity and Cross-Cultural Fandom of the Genre*, edited by Antonia Levi, Mark McHarry and Dru Pagliassotti (2010, McFarland & Company). She writes on p204:

"The unexplained and unquestioned presence of homosexual and transgender relationships in CLAMP's Tokyo Babylon *spoke to playfulness and possibility. The transgressive act of these women authors, creating and appropriating space in the male dominated manga industry took me back to the cold Canberra rugby fields and the nerdy girl hiding in the library. The graphic sexual images in yaoi shock the nerdy girl, but they fascinate the straight woman. How had performing wife, mother and researcher taken me back to that library? When had manga reading for my pleasure been taken from me? When, and why, had I* allowed *it to be taken from me? When did getting fucked become getting fucked over?"*

One of the other elements of *Tokyo Babylon* that stands out is the artwork, and as mentioned before, I adore the costumes given to the main characters. The Dark Horse books bring these outfits to life with the special colour pictures that are displayed in both of their releases. Below is list of my personal favourites:

- Hokuto in a heart-themed outfit. It includes a large pair of red-heart earrings, a pink top with a heart-shaped keyhole, a heart belt-buckle, and heart-shaped buckles on her pink high-heeled shoes. She sits on a red, heart-shaped cushion and has a pair of purple feather boas also.

- Subaru in a lilac suit, with matching tie, boater and gloves. The picture is of him as he has dived into water, and he is thus surrounded by bubbles and fish.

- An Alice in Wonderland-inspired set, with Subaru as the Mad Hatter in a pink suit, Seishiro as the White Rabbit with an oversized pocket watch, and Hokuto in a blue outfit which has her wearing an enormous blue bow on her head. I assume she is meant to be Alice, but it is hard to tell.

- Subaru and Seishiro in more religious, Christian-themed outfits, both wearing crosses and with one large cross slung over Seishiro's shoulder as Subaru lays on the ground. Subaru is in white while Seishiro is in black, and is also displaying a grey, sightless right eye.

The outfits in *Tokyo Babylon* still inspire fashion today. In April 2021, the magazine *SPUR* featured a fashion shoot with outfits inspired by the series, with models displaying Gucci, Prada and Louis Vuitton. Strangely however, while Subaru's peculiar outfits are often talked about, Seishiro's more simplistic look also has its own appeal, which adds to his threatening nature. By normally dressing in a suit, tie and overcoat, he looks like anyone else you would see in the street, which adds to the menace. You might think in a fantastical series the enemy would be someone dressed wildly, but what is scarier is a threat that looks more or less like yourself.

Along with the manga, *Tokyo Babylon* has had several adaptations. Between 1992 and 1994, a two-part OVA was released, much like *RG Veda*. However, while *RG Veda* adapted the middle of an existing story, the *Tokyo Babylon* anime consisted of two original stories and thus it is the more watchable of the two. Sadly, the anime is now out of print in English, so only second-hand (region free) DVDs and VHS tapes are available.[11]

Tokyo Babylon was also the first CLAMP series to be turned into a live action film. *Tokyo Babylon/1999* was released in 1993 and is partly based on the story about the party phone line, in which a group of teenage girls use this line and magic to get revenge against those they hate. It has never been given a proper English-language release.

As for what happened next, there have been some recent developments. Developments that occurred long after I had finished writing this chapter. In October 2020, the official CLAMP fans website began posting new art of CLAMP's characters, normally once a day, every day. The last characters happened to be Subaru and Seishiro. Then, on 19th October, they posted a link to a YouTube video saying: "–7 more days". The image on the video, that would eventually debut on 25th October at 15:00 GMT (26th October midnight in Japan) was a white background with the number 7 and the word "START" written there. The next day the image changed, to an orange background, the number 6 and the word "PAIR". Fans of *Tokyo Babylon* realised that the number and colour related to particular volume covers of the series. Volume 7 was in white, Volume 6 was in orange. The other word was the name of a chapter in that volume. When the video was finally released, it was a trailer for a new anime, *Tokyo Babylon 2021*.

This new series was originally scheduled for April 2021 and set in the year 2021 rather than the original 1990s setting, but issues quickly arose, and for once they were not related to Covid-19. While there have been many CLAMP fans happy about this news, some also treated it with caution. Some disliked the fact that it was being set in a different time period, while others took issue with the company making the series, GoHands, with people criticising it in the past over a lack of quality when it came to their previous shows. Most of them referenced a 2017 anime called *Hand Shakers*, reviews of which were bad to say the least. James Beckett of the *Anime News Network* reviewed the entire series, rating the first two episodes "D-". After it finished its 12 episode run, it was still at the same rating. The episodes in between got no higher than "C-", with one going as far down as "F". Beckett ended the review of the last episodes with the words: "Goodbye, *Hand Shakers*, and good riddance." Beckett and another *ANN* writer, Nick Creamer, named *Hand Shakers* the worst anime of 2017. In 2019, *Hand Shakers* got a sequel, *W'z*.[12] Beckett reviewed it again and his reaction was predictable, naming it the worst anime in all of 2019.

Some fans quickly complained about the way the central characters in *Tokyo Babylon 2021* looked, and I for one did think they got Seishiro wrong, not making him broad-shouldered enough. There is also the question of how this new anime relates to the rest of CLAMP's work, because Subaru and Seishiro's story would continue in manga form. They are two of CLAMP's most compelling characters, and their relationship is one of the most gripping in the CLAMPverse. I think perhaps the best way to sum it up to British readers would be this: imagine if there was an announcement for a new series of adaptations of the works of Shakespeare, to be made by Channel 5; you worry the latter is going to outweigh the former.

These worries increased, because when GoHands released the designs for the three main characters, it was pointed out by people that their designs were taken from sources they did not reference. Hokuto was seen wearing an outfit that originally appeared in a photo, worn by Yeri from K-pop group Red Velvet in 2019. Subaru was seen in an onmyoji outfit that first appeared on a doll made by the company Volks in 2017. GoHands confessed that they had plagiarised the outfits. The promotional artwork and trailers that had already been released were then taken offline, with the company having to redesign the outfits from scratch and postponing the entire series to a later release date.

On 28th March 2021, it was announced that even more cases of plagiarism had been uncovered in *Tokyo Babylon 2021*. The result of this was that production of the anime was completely cancelled, with plans to restart an entirely new production afresh. For most CLAMP fans, this came as a relief, with the hope that the new production will be a vast improvement. In August 2021, it was reported that GoHands launched legal action against entertainment company King Records for non-payment of approximately ¥450 million ($4.1 million) regarding the cancelled production of the series. These proceedings have revealed the series would have run for 21 episodes. CLAMP themselves posted a statement on Twitter saying that they hope to take part in any future projects in other media once they are authorised.

•

While the dealing of important social topics is one of the things that make *Tokyo Babylon* stand out as a series in its own right, the relationship between Subara and Seishiro is also a draw for readers. This is best shown in the next major series CLAMP created, one that CLAMP began while *Tokyo Babylon* was ending. It is also my personal favourite of all of their works. It is shocking, grand and wonderfully illustrated. Also, while *Tokyo Babylon* dealt with social issues, this one dealt with an issue that while less to do with real-life problems does relate to one problem that concerns us all, even if it does not transpire the way it does in this manga… the end of the world itself.

---

1 – To put that into some form of context that British people might understand, if you were playing the Japanese version of Monopoly, Ikebukuro would be where The Strand is, the first red property. Anime and manga fans will be most familiar with Ikebukuro being the setting for the light novel series *Durarara!!* (pronounced to sound like a revving motorbike) and its adaptations. It features among other things probably the most

famous Irish character in anime, Celty Sturluson, a dullahan/headless horsewoman who has tracked down her stolen head to Ikebukuro. Her headless horse now possesses a motorbike and thus she travels around the city as a courier wearing a yellow helmet with tinted visor to stop people from spotting her missing head.

2 – I assume that she is referring to Babylon the ancient city, rather than the Whore of Babylon in the Book of Revelation, although supposedly the Babylon in Revelation is meant to be a code for Rome, the Empire that was persecuting Christians at the time.

3 – For any car fans reading, while Subaru does wear blue outfits, sadly he is not seen wearing gold gloves and boots to go with it. Although I'm no car expert – I can't even drive at the time of writing this – a little research shows that the Subaru Impreza with the trademark blue body with gold alloy wheels did not come out until after *Tokyo Babylon* ended. Don't worry if you are a car fan, mind, you'll soon find something of interest when we cover *Magic Knight Rayearth*.

4 – In Monopoly, Shinjuku would be where Bond Street is, in the last green space.

5 – However, when listening to the *CLAMPcast in Wonderland* podcast it was pointed out that this outfit worn by Subaru does look very similar to the one worn by Michael Jackson in the video for *Thriller*. Just put on the hat, two black gloves instead one glove covered in rhinestones, and use the Jackson after his skin changed colour and you are getting there.

6 – And yes, I do know that some people will object to the nine-year age difference between the two male lovers, one of whom is sixteen, even if nothing actually physical is shown in the manga itself. These age gaps often appear in manga, particular 'shojo' manga aimed at young women, of which most of CLAMP's work is. Mind you, it puts the whole 'looking like Michael Jackson' thing into a different context – glossing over the fact that our 'Jackson' is attracted to someone older than him.

7 – I later learned, thanks to a sketch from the comedy kids TV show *Horrible Histories*, that there is a Japanese folklore monster (yokai) called the 'jubokko', which looks like a tree and consumes human blood. Whether there is a connection between this and the story Seishiro tells, I am unsure.

8 – Hanging is the method of execution in Japan, and it is normally used in cases such as multiple murders.

9 – Or to put it another way, the villains I tend to find least interesting are the ones that would do your stereotypical evil laugh. For me, the best villain to do an evil laugh is the ironically named Mr. Gently Benevolent from the BBC Radio 4 Dickensian sitcom parody *Bleak Expectations*. This sitcom was my specialist subject the first time I appeared on *Mastermind*. I was leading at the end of the specialist subject round, but when I came to general knowledge I was last, but only two points behind the winner. The second time I did the show, my specialist subject was the Four Gospels, where again I was last. I'm not aware of anyone coming last on *Mastermind* twice, but do feel free to correct me if I'm wrong.

10 – I must admit, Seishiro is also the one character by CLAMP I would most likely cosplay. I like dressing as the more shady characters, and he doesn't need much in the way of an expensive outfit: just a suit, glasses, and in my case a black wig or some hair dye. Hardest part to find would be a pack of Mild Seven, his favourite brand of cigarettes, which no longer go by this name (they are now called Mevius). I might need someone to make a fake Mild Seven packet.

11 – The image that is used as the DVD cover for the *Tokyo Babylon* DVD release was also used as the cover for Helen McCarthy's book *500 Essential Anime Movies: The Ultimate Guide*, published by Ilex in 2008.

12 – I have no idea how you pronounce it.

CHAPTER 4

Try to feel it. Try to shout it. Cast off everything. Let your heart burn. - *X*, aka *X/1999* (1992-2003)

In 2012, Stephen Fry's BBC Radio 4 documentary series *Fry's English Delight*, which examines aspects of the English language, broadcast an episode called 'The Story of X', examining why the 24th letter of the English alphabet is the most interesting letter of all.

As you can see, or rather hear, given that it was radio, the letter does have several elements that make it interesting. X can be used to signify kissing; the Greek letter 'Chi', which looks like our 'X', was an abbreviation of 'Christ', hence 'Xmas' for 'Christmas'; for the Ancient Romans it is the number 10, while a horizontal line through the 'X' denotes the denarius unit of currency; it can be used as a signature; mathematician and philosopher Rene Descartes was responsible for using the small version of the letter to mean both the horizontal axis in graphs and to mean unknown quantities in algebra; this unknown aspect of the letter is why Wilhelm Röntgen called the rays he discovered 'X-rays', and the fact that these rays allowed to see bones meant the letter became associated with the taboo, with all things X-rated, and things that are, albeit misspelt, eXploitative, eXciting, eXtreme, eXclusive… X cetera.

In the same programme, Fry interviewed film critic Mark Kermode, where they talked about X-rated films such as *The Man with the X-ray Eyes* and *The Quatermass Xperiment*, which made use of the fact that these were, at the time, eXtreme adult films. While this is in my view the best episode of *Fry's English*

Delight, I know of two other 'X' things, both of them Japanese, that did not make this 30 minute programme.

One is a band. X, now known as X Japan in order to prevent confusion with other bands with the same name,[1] are possibly the biggest rock/metal band to come out of the country.[2] X Japan are certainly a band I would recommend that people should read up on, mainly due them being described in 2017 by *The Times* as: "The world's unluckiest band", a fact made more apt due to the print edition of the article having a photo accompanying this headline that only showed four of the band's five members.

Like CLAMP, little, in terms of books, has been written about X Japan in the West, but there is a documentary film about the group called *We Are X* that is worth watching, partly because the story of the group does feel like *Spinal Tap*, but with the tragedy they not only going up to 11, but possibly passing 12 and reaching unlucky 13. Put it this way, what you are about to read about them is all true.

The band's front-man, principal songwriter, drummer and pianist, Yoshiki (all the members are known by one-word names) faced tragedy at a young age, his father committing suicide when Yoshiki was aged ten. Two members of X Japan also killed themselves. Taiji, the original bass player until he was fired from the band in 1992 for reasons never made clear (although he later appeared in some reunion shows), was arrested after an air-rage incident in 2011 and was later found to have hanged himself in his police cell. Back in 1998, Hide, the original lead guitarist, was found to have died in his apartment, with a towel wrapped around a doorknob indicating that he had strangled himself.

In *We Are X*, the band say that they believe that Hide died accidentally while doing a neck stretching exercise while drunk. However, at the time the death occurred it was officially reported as suicide. This in turn led to three copycat suicides. Hide's funeral was attended by over 10,000 people, during the middle of a massive heat-wave in which 197 people collapsed, and 56 had to be taken by ambulance for treatment. Not only that, but one fan who laid flowers at the temple where Hide's funeral took place slit her own wrists. A car full of fans wanting to make it to the funeral drove through the night without sleep, which led to the driver falling asleep at the wheel, crashing, and causing a motorway pile-up that resulted in another death and seven more people seriously injured.

Not only this, but the death of Hide took place five months after X Japan had split up because Toshi, the singer, had left the band because he had been brainwashed by a cult. He eventually recovered and the band reformed in 2007. This ten year gap however is nothing compared to the gap of over 20 years that there has been since X Japan last put out a brand new studio album. The fifth and most recent album, 'Dahlia', came out in 1996, and while the band say that they have completed their sixth album, and there is even a Wikipedia article entitled: 'Untitled X Japan album' all about it, at the time of writing it has still not come out. Also, of their five studio albums only two of them are available in the UK to download and stream.

The band have faced other problems too. Yoshiki has had many problems with his health, including carpal tunnel syndrome, tendonitis, torn ligaments, asthma so bad that he has to have oxygen tanks on the side-stage should he collapse during a gig, and years of constant headbanging resulting in injuries to his neck so severe that they, "would force a professional rugby player to retire." Yoshiki ended up having to have emergency cervical artificial disc replacement surgery. Meanwhile in 2016, the band's rhythm guitarist, Pata, ended up in intensive care following a life threatening condition of the colon and a severe blood clot. This resulted in X Japan having to postpone a concert at Wembley Arena by a year.[3]

Of course it is not all bad luck. They are Japan's biggest band, with Yoshiki one of the biggest music stars in the country. As well as being in rock/metal, Yoshiki is also a name in the world of classical music. This resulted in him composing a piece of music especially for the Emperor Akihito's 10th anniversary of his rule, and more recently he wrote the music for one of the themes for hugely popular anime series *Attack on Titan*.[4] His work in both classical and rock/metal makes him one of the few people who can claim to have worked with both Sarah Brightman and, rather unluckily for him and indeed many others since I've written this, Marilyn Manson. Yoshiki also has his own brand of wine, kimonos, and is one of the few real-life people in the world to have a Hello Kitty character based on him, Yoshikitty. X Japan themselves have performed on some of the world's biggest stages, including at the Coachella festival in 2018. However, typical of their luck, they ended up performing at the exact same time Beyonce was headlining on the main stage. Given all this, I would say this: Having gone through everything I've listed above, you might want to give X Japan at least a little listen.

One other reason for listening to them is this: Due to the similarity in name, X Japan became involved with CLAMP's next manga, *X*, also known as *X/1999*, partly because that was the year it was set in, and partly because English-language publishers couldn't market a comic aimed at young adult readers with an explicit title like *X*. The series would become CLAMP's biggest hit up to that point. So big that the series even carried on beyond 1999, which is particularly interesting given that the series is all about the apocalypse occurring in that year.

X was published in *Monthly Asuka*, the same magazine that published *CLAMP School Detectives*. Indeed, both series began in the same year, with *X* debuting on 24th March 1992. The series would be collected in 18 tankobon collections, although arguably you could say it went up to 25, as *Tokyo Babylon*'s leads

Subaru and Seishiro are two of the main characters in *X*. *X* is so well known that when Dark Horse published *Tokyo Babylon*, they advertised it as the 'prequel' to *X*, although it does feel that calling *X* the sequel would be more accurate.

In terms of publication in English, *X* also stands out in that it is the only one of the early CLAMP titles not released by TokyoPop. *X* was originally published, and to this day is still published, by Viz Media. Originally, they released individual chapters in a magazine called *Animerica Extra*, then in 2003 they released the individual tankobon volumes, and between 2011 and 2013 they collected the series into six 3-in-1 editions, which are also available digitally.

One of the most interesting aspects of these collections is the cover, created by Mokona. Now while certain clichés tell you not to judge books by them, in my view the cover of *X* is not just the best of CLAMP's covers, but one of the best book covers around generally. All of CLAMP's other works make the most of their amazing art and rightly so, but for *X* the cover consists almost entirely of nothing else except a massive letter 'X' on a plain black background. Apart from the 'X' there was also the name of CLAMP directly under the big letter, the word 'CLAMP' being the second largest text on the cover. It also included the volume number, the name of the publisher, the publisher's logo, and the tagline of the series: "Their destiny was foreordained, 1999". The back cover contained one of their more colourful illustrations, but nothing too big could go on the cover however, as they needed to make room for barcodes which were only just arriving in Japan. When *X* was first published in English, Viz reversed it and decided to put the colour illustrations on the front cover and the massive 'X' on the back, as well as giving each volume a subtitle relating to a term from orchestral music (see Appendix C).

The Viz 3-in-1 editions not only went back to the original

cover order of the 'X' on the front, but were designed to be even simpler. They featured just the 'X', 'CLAMP' beneath this, and under that the number of the book in Roman numerals (I to VI) and '3-in-1' next to it. Viz's name does not appear on the front cover, only on the back cover, which includes a small inserted colour illustration from the series, and on the spine. The spine also contains an artwork for the series, which when you place all six books in order, form a single continuous drawing of all the main characters in the story.

The title itself obviously holds some mystery. This is partly because there isn't really an equivalent of the letter 'X' in Japanese. When asked in the *CLAMP no Kiseki* interviews about what the 'X' meant, Ohkawa said: "Well, first of all, it represents an unknown number, an undefined that you need to solve for in a numeric equation. Secondly, it's an oblique image of the cross, really. There are so many meanings that it holds. It stuck pretty quickly for one of our titles. We showed it to our editor and that was that, 'X' was decided."

The idea of writing a story about the possibility of the world ending in 1999 was one of interest at the time. The most notable example was the claim that Nostradamus believed that the world would end in July 1999. While none of CLAMP believed these ideas, the idea of a story of the apocalypse occurring in 1999 appealed to them. Also, like with *Tokyo Babylon,* they could continue to cover social issues, particularly with things like the environment and natural disasters such as earthquakes.

X includes many of the recurring elements of their past work: not just using characters that appeared in previous series, but the subject of faith also comes up again. Their idea of the apocalypse is mostly an environmental one, but religion once again frequently appears: Buddhism, Shinto, Catholicism, Taoism, the Kabbalah, Freemasonry, and the occult are all referenced in *X.* Going back to Ohkawa's comments on the title, part of the reason *X* is so called is because the cross-shaped X references the cross in Christianity. The two central groups in *X* reference the Book of Revelation. There is also not just religion, but other moral and ethical aspects the story brings up, which we'll discuss later. But for now, let's examine the story itself.

X (1992-2003)

Taking place in what was then the near future, *X* begins with teenage schoolboy Kamui Shiro returning home to Tokyo in the year 1999, after being away from the city for six years. His first day at his new school is troublesome, mainly because of what he encounters on the first day: strange guys in suits and shades. Kamui quickly finds out these are summoned spirits and gets rid of them. When he enters the school, Kamui learns that he is in the same school as his two greatest childhood friends, brother and sister Fuma and Kotori Monou, whose father Kyogo is a priest at a shrine where they both work and live. However, Kamui has become much colder and distant during his six years away. Kamui is now living on his own for one thing, his mother Toru having died. Before dying, Toru asked her son to promise that he will change fate and return to Tokyo.

It is not long before Kamui is in more supernatural fights, including one with a schoolgirl who can produce a sword from out of her own hand. Kamui begins to realise that someone appears to be watching from a distance. Actually, 'watching' is the wrong word. One person tracking Kamui is a woman named Princess Hinoto. She is a 'dreamgazer', who has the power to see the present and future in dreams, but she, like all dreamgazers, suffers from poor health. In her case, Hinoto is blind, deaf, mute and cannot walk. She can use her dreams to communicate (in the manga this is highlighted by the use of a different font from the other characters). Hinoto herself is employed by the government and lives in the basement of the National Diet Building, the home of the Japanese parliament. Hinoto is not the only one who can see dreams. So can her younger sister Kanoe, although she cannot see into the future without assistance. Thus, she instead spies on her sister for her own sinister purposes. Kanoe is working in the basement of the Tokyo Metropolitan Government Building, the home of the city's civil service, while during the day she works as the secretary to Tokyo's governor.

Kamui finds himself being followed by supporters of both Hinoto and Kanoe. Worse than that however is that Fuma and Kotori find themselves sucked into the chaos. Kamui sees horrific, violent visions. They show Kotori being murdered and not just Tokyo but the entire world being destroyed. Kamui swears that he will kill anyone who harms Fuma or Kotori in any way. However, the first person to truly suffer is Kyogo. His shrine contains a sacred sword which he tries to protect, but the sword is taken by an androgynous person called Nataku, who delivers Kyogo a mortal wound. After this, Hinoto dreams that there will be two sacred swords and two Kamuis, with one seemingly angelic and the other devilish.

Soon afterwards Kamui receives a visit from Tokiko Magami. She is the nurse at Kamui's school, but she also reveals herself to be Kamui's aunt, the younger sister to Kamui's dead mother Toru. According to Tokiko, Toru said that she would give birth to a child that will be, "for the sake of the Earth itself." (Book I, p474) Kamui later learns that his mother's family are 'shadow sacrifices', a kind of scapegoat who give up their lives to help others. Around the same time, Fuma is being sent visions by Kanoe showing Kamui as evil and killing his sister. Kamui, Fuma and Kotori all find themselves encountering people on both sides of the fight.

Eventually, those supporting Hinoto convince Kamui to meet her. In their meeting and through her visions, Kamui comes to learn more about the truth regarding the perilous situation that he and the whole world find themselves in. There are two groups of people coming together in Tokyo. Hinoto's group are the Seven Seals, aka the Dragons of Heaven. Kanoe's group are the Seven Angels, aka the Dragons of Earth. The Dragons of Earth believe that humanity is a plague upon the world that will one day destroy it. Thus, they believe that the only way to save the world is to wipe out humanity. The Dragons of Heaven meanwhile, believe that humanity can help mend and protect the world, and are fighting to keep the human race alive. Currently, the thing that protects Tokyo and thus also the Earth are 'kekkai', a series of spiritual barriers, the name of which comes from the sectioned-off area of Buddhist temples. The Seven Seals protect them, while the Seven Angels are trying to destroy them, which in turn will allow them to destroy humanity using a series of destructive earthquakes. The Seven Seals can also create their own kekkai to protect particular areas when they go into battle with the Seven Angels, but if the Seal dies in battle then all the damage caused in the fight will still happen. Regarding earthquakes, CLAMP were not the first Japanese authors to use them as the method for the destruction of their homeland. The 1973 novel *Japan Sinks* by Sakyo Komatsu also sees the entire country being destroyed by devastating earthquakes. This novel was adapted in 2020 into an anime for Netflix called *Japan Sinks: 2020.*[5] Anyway, the story…

It is Kamui's fate to side with one of the two groups. He will either become a Dragon of Heaven and will save humanity, or a Dragon of Earth and destroy it. Kamui is reluctant to join either side. At the same time however, Fuma also becomes involved in the conflict. He helps to protect Kamui when he is involved in a fight with one of the Seven Angels – this Angel being a familiar-looking gay assassin who is wearing a pair of shades to conceal his blind right eye. However, Fuma seems to be becoming increasingly disturbed in his way of thinking, claiming that their fates are twinned. After this, they find Tokiko has been violently attacked. It is her fate, as the last surviving shadow sacrifice, to help Kamui by dying and giving birth to a second sacred sword. Before her spirit disappears, Kamui is told to keep the sword safe and store it in a particular place: the CLAMP School, or CLAMP Academy as it is called in Viz's translation. However, the increasingly weird Fuma claims that a second sacred sword means that there will be a second Kamui too. The new sword is collected by the Academy's current chair, the now adult Nokoru Imonoyama, with the help of his fellow *CLAMP School Detectives*, although Nokoru is the only one who speaks. One of the things protecting the sword in the school is their subway system. Turns out it travels around the school in the shape of a pentagram, providing protective magic.[6]

Kotori meanwhile is visited in her dreams by another dreamgazer who shows her more visions, but this dreamgazer is working for the Dragons of Earth. Eventually, the matter of which group Kamui joins is decided. While he is not interested in saving the world, the one thing he knows that he wants to protect is his friendship with Fuma and Kotori. As he wants to protect some people, even if it is just these two, that means he must become one of the Seven Seals, a Dragon of Heaven. However, due to their twinned fates, Fuma automatically becomes a Dragon of Earth and joins the Seven Angels. The sacred sword seems to obey Fuma, resulting in Fuma believing that he is the real 'Kamui'. Thus, he strikes Kamui, stabbing his hand. Kotori meanwhile finds herself tied to some rubble in the shape of a cross, and is risen up into the air like Christ at the crucifixion. Fuma declares that Kamui cannot stop the change that he and the Angels are bringing, and commits the most dreaded deed – using the sacred sword to kill his own sister. Before Fuma kills

Kamui however, other members of the Seven Seals come to save him.

The aftermath of Kotori's death sees Kamui and Fuma taking separate paths. While Fuma begins his work with the Seven Angels and begins to help them destroy the kekkai, Kamui vows to save Fuma, which in turn will save humanity. However, things become even more problematic for the Seven Seals when Hinoto sees visions of her own death at the hands of Kamui, leading to a more destructive, evil side to immerge from her psyche, wanting to save her life above those of everyone else. All of this presents new challenges, conundrums and dangers for Kamui and his friends.[7]

Of course, one thing yet to be discussed is who all the members of the Seven Seals and the Seven Angels are. While we know that Kamui is in the former and Fuma is in the later, it should be clarified that Hinoto and Kanoe are not in either group, but are supporting their sides for the most part.

Aside from Kamui and Fuma, there are some other people we already know that are in the two camps. Two of them are Subaru Sumeragi and Seishiro Sakurazuka. Subaru is still hunting down the man he loved because of what he did to his twin sister Hokuto, who also appears in *X*, albeit in the dreams of others. He joins the Seven Seals, while the assassin Seishiro is one of the Seven Angels. Things have obviously changed for both men over the passing years. Subaru's dramatic clothes have toned down a bit, although he does like a long white coat to match Seishiro's long black coat, but his empathy still remains, on the whole. One telling moment on how he has changed is a moment when he bumps into someone on the street and does not say sorry, so his complete selflessness has gone. However, his general sense of selflessness becomes a determent to him when he finally does battle with Seishiro. As mentioned, Seishiro is now seen wearing a pair of shades in order to prevent his blinded right eye from showing.

There are two other dragons that we have already referred to. One is Nataku, the Dragon of Earth who steals the first sacred sword and kills Fuma's father Kyogo. Natakua is a clone of ambiguous gender, created by a man named Motoharu Tojo, the head of Tojo Pharmaceuticals, the largest pharmaceutical firm in the country. Tojo's HQ is underneath one of Japan's most famous skyscrapers, the Sunshine 60 building – a building that just happened to be built on the site of the former Sugamo Prison, which held and was the site of execution of several Japanese war criminals including Prime Minister Hideki Tojo. Note the similar names.

Nataku was created from genetic material from Motoharu's son Masaki, and his dead granddaughter Kazuki. As a result of this, Nataku is technically sexless. Motoharu wants to destroy the sacred sword so the end of the world cannot happen, thus sending Nataku out to find it, but his plan to destroy it fails. Nataku fights in battle with a long scarf which Nataku can manipulate into various shapes.

We also mentioned the girl who can create a sword from out of her own hand. This person is a Dragon of Heaven, Arashi Kishu. She was found abandoned as a child and raised by priests at the Ise Grand Shrine, a shrine devoted to the Shinto sun goddess Amaterasu, and is one of the holiest places in the Shinto religion. She fits into the mould of what in some fandom circles is referred to as a 'tsundere' – someone who on the surface appears cold and unwelcoming, but as the series progresses opens up and becomes friendlier.[8]

One person Arashi opens up to in particular is another Dragon of Heaven, Sorata 'Sora' Arisugawa, who has several powers including controlling electricity. Taken away from his mother as a child, Sorata was raised by Shingon Buddhist monks, this branch of Buddhism being one of the oldest in Japan. The monks declared a prophecy that Sora will protect Kamui with his life, but will also die for a woman. Sora soon falls for Arashi, and slowly Arashi also starts to love him back. While his fondness for women is clear, his friendliness towards men has led to other people, including the women at *CLAMPcast in Wonderland*, to claim Sora is bisexual or pansexual.

Among the other Dragons of Heaven are Karen[9] Kasumi, who is a devout Catholic. While her first name is now used to mean someone considered to be entitled, Karen is no 'Karen'. Karen's powers allow her to control fire, but her harsh, strictly religious mother believed that this was a sign that Karen was a devil, which led her to violently abuse her own daughter. The mother was killed in a car crash, and now in adulthood Karen is a sex worker. To be precise, she works at a 'soapland', which is a kind of massage parlour. She often goes into battle in her revealing outfits, despite her religion.

Karen is most commonly seen working with another of the Seven Seals, Seiichiro Aoki, who has the power to manipulate the wind. He is also arguably the most normal of all of the major characters, being the only one with a close family. His nephew, Daisuke Saiki, is someone who works closely with the Seven Seals and has some of the same powers as Seiichiro. Seiichiro works as an editor at a manga magazine. To be exact, he works at Kadokawa Shoten, the company that published the magazine that *X* appeared in. Seiichiro Aoki also happens to be the name of the real-life editor who CLAMP worked with on several of their manga including *X*, and he has a credit in the comic.

The last of the Seven Seals is Yuzuriha Nekoi, who is presumably named after CLAMP's Nekoi. She is the descendent of the keepers of the 2,000-year-old Mitsumine Shrine, and while the 'neko' in the name means 'cat' in Japanese, she actually works with dogs. To be exact, she works with one very special dog, Inuki. Inuki is a dog spirit who has various powers that Yuzuriha can use. Most people cannot see Inuki, and so as a child other children mocked her, thinking that Inuki was an imaginary friend. Thus, Yuzuriha is very happy whenever someone else is able to see Inuki themselves.

One person who does see Inuki is a man named Kusanagi Shiyu. Kusanagi is a member of the Japanese Self-Defence Force.[10] The fact that he is able to see Inuki leads to him becoming close friends with Yuzuriha. Kusanagi has a great affinity with nature, believing what humanity is doing to wildlife is wrong, that the conflict between humanity and nature should be done with as little violence as possible, and that no one should be killed in the conflict. You might think this is strange for someone in the armed forces. What makes it even stranger is that Kusanagi is actually one of the Seven Angels, whose ultimate role is to destroy the human race.

Alongside Kusanagi, Seishiro, Nataku and Fuma, the other three Dragons of Earth include Satsuki Yatoji, who may well be named after Satsuki Igarashi. The only woman in the group (although as stated, Nataku's gender is somewhat unknown), Satsuki has no love for humanity or nature. What she loves is technology and she is extremely 'rational'. Specifically, she loves a supercomputer called the Beast, inscribed with the number 666.[11] Satsuki uses the Beast to spy on the enemy and can also fight using it. Satsuki's rationality comes across most strongly when she is in a battle with Yuzuriha. Satsuki asks why it is wrong for her to kill people, when people kill animals and plants all the time. Yuzuriha's best argument is that people are, "not all like that", which in a modern day perspective feels a bit like an argument when someone says: "Not all men…"

One of the few people that Satsuki appears to have any feelings for is another one of the Seven Angels. On the surface, the civil servant Yuto Kigai appears polite enough, congratulating happy couples on births and marriages as he gets them the right certificates for them to fill. Deep down however he appears to have no moral compass at all. He is happy and cheery even when he is fighting, having the ability to control water and battling with a special weapon that is hard to describe. On the surface it looks like a dagger and whip, but the ends appear to have Buddhist artifacts attached to them. Yuto is also having a physical relationship with Kanoe.

The last of the Seven Angels is Kakyo Kuzuki. Compared to Yuto, he is totally miserable. He has good reason too. Like Hinoto, he is also a dreamgazer and he too is ill. In his case, he is in a coma. This was due to the fact that his powers resulted in him being kept prisoner by a political group. He once tried to stop someone from being killed, but when he tried this one of those in the political group shot him. He has been in this coma ever since. Now Kakyo just wants to die, a wish that Fuma promises he will grant him in exchange for doing his bidding.

•

In terms of overall subjects and themes, *X* is probably the most complex of all of CLAMP's works. The subject of impending doom and humanity's role in it is obviously vital to helping understand the story, but interestingly it is probably the Seven Angels that help explore these notions more than the Seven Seals.

For example, with Kakyo wishing for death, this appears, to me at least, to relate to the subject of assisted suicide. Kakyo wants Fuma to kill him and Fuma will do so, provided Kakyo does what he is told and helps his cause. The issue of assisted suicide again relates to the occurring social issues that appear in both *X* and *Tokyo Babylon.*[12] Similarly you have Kusanagi, a man with a love of nature which raises issues with the environment and humanity's relationship with it, while in the character of Satsuki we see the threat from technology. Let's not forget that in 1999 there was worry from some people about the dangers of the

Millennium Bug. You can also argue that Nataku relates to issues of technology, given that the character is a clone, so there is the issue of technology's relation to the human body.

As well as the social issues, religion is a subject that comes up again and again in the story. So many of the main characters work in religious jobs. The Monou family maintain a shrine. Arashi and Yuzuriha also lived and worked at Shinto shrines, Sora was raised by Buddhist monks, Karen came from a strict Catholic background, Subaru and Seishiro's work dealing with the occult has already been discussed, and we learn from Satsuki's past life that she worked with scientists who were related to the Kabbalah and Freemasonry. In one scene, Satsuki destroys an area of Tokyo in the shape of the Yosher-Upright shape of the sefirot, the ten main attributes to Kabbalah as drawn in three columns. It should be stated that references to the Kabbalah seem to relate to more new-age or occult ideas of faith rather than actual Jewish mysticism. Another thing that on surface appears to be Jewish, but isn't, is the symbol commonly given to the Seven Angels: a candlestick with six branches coming off it. It may look like the menorah, but it is actually related to a Taoist candlestick, the seven branches representing the seven stars you find in the constellation of Ursa Major. The constellation is also the symbol for the Seven Seals.

The names of the two groups also come from the Bible. The Seven Seals and Seven Angels are references to the Book of Revelation. Chapter 5, Verse 5 references the Lamb being worthy to break the seven seals on a scroll, which are broken in Chapter 6 and Chapter 8. In Chapter 16 we witness seven angels pouring out seven bowls, which cause seven plagues.

Even the name of the central character directs to faith. 'Kamui' comes from 'Kamuy', divine beings from the mythology of the Ainu people, the aboriginal people of Japan's northern island of Hokkaido. The name 'Kamuy' is more familiar to manga fans from *Golden Kamuy*, a period adventure series by Satoru Noda. One of the main characters in the story, Asirpa, is an Ainu girl, and in the British Museum's exhibition of manga in 2019, she was the main character used to promote it.

One of the key features relating to this was the growing rise in various doomsday beliefs in the run-up to 1999, and a real fear by some people the world might end that year. Japan was in the middle of an occult boom in popular culture. Cults and new religions were gaining traction – remember what happened to Toshi in X Japan, when joining a cult resulted in the band splitting. Meanwhile, raising awareness of climate change also added to this idea of the end times soon coming. The theory of Gaia, that the world is a single living organism, started to gain traction, with one idea concerning it being that humanity might be akin to a disease, and when you get a disease, one of the ways to fight it off is by developing a fever to burn it away. Some people believe that the Earth warming up is like the world's equivalent of burning away the virus of humanity.

This also relates to the subject of destiny and fate. Everyone in the story is trying to control Kamui's fate as to whether he will save or destroy the world. As far as CLAMP are concerned, they have said in the past that they do not think that any kind of supernatural force controls your destiny, which may explain why Kamui tries to rebel against the notion.

Another thing that needs to be highlighted is the artwork, primarily because of the audience. Most of CLAMP's work is obviously aimed at women and girls, manga aimed at girls being known as 'shojo' comics, especially when it comes character design, especially many pretty male characters: Kamui and Subaru are attractive guys; not in a ripped muscle-boy way, but in a cute, charming way. However, the subjects covered in *X*, primarily the end of the world, and the violent, action-filled gory detail that entails, is normally seen as a more male-orientated subject, that would fit the 'shonen' comics. *X* ends up appealing to all genders as it covers what are generally male subjects in a female way, and, let's not forget that this, like *RG Veda*, features characters that are neither male or female.

This is a big deal, given that manga demographics have much more of a gender divide than Western comics. CLAMP works are one of the few that appeal to people of all genders. To quote Cristal Marie's *A History of CLAMP (and The Future of Netflix)* YouTube video: "CLAMP is one of the key studios responsible for evolving the trend where shonen became more bishonin friendly, aka pretty boy friendly. Marketing for shonen has since become a lot more complex."

The art in *X* is some of the greatest in all their works. If you get the 3-in-1 editions, they contain special colour drawings, with the back of the books containing written details on each piece. Meanwhile, the art in the actual manga is also some of their most stand-out work. Sometimes we see tender moments between the characters, but then you get to the battle scenes, with the characters using supernatural abilities, duelling with swords and using sophisticated technology in the fights. The images used to convey what might happen to the world are breathtaking, with images in the dream sequences of dragons fighting each other to represent the two factions, and even good and evil versions of Kamui fighting each other. Some scenes are particularly shocking for a shojo comic, especially the moment in which Kotori is killed. There is also a duel between Subaru and Seishiro in Vol. 16 which is one of the greatest and most tragic moments in all of CLAMP's catalogue.

One of the things you see when reading *X* is that the opening page is an illustration in the form of a tarot card from the Major Arcana. For example, the first volume begins with a drawing of The Magician card, with Kamui as the magician. The second sees Hinoto as the High Priestess and so on. These illustrations ended up becoming used in an actual set of tarot cards which featured colour illustrations from *X*.[13] This deck appears to have been released between the 14th and 15th volumes, as the 15th card, The Devil, and all the others beyond it differ between the deck and the manga. In the deck, The Devil card shows Fuma. In the manga, it features Yuto – in a leather military-style outfit in a BDSM scene, with two blindfolded, tied-up naked women at his feet. Given the clear reference to feminism in *CLAMP School Detectives*, it would seem that CLAMP appear to be on the more sex-positive arm of the movement, which is something that will be touched upon in the next chapter when we discuss the one-volume adult manga *Miyuki-chan in Wonderland*.

X also helps to expand the CLAMPverse even more. One of the best indications of this occurs at the end of Vol. 12. As the manga progressed, at the end of each volume there was a short bonus chapter focusing on one of the main characters, normally told in flashback, but with some exceptions. One exception is Seiichiro's chapter. While it is mostly in flashback, at the end we see him on the phone to his wife, Shimako, after he has been shopping. One shop he has been to is called 'Piffle Princess', which is a shop that appears in many other CLAMP series and helps link the multiple stories together.

Having said this, whether all the universes are connected is a complex matter. CLAMP have said in the past for example that their fantasy stories, such as *Magic Knight Rayearth*, take place in separate universes. As that series does begin on a version of Earth then that would mean their Earth is different to the one in *X*. It's all very complicated.

At the risk of revealing more spoilers, I feel the need to talk about the finale of Vol. 18, the last collected volume of manga. Over the course of the series, Hinoto's evil side begins to gain more influence over her, there have been members of the Seven Seals and Seven Angels who have suffered terribly, including deaths, and yet another character loses their right eye. There is even a moment where one character changes sides to the rival faction (see Appendix A to find out who). Kamui has a heart-felt talk with Karen as the chaos continues, and Hinoto thinks: 'It is time for the final battle to begin.' As for the final, it is difficult to say, because that line from Hinoto is the last line translated into English in the manga *X*.

There were five chapters that were not released in a tankobon. These were originally released in a special edition of *Newtype* magazine called *CLAMP Newtype Platinum*, and today you can see these chapters in the book *All About CLAMP*, which is an art book of colour illustrations from almost all of CLAMP's series at the time of publication in 2009. However, as it is only available in Japanese, you can only go on the images to figure out the plot if you can't speak the language, which I can't. I long for the day when someone might translate these chapters and make them available to buy legally, even if it was just digital versions. Fortunately, *CLAMPcast in Wonderland* has done an episode about these chapters so there is some info for English-speaking readers.

These extra chapters see Kamui taking the sacred sword out of its secure place at the CLAMP Academy, a deadly battle between Hinoto and Kanoe in the dream world, and the beginning of the ultimate battle between the Dragons of Heaven and the Dragons of Earth. We see Kamui on his back, and Fuma lifting up his sacred sword to stab him, and then… we don't know what happens next. We don't know, because since 24th March 2003, 11 years after the series debuted, *X* was put on a permanent hiatus and has never returned to this day.

X had actually been through a few hiatuses over the course of the run. In 2004, in an interview with *PUFF Magazine,* it was stated that the main reason for these breaks was the real-life situation in terms of society at the time. In January 1995, there was the Great Hanshin earthquake near Kobe that resulted in the deaths of over 6,000 people. In March 1995, a terrorist attack on the Tokyo underground system using sarin killed 12 people, with responsibility blamed on the Aum Shinrikyo doomsday cult. In 1997, the 'Sakakibara Incident' occurred, where a violent double child murder occurred again in Kobe. In the interview, Ohkawa mentioned that: "We received a letter from a person residing in Kobe at the time, saying that they, 'couldn't bear to read [*X*],' which really made us ponder our future."

Some people put forward other theories as to why the series stopped. Some say it was because CLAMP were too busy working on other titles and so just stopped working on *X*; others suggest that they did not have a clear ending for the story. One common theory is that the publisher halted publication because they believed *X* was too violent, to which the sane response has to be: "Why would you publish a story about the apocalypse if you were worried it might be violent?"

Whatever the reason is, the fact that *X* remains unfinished after nearly 20 years is a tragic one. There is still so much to know. Is humanity saved or not? Does Fuma kill Kamui, or is Kamui saved? Does Kamui help Fuma return to his senses? Does the evil side of Hinoto triumph or not? Do more characters swap sides, or do those who have swapped return to their original camp? Over the course of the story Yuzuriha and Kusanagi's relationship grows, but she never realises that he is the enemy, so what happens in their relationship? Kusanagi is never seen fighting in the manga, so does he actually get involved at all? People have argued that maybe the two sides are better off uniting, instead of fighting, to save the Earth, shunning the idea that the best way to help the planet is to stop humanity. The women on *CLAMPcast in Wonderland* have argued previously that the demands of capitalism are more to blame for climate change than humanity in general. They also point out that even if everyone on Earth is killed, what happens to people who are not on Earth when the apocalypse happens. Would astronauts survive? Personally, I would guess that Satsuki would find a way of using Beast to bring them down technologically.

CLAMP themselves know the ending, because as they have said in the past they predetermine all the endings of their work, but given how rarely they speak in public, finding out what is going to happen from them directly will be tricky.

In terms of answers, there are a few places we can go to. One is the anime adaptations, both of which were made by the same studio, Madhouse. These adaptations consisted of a film in 1996, and the other a TV series that aired between 2001 and 2002. The TV series was directed by Yoshiaki Kawajiri, who is most famous for dark, moody works, including the horror OVA *Wicked City* (1987) and the feature film *Ninja Scroll* (1993). As both of these series were made while the manga was still being written, we know that neither are really the true ending, but it is better than nothing. As well as the anime, two video games based on the series were also released in 2002 – *X: Card of Fate* and *X: Unmei no Sentaku* (*X: Fateful Choice*), but neither made it outside of Japan.

Of the two, the film is less faithful to the manga due to it being made when the manga was relatively young. It does deviate from the plot somewhat, featuring characters that do not appear in the original manga. When the film came out, Kakyo had not yet appeared, so a totally new Dragon of Earth called Shogo Asagi took his place instead. In the film, he controls water and appears to mainly cause destruction just for the sake of it.

The film was directed by Shigeyuki Hayashi, a man who is much better known under his one-name pseudonym Rintaro.

It was the first film he had directed in nine years, his last work prior to *X* being *Labyrinth Labyrinthos*, a segment in the three-part anthology film *Neo Tokyo*. Rintaro would go on to find greater fame as the director of *Metropolis*, an anime film adaptation of a manga by Osamu Tezuka, the manga itself being loosely inspired by Fritz Lang's 1927 sci-fi classic. Another notable member of staff was art director Suhichi Kusamori, who worked with Rintaro on both *X* and *Metropolis*. Kusamori has also worked on some of the most famous anime films ever, including Studio Ghibli's *Grave of the Fireflies* and the cyberpunk classic *Ghost in the Shell*. He would also work on other CLAMP projects, including a film based on their manga *xxxHOLiC*, and on the TV series *Blood-C*, for which CLAMP provided anime designs and scripts, but it is part of a much longer-running series and thus is something not really covered by this book.

The film is perhaps more interesting, given the music. This is where *X* the manga gets its connection with X Japan the band, because the end theme for the film is the band's song 'Forever Love'. This might seem a little odd for fans of the band, given that one of X Japan's most famous songs is called 'X'. However, the song 'X' does appear in a short anime that was used as a music video to promote the manga when it launched in 1993. Several other X Japan songs were also used in other videos to promote the film, namely 'Silent Jealousy', 'Kurenai' (Crimson) and 'Endless Rain'. These videos were bundled into a collection written as X^2, but weirdly it was pronounced 'Double X' in English.

In terms of success, the exact takings of *X* appear to be unknown. However, according to IMDb, the film had a very limited opening in the USA. When it debuted on 12th March 2000, four years after *X* debuted in Japan, it made just $6,672 on its opening weekend at the box office. The final gross figures in the USA was $143,355, while the total gross figure worldwide was $266,914. However, the figure does not take into account sales from related side products.

In the *All About CLAMP* book, there is also a bonus little comic which jokingly continues the story of *X*. With Kamui about to be stabbed, he has his eyes closed, and when he opens them, he suddenly finds himself in the later CLAMP manga *xxxHOLiC*, which began in the same year *X* went on hiatus.

However, perhaps the best idea for an ending appears in an earlier CLAMP manga. In *Man of Many Faces*, the last two chapters see the main couple, Akira and Utako, as adults. In those chapters, Akira is a 20-year-old now studying at the CLAMP School's university, doing a medical degree. However, that manga begins with Akira being a 9-year-old, with him later turning ten in the second of the two volumes. As that series ran between 1990 and 1991, that would mean that ten years have passed in *Man of Many Faces*, and thus these future chapters take place in the new millennium. Given that, it would appear that humanity does have a bright future and survives the events of *X*. Nevertheless, it would still be better overall for CLAMP to finish the story as we have been waiting for so long, although CLAMP fans are not alone in waiting for long periods of time… X Japan fans have been waiting over 25 years for their next album to come out.

Concerning the theory that they stopped it because they were working on other manga, while that is unlikely, it is true that CLAMP were certainly busy on other projects. When *X* began, the only series that CLAMP had then completed was *Man of Many Faces*. At one point the quartet, all of whom were at that time still in their mid-20s, were producing over 100 pages of manga per month across their various works. As *CLAMP School Detectives* and *Duklyon* ended in 1993, the group began working on a whole batch of other projects. Some are just as, and even more popular, than *X*. Other series were short-lived, but are nevertheless of interest. In the next chapter, we will look at some of these shorts.

Regardless of all this, if I ever got to meet CLAMP, I think there is at least one request I would make: "**PLEASE FINISH X! PLEASE!** We've been waiting nearly 20 years! Just tell us how it bloody ends!"

---

1 – There are also two different punk bands also called X, one in the USA and the other in Australia.

2 – As to which of the two genres they belong to, this is a matter of debate. Part of me hopes that they belong in the rock group, mainly because of the glam-like elements of the group ('visual kei' as it is known), particularly in their early days. Glam rock is cool, glam metal not so – and what with guitarist Hide's fondness for having topless women performing with him when he did his solos, I fear the later. Sadly, X Japan are not a group covered in Andrew O'Neill's otherwise brilliant book *A History of Heavy Metal*, but then again neither are Babymetal, now the most well-known Japanese metal band globally, and in 2019 (after the publication of O'Neill's book) the first Japanese band to perform at one of the main stages in Glastonbury. Japanese bands that are covered include the black metal band Sigh and the grindcore band Flagitious Idiosyncrasy in the Dilapidation. Other Japanese metal bands that I like include BlackLab, a doom duo who, like 25% of CLAMP, come from Osaka, and, like 100% of CLAMP, are all women.

3 – A gig that I am happy to say I was at. At the gig, a new song called 'Kiss the Sky' was performed, which the crowd sang along to. Supposedly it will be on the long-awaited sixth album, so I might be on a rock/metal album… eventually.

4 – For Brits, getting a massive musician like Yoshiki to write the theme for a big anime series like *Attack on Titan* is like Channel 4 holding a press conference to say: "We are going to give *The Great British Bake Off* a brand new theme song, and here's the person who is going to sing it…" and then in walks Adele.

5 – In January 2020, my hometown of Stockton-on-Tees was hit by an earthquake. Well, I say 'earthquake'. It had a magnitude of between 2.8-3, which the Japanese would consider pitiful. All I remember was a brief shake and a noise waking me up. Looking back on it, the 'Tees Tremor' as it became known was probably the least destructive thing to hit the region that year.

6 – Turns out that sometimes there is a purpose to being extravagant.

7 – Oh, speaking of conundrums, do you remember in the preface when I said I worked as a *Countdown* conundrum setter? That was a hoax, aka a 'mountweasel', that I created in order to trap any lazy journalists to see if they would actually read the book, or just read the preface in order to get information about me. If you are someone who failed to read that this fact was false and you ask me what it was like to work on *Countdown*, you are a cunt.

8 – The opposite of a 'tsundere' is a 'yandere', someone who on the surface is very friendly, but deep down is horrible, even to the extent of being violent and murderous. A personal favourite example of this kind of character is Yuno Gasai from the gory thriller *Mirai Nikki* (*The Future Diary*).

9 – Pronounced 'KAR-en'.

10 – The Japanese Self-Defence Force (JSDF) is the Japanese version of the army. After World War II, the new Japanese constitution forbade the Japanese army from being deployed abroad, and thus the army is there only to defend the country. As a result of this, Japan is considered one of the most peaceful nations in the world. However, recent Prime Ministers Shinzo Abe and Yoshihide Suga have been attempting to change the constitution to allow the Japanese army to be deployable elsewhere. This is an extremely controversial move in the country, and the current PM at the time of writing, Fumio Kishida, appears to be less hawkish regarding this policy. Kishida has also pledged to support the anime and manga industry since he came into power.

11 – Although it should be said that according to the oldest discovered copy of the Book of Revelation, the Number of the Beast is 616, not 666.

12 – In Japan, assisted suicide appears to be allowed in some cases, but there are no official laws concerning the subject.

13 – I ended up buying a deck. I don't believe in predicting the future with them, so instead I use them to play patience/solitaire/klondike with them, which is a lot more difficult than the normal version. I play using both the Major and Minor Arcana, with the Major cards only being allowed to go on themselves. Swords and wands go on cups and pentangles (long things on round things). I play with nine increasingly-sized stacks and draw three cards at a time. I've never won.

CHAPTER 5

Love, Lust, Korea and Snow – CLAMP's four one-volume wonders (1992-1995)

In this chapter, we will be covering four different CLAMP series that when they were collected in tankobon only lasted one volume each. The reasons why they are only this long vary from title to title. Most were only intended to be one volume, but some series were ended early.

This jumble included the supernatural series *Shirahime-Syo: Snow Goddess Tales*; *Legend of Chun Hyang*, which is an adaptation of a Korean folk story; the smutty *Miyuki-chan in Wonderland*; and the more romantic *The One I Love*.

As with most of the early CLAMP titles, these four series were eventually released in English by TokyoPop. Today, all four are now available from Viz Media, as e-books only.

Shirahime-Syo: Snow Goddess Tales (1992)

Shirahime-Syo was a short-lived series for one simple reason: It was being made for a magazine that was ceasing publication. It took just ten days to make. In the *CLAMP no Kiseki* interviews, Ohkawa explains the origins:

"At the time, Kobunsha was publishing a magazine called Val Pretty. Its editor came to us and said, 'The magazine is being discontinued, but will you draw a graphic novel for us?' I remember that the issue of the magazine itself with the announcement (of Shirahime-Syo) was the final one before it was suspended."

Inspired by the TV show *Manga Japanese Legends*, today *Shirahime-Syo* is remembered primarily for its art. Due to the story being inspired by folktales, CLAMP went with a more traditional medium to create the comic, using brushes and ink.

•

Set in unspecified periods of the past, the story begins with a man meeting a pale-skinned woman, Shirahime, during a snowstorm. The man warns the woman to find shelter as the Snow Goddess will soon be arriving, for it is said that snow is caused by the Snow Goddess shedding her tears.

Following this brief introduction, we are then told three separate short stories, each with a snowy backdrop. The first, *On Wolf Mountain*, follows a girl called Fubuki. Her father was killed by a wolf, so she decides to hunt it down and kill it as an act of revenge. While searching for the wolf, she is attacked by a pack of wild dogs, but before they can harm her, Fubuki is saved by the very wolf she is trying to hunt. The wolf continues to protect her, and eventually she becomes more attached to the animal, giving it a rather familiar name: Inuki.[1] However, as you might suspect, the story ends in tragedy and tears, as well as snow falling.

The second tale, *The Ice Flower*, is the shortest and, in my view, the weakest of the three stories. An unnamed man is with his lover, Kaya. As they stand by a frozen lake, the man is about to go away but promises to return and marry her. The man does indeed return, but it has taken him 30 years to do so, so he is shocked to discover what has happened to Kaya when he arrives at the lake from which they departed.

The third story, *Hiyoku no Tori* (*Wings Side-By-Side*), follows an unnamed soldier who has left his fiancée, Yukino, to join a battle, but, like in *The Ice Flower*, he promises to marry her when he returns. However, after the battle he gets lost. In the wilderness, he sees two herons, a male and a female, happily together. The soldier is so angered by this, thinking that it is unjust that the herons can be together but he can't be with the one he loves, that he shoots one of the herons with an arrow. After this, he still struggles to find his way home, and has disturbing dreams of a woman holding a skull, which he eventually comes to realise represents the living heron.

After the three stories are told, we return to our opening scene, where the pale-skinned woman reveals her true identity. As you have probably figured out, she is the real Snow Goddess, but she tells the man that the snow is not caused by her tears, but the despair of man.[2]

•

As stated, the artwork is the main reason the series is remembered. The following extract from the *CLAMP no Kiseki* interviews gives the best insight into the situation, when all four members were asked: "Why did you use a brush and ink as the media?"

Ohkawa: *To give it more of a folktale atmosphere.*

Nekoi: *We didn't use screentone at all, so the characters' clothes, the backgrounds and everything were painted with diluted ink.*

Igarashi: *But the manuscript paper got soaked through (since it had been painted with ink), and we had a rough time drying it out.*

Mokona: *There were almost no rough drafts, and once the frames were drawn, everything up to the background was executed all in one shot. We had only one chance at everything, but because of that, we finished it faster. That was an advantage we hadn't thought of... *laughs**

As well as this, the interviews also mention that many of the things that would now be done with more advanced technology, such as the process of plate-making and half-toning, were done by hand. CLAMP were also forced to work to a very tight schedule, with Ohkawa commenting: "When the editor asked us to do it, we had only ten days to finish the art. *laughs*"

The quality of the art clearly stood out, using the more traditional methods. When the collected volume was published, the cover was on traditional Japanese paper with an embossed inlay finish. Even when it was first released in English by TokyoPop, they originally sold it as a hardback rather than the more normal paperback.

When the story was released, Ohkawa commented that opinion from readers was divided, but this is apparently common whenever CLAMP did something new. Mokona meanwhile said: "Seeing the brush strokes, there were some readers who thought the art was crudely done, but on the other hand, there were readers that understood that it was a new technique. Also, apparently there were some people whose interest this piqued for the first time, and they wondered, 'What kind of works did these authors draw before?'"

Shirahime-Syo certainly shows a more experimental side to CLAMP with their willingness to create a new work using different materials. The quality of the stories is mixed. For me, the first of the three is the best, but then again the whole wolf-thing might just be influencing me.

Legend of Chun Hyang (1992-1994)

The next of these one-volume series is *Legend of Chun Hyang*, which also began in the same year as *Shirahime-Syo*. There was only a four month gap between the releases of both series. *Chun*

Hyang was originally serialised in the magazine *Serie Mystery Special*, published by Hakusensha. It is CLAMP's only work from this publisher.

In one clear aspect, *Chun Hyang* bears similarities with CLAMP's debut work *RG Veda*, in that it is based on a famous tale from abroad. In this case, this story is adapted from *Chunhyangga*, a folk story from Korea that is a form of 'pansori', a story told in musical form. Also, like *RG Veda*, CLAMP's version is not a strict adaptation of the original. Obviously, the fact that this story is Korean rather than Indian means that there is a bit less of an issue with the whitewashed/Nipponwashed cast, but for those more interested in the original, CLAMP's version does deviate.

However, CLAMP do at least acknowledge the differences between their version and the original. The manga starts with the following passage: "A long time ago there lived a very beautiful maiden named Chun Hyang. Although she was born a commoner, she was accepted into marriage to the nobleman Mong Ryong. When fate separated her from her betrothed, Chun Hyang refused the advances of suitors, and for that she was put in jail. Her one true love would be Mong Ryong. In her native Korea, Chun Hyang's story has passed into legend. Chun Hyang endures as a symbol of chastity and continues to be honoured to this day. However… this Chun Hyang is a little bit different."

The bit after the ellipsis[3] is on a new page showing CLAMP's version of Chun Hyang, a rather feisty 14-year-old. Indeed, this Chun Hyang is not just a teenager, but as the front cover of the English release demonstrates, one who is skilled in fighting.[4]

•

The story is set in the land of Koryio, which is home to around 300 towns and villages that are ruled by the Chun-An government. Each of these settlements is ruled by one of 321 officials known as Yang Ban, who are sent by the government, with each Yang Ban serving a ten year term in each post. While they are meant to make sure each area is prosperous, there are obviously some troublesome Yang Ban.

In the small town of Ryon Fi, the local Yang Ban is an exploitative troublemaker, who is happy to kill those who defy his vile rule, with his son being equally problematic and happy to do horrible things knowing his father will protect him. When the Yang Ban's son tries to force a woman to come to his castle and, "have some fun", Chun Hyang suddenly appears on the scene and sends him away with her martial arts and fighting skills.

After this, Chun returns home where she lives with her one surviving parent, her mother Wall Mae, the town's most respected Mu Dang (medicine woman), who is also capable of using magic. In their garden however they find in a tree a mysterious stranger, a man who claims to be a traveller and whose name is Mong Ryong. Despite hardly knowing him, Wall invites Mong to stay for a while, but Chun is not interested in him. Chun does however tell Mong of the troubles in the town, and hopes they will be visited by the Am-Hang-Osa, the highest official in the Chun-an government, who will be able to put a stop to the current Yang Ban.

As this is going on, Wall is visited by the Yang Ban's son and an army of guards, who force her to visit the Yang Ban. Upon discovering this, Chun and Mong decide to go to the castle themselves to get her back. But when they arrive it is too late. Chun discovers to her horror that her mother is dead, having committed suicide by stabbing herself. Chun is so angry that she goes to kill him, but when the Yang Ban says that he will punish the townsfolk if Chun tries to defy him, Mong takes out a secret weapon, a jewel-encrusted medallion in the shape of a five-pointed star – the official sign of the Am-Hang-Osa, which is Mong's real job. Mong then authorises Chun to have the power to get her revenge and she slays the Yang Ban. Afterwards Mong offers Chun the chance to follow him on his travels around the country. She agrees, but makes it clear that she does not like him. That concerns the first chapter in the story.

In the second chapter, Chun and Mong help out a different village where it has not rained for many months, the cause of which is a Mu Dang brought in by a new corrupt Yang Ban for our heroic duo to deal with, while the third chapter is a prequel to the first, following Chun at the age of six, and… that's it.

While this chapter of my book is concerned with series that lasted only one collected volume, in the case of *Legend of Chun Hyang* it was not meant to be such a short run. The manga ended after three chapters because *Serie Mystery Special* magazine stopped publication, and the series was not picked up again. Thus, it ends abruptly.

•

It's a shame that *Chun Hyang* ended up going the same way as *X*, although actually *Chun Hyang* was the first of CLAMP's works to end early. They too were upset by it, with Mokona saying in the *CLAMP no Kiseki* interviews that they would have liked to have continued making it. It too has similarities with *Shirahime-Syo*, in that the first chapter was also done with a brush, but for the other chapters they resorted to more modern methods.

However, the biggest similarities are with *RG Veda* and the way that CLAMP changed the source material. The magazine's editors wanted an element of mystery to the story rather than just romance. Regarding Chun, Ohkawa says: "The original Chun Hyang was difficult to capture in a visual format. It was a compendium of feminine virtues and that is always a bit tedious when telling a story using images. *laughs*" Another major difference is that in this one volume Chun is not in love with Mong, but presumably they would have fallen in love if the story had been allowed to continue. CLAMP's version of the story also differs in that their version of Mong knows how to use magic, while he doesn't in the original story. There was some serious research in making the manga as well. Ohkawa mentions in the interviews that in order to correctly illustrate the traditional Korean costume known as the 'hanbok', she had to wear one herself.

Possibly the oddest aspect of the story is the way the chapters were scheduled. It was only three chapters long, but they were spaced so widely. Depending on the publication, new chapters of a manga most often tend to come out weekly or monthly. The chapters of *Chun Hyang* ended up coming out yearly, one in 1992, the second in 1993, and the prequel chapter in 1994.

Chun Hyang ended up as a lost story. It is a shame, as it might have ended up being a much bigger hit rather than just the one volume. It is a great pity.

Miyuki-chan in Wonderland (1993-1995)

If you had been one of the lucky people to have visited the British Museum's manga exhibition in 2019, one of the first images you would have seen upon entering the exhibition would have been of the cover image of CLAMP's manga *Miyuki-chan in Wonderland*. While on the surface this seems appropriate given this manga's connection to a British work, and indeed Lewis Carroll's *Alice* stories are popular in Japan and are subject to many anime and manga adaptations, in another way it is also very inappropriate for one simple reason: *Miyuki-chan* is a sex comedy. *Miyuki-chan* is also the first time CLAMP went into 'yuri' – lesbian manga.

This is something that the British Museum must have known about. In the hefty official book that accompanied the exhibition, *The Citi exhibition: Manga*, edited by Nicole Coolidge Rousmaniere and Matsuba Ryoko, a section entitled 'Through the Looking-Glass and into Manga' by Amanda Kennell comments that the series: "…traces the journey of the titular Miyuki through a Wonderland full of beautiful lesbians, all of whom are lecherously attracted to poor disinterested Miyuki."[5] I later learned on an episode of *No Such Thing as a Fish* (Episode 349, 'No Such Thing As Tug of War for Clowns') that Japanese erotic art known as 'shunga' is the second-most searched for thing on the British Museum's website, getting 40,000 hits in 2017, and only beaten by their Egyptian exhibition, i.e. mummies, at 53,000. More people search for shunga than for the Museum's opening hours. People know the Museum has smut, they just don't know what time to see it.

Of the four series covered in this chapter, *Miyuki-chan in Wonderland* is probably the most interesting of the quartet, partly because of the stark change of tone and subject matter to what they had done previously. It shows how diverse CLAMP are, having previously written children's stories like *Man of Many Faces*, they are also capable of making something more erotic. It is also interesting because, perhaps not surprisingly, it is probably the most derided of all of CLAMP's works by the critics.

However, the series was not originally intended to be released as a volume. Originally published in *Newtype* magazine, CLAMP were proposed to do another series after another manga artist was taking a year-long break. Igarashi said in the *CLAMP no Kiseki* interviews that: "We didn't think it would be compiled into a tankobon, either." The main thing CLAMP wanted to do was draw some sexy ladies and that was about it. Ohkawa added that: "We didn't want a single boy to appear. *laughs*" Indeed, only one boy is mentioned in the entire manga, and that is in the final chapter. Thus, weirdly, all of this sex comedy series passes the Bechdel-Wallace test, in that only women appear in the scenes and don't talk about men.

•

Each chapter of *Miyuki-chan in Wonderland* sees the title character, a teenage schoolgirl, being sucked into a parallel world populated only with other women, all of whom are attracted to her. Eventually she wakes up at the end of every chapter to find everything appears to be a dream, but the last image always indicates that something really has happened, such as an arm or leg suddenly appearing.

In the first chapter, Miyuki ends up in a version of Wonderland after falling down a hole when she bumps into the White Rabbit, who appears in the guise of a bunny girl who for some unexplained reason is skateboarding.[6] There she meets sexy female versions of the characters in *Alice in Wonderland*, including a fishnet-wearing Mad Hatter, and a dominatrix-like Queen of Hearts who flogs Miyuki and forces her to call the Queen "Mistress". This chapter is followed by one in 'Looking Glass Land', which among other things, leads to a scene where Miyuki says: "I've never been turned on by chess pieces before."[7]

In the other chapters, Miyuki is sucked into a TV in the middle of the night after she fails to be awake for a late-night re-run of the film *Barbarella*; she turns up late at her part-time job at a restaurant and dreams of having to take part in foxy boxing with the rest of the staff; enters the world of a Mah-Jongg manga and has to play a strip-version of the game; finds herself in a role-playing video game where among other things she is attacked by a female incubus,[8] and finally, in a promotional device, she is sucked into the anime film version of *X*, meeting various female characters from CLAMP's apocalyptic manga, including sex worker Karen, who strips her and gives Miyuki lingerie to wear, which is then cut up by Arashi. It is also in this final chapter that we read the only reference to a man, where Miyuki mentions Kamui.

•

It does feel weird reading *Miyuki-chan*, partly given the context of the other works CLAMP have made. They are no strangers to making content that is not suitable for everyone. You wouldn't show the violent *X* to a child, for example. However, for some reason people seem to be more offended by the sexy works CLAMP have done rather than the violent stuff. Of course, the fact that Miyuki is still a teenage schoolgirl may be part of the reason for this. While she is never seen having intercourse or being entirely naked, the fact that so many sexy women doing lewd things surrounding her, including stripping and whipping Miyuki, does make reading the comic rather uncomfortable. It is even more uncomfortable when you realise that Miyuki is not consenting to any of this. She ends up the unwilling victim.[9]

What makes it more uncomfortable though is something mentioned in the *CLAMP no Kiseki* interviews. When asked the question: "Did you take someone as a model for Miyuki's character?" Ohkawa answered: "We weren't inspired by anybody in particular, but Nekoi's sister is called Miyuki. When she told us, 'I would like you to use my name [in a series],' we didn't think twice. Oh well, it slipped out of me. *laughs* I don't know if it's okay to reveal the identity of the person whose name we used as an inspiration. *laughs*"

I would argue that it isn't okay in this instance. I imagine that if anyone wrote a piece of erotic fiction in which any of the characters happened to share a name with a close family member of the author, it is, at best, going to make for some awkward family conversations. Even worse is if that fact becomes common knowledge among the public. Put it this way, if it turned out that *Fifty Shades of Grey* author E. L. James had close siblings called either Anastasia or Christian, that would have attracted a considerable amount of attention.

It should also be stated that out of the four manga in this chapter, *Miyuki-chan* is the only one to get an anime adaptation. It is very brief, just two OVA episodes covering the first two chapters, each only 15 minutes long. While released in North America, it has never been released in the UK.

However, as mentioned earlier, another thing that is notable about this manga is the reviews. It would be wrong to say that they were all negative. Reviews were mixed, but some really hated this. Now, when it comes to reviews, I am something of an expert, not just because I write them for both online and in print, but I also collect them. Every year since 2010, part of my work for the British Comedy Guide involves me collecting all the reviews from just about every newspaper and website around during the Edinburgh Festival Fringe, the world's largest arts festival. I collect approximately 5,000 reviews every August. It can be an exhausting, tedious, depressing and draining job, especially given how shoddily written some of the reviews are or just how vile some websites can be, and while the comedy press is often bad outside of the Fringe too, during August the workload is immense. My general view is that my job involves collecting the opinions of arseholes (critics), talking about other arseholes (comedians) for the benefit of more arseholes (the public, i.e. you). While I have got some recognition in the industry for my review collecting, I am now being given some extra help in this line of work, and I am now a judge for the increasingly prestigious Malcolm Hardee Awards, but my name is generally not that well known, so far as I'm aware.

Anyway, an overview of the reviews shows how diverse the opinions are. During my Fringe review collecting, one of the most positive aspects is showing the diversity of opinion. This is best shown when a show gets a 'rainbow review', i.e. a five star, four star, three star, two star and one star review from various publications. For the purposes of illustration, listed below are some extracts of reviews of *Miyuki-chan in Wonderland* that I have come across.

A review of the manga from *Anime Fringe* by Patrick King: "The visuals are what really make this book worth it. CLAMP has a knack for creating some beautiful illustrations, and this title is no exception. If you're looking for a book full of random drawings of beautiful women in various states of undress, then look no further – there's not much more to *Miyuki-chan in Wonderland*."

From *The Anime Review* covering the anime version: "For people who want eye candy, it's all there in its glory – the only good thing I can even say about it is that your eyes will not be sore from watching it, and that's why it doesn't suffer an even worse grade. Fans of CLAMP might be satisfied. The rest of us, however, will want our money back." Rated 'D'.

An anime review from Christopher Macdonald on the *Anime News Network*: "Uhh, weird. To be honest, the above simple phrase is probably an extremely good review of *Miyuki-chan in Wonderland*. Anyone who has seen *Alice in Wonderland* knows just how disjointed and nonsensical the movie is. *Miyuki-chan in Wonderland* is somewhat akin to *Alice in Wonderland* on amphetamines… Honestly, *Miyuki-chan* is recommended viewing to anyone, regardless of their tastes, it's a bit like that crazy trip that you have to take just once in your life."

In a manga review from Katherine Dacey on *Manga Bookshelf* in an article entitled, 'The Manga Hall of Shame', she writes: "This odd one-shot represents the nadir of this talented quartet's work.[10]

...The stories are short and repetitive, barely spanning 100 pages in total, and are so inane that they don't work as pornography or parody. Strictly for the CLAMP completist."

Mason Templar, who reviewed all of CLAMP's titles that had been released in English at the time of publication for Jason Thompson's *The Complete Guide to Manga* published in 2007 wrote: "If you buy it at all, buy it as an art book, as the book does showcase lead CLAMP artist Mokona's full range of sexy women." He goes on to say that Miyuki's best role is in cameos in a later CLAMP work, *Tsubasa*, and gave the series a rating of one out of four.[11]

Finally, in *The Anime Encyclopedia*, Jonathan Clements and Helen McCarthy describe the anime as: "A pointlessly kinky retelling of *Alice in Wonderland* in which all the characters are sapphically inclined females", and when talking about how each chapter ends with everything being a dream, they say it is: "A one-note gag that falls crushingly flat when the clever designs are forced to do more than look good on paper."

You will have probably noticed that all of these reviews are from Western critics. It is obviously hard for me, as someone who doesn't speak Japanese, to engage the views of what Japanese people think of the series. That and the fact that reviewing manga doesn't really seem to be that big a thing in Japan anyway, so far as I know. The view in Japan appears to be that if something is not good, the readers will let the publishers know in their surveys or just won't buy the books or watch the shows.

I am okay with saying that *Miyuki-chan in Wonderland* is not CLAMP's finest hour, but as for it being the worst of their titles I'm not sure, for the following reasons:

1) As previously mentioned in the *CLAMP no Kiseki* interviews, CLAMP were not expecting it to be released as a single volume, so you might want to cut them some slack about reviewing it because they didn't expect it to come out.
2) As some of the reviews acknowledge, the manga still has some good art in it.
3) You suspect that some of these critics are just being snooty about such an esteemed group like CLAMP working on something that is so close to pornography.
4) I suspect there could be sexism going on. If CLAMP had been drawing sexy gay guys, I suspect there would be less complaining, as no one complains much about boys' love and yaoi comics. The fact that it is female characters being sexualised is always going to attract more anger from people, even when the work is being created by other women.

Having said this, the series is certainly still one of the weakest in terms of plot and writing, and yes, while the erotic art is well executed, in comparison to other erotic art, it is no *Stay Up Late* by Brian Swords of York, Pennsylvania.[12] At least *Miyuki-chan in Wonderland* is still available to read in English if you do want to look at it.

Also, as previously mentioned, Miyuki does appear in CLAMP's other work. Aside from *Tsubasa*, one of her most high profile appearances was in the anime version of *CLAMP School Detectives*, which begs the question: "How many kids watching this show knew that it also starred someone from a porn comic in it?" In one of the episodes Miyuki is in, she visits the CLAMP School during its annual festival, bringing along a pet ferret which runs away. Naturally the boys end up helping Miyuki find the ferret, but the animal keeps running away from the boys. Nokoru realises the reason is because the ferret hates boys. Seems that even the animals Miyuki hangs out with are lesbians.

The One I Love (1993-1995)

Now we come to the book that whenever I think of it, the first thing that pops into my head is 'You're Still the One' by Shania Twain.[13]

Released in the magazine *Monthly Young Rose*, published by Kadokawa Shoten, *The One I Love* is the one CLAMP title that differs the most from the others. For starters, it is not one single story, but 12 short ones, each just seven pages long. Also, each of the stories is accompanied by an essay written by Ohkawa. It was also the first time that Nekoi would be the main illustrator.

•

Each of the dozen stories in *The One I Love* focuses on a different unnamed woman and their current romantic struggles. Some tales are based on real-life stories involving things that happened to CLAMP themselves or to people they knew.

The stories cover, among other things, a couple who have had a fight, a bride on her wedding day, a girl worried about the strain her boyfriend's work as a manga artist is having on their relationship, and a girl recalling her childhood sweetheart.[14]

•

It is obviously difficult to talk in detail about each story, because each individual story is so brief. Because of this *The One I Love* is so far the only one of CLAMP's titles that appears to have no cross-over with any of their other series.

Fortunately, if you want detail, there are the essays at hand. Unfortunately, the nature of these essays does make reading this manga somewhat slow. While critics say that *Miyuki-chan in Wonderland* is the worst CLAMP book, at least it is relatively quick to read in comparison to *The One I Love*, which is my least favourite work in the CLAMP canon.

Like *Miyuki-chan*, opinion is divided about the quality. Templar's review of it in *Manga: The Complete Guide* gives *The One I Love* a slightly better rating than *Miyuki-chan*, but only by half a star, and goes so far as to say that the way the stories conclude with the women being the ones changing their behaviour for seemingly perfect men is, "almost anti-feminist in execution." I think that this is going too far myself. It's perhaps clichéd, but anti-feminist seems an over-exaggeration.

Personally, I would echo the comments of another reviewer, Liann Cooper of *Anime News Network*, who suggests that, "The anthology is probably best read in small doses." The fact that this manga is actually an anthology of small stories means that it is easy to dip in and out of. If you don't like one story, the next one might take your fancy.

For me, the best story is the 11th in the collection, 'Apart', which deals with the subject of a long-distance relationship after the boy moves to a different town, but they are able to keep the relationship going with him saving up the money for a train ticket to see the girl narrating the story once again. It ends with words that to me struck a chord: "It's not distance that ruins a relationship. As long as you want to see each other, love can last. Your heart doesn't grow distant because you're apart. If your heart grows distant, it might be for other reasons. As long as you want to see each other, your hearts will be close together." The accompanying essay says that the real-life long-distance relationship that inspired this story ended up in marriage. Personally, I found this story to be rather moving.

•

The four series covered in this chapter have varying degrees of quality, with some critics going so far as to describe one or two as the worst in CLAMP's catalogue. However, all four also have some merit.

Shirahime-Syo witnessed them experimenting with new artistic methods. *Chun Hyang* also features this artwork, and may well have been a major hit if the magazine behind it hadn't folded. *Miyuki-chan* demonstrated CLAMP's ability to create more adult work. *The One I Love* allowed them to work on smaller-scale projects and deal with personal issues.

Another thing to remember about these series is that they were being made while CLAMP were still working on *X*. Not only that, but *Chun Hyang*, *Miyuki-chan* and *The One I Love* were also being made at the same time that another CLAMP title was in production, which is the subject of the next chapter. Not only is it the series that truly propelled them into the public consciousness, it is a series dealing with a genre that was at the time in its infancy, but has since come on to dominate anime and manga itself. It also features a lot of things named after cars.

---

1 – Remember that this story came before the appearance of Inuki the dog spirit in *X*, so *Shirahime-Syo* is the first time we see this name being used.

2 – Except in Britain, where snow is very much the cause of man's despair, the cause of derision from countries who cope with much bigger snowfalls than us, and the cause of very feeble excuses for trains being delayed. For those outside the UK, look up the Wikipedia article on 'The wrong type of snow'.

3 – That's the technical name for the dot-dot-dot punctuation mark in case you don't know, and sorry if that comes across as patronising.

4 – Before I go on, I should say that I know that is perfectly innocent because the original story was written hundreds of years ago in a different language, but there's still a small part of me that, as a disabled person, feels uncomfortable either reading, writing or saying 'Mong' so often. I'm not saying we should censor it, I'm just saying that every time I bring it up, I have to remind myself that in this context it's perfectly fine, while another part of me butts in and thinks: 'Is it…?', with these two parts of my brain going back and forth in this trivial way.

5 – I do wonder why the Museum went with this series as one of the first things you saw at the exhibition. Part of me wonders if this was some joke by some dodgy museum curator, or perhaps they didn't know what the manga was about at first, thinking it was entirely innocent and didn't know about all the sexy stuff until it was too late to change it.

6 – I was later told by Robin Kaplan from *CLAMPcast in Wonderland* that this is a reference to the opening anime for the *Daicon IV* Nihon SF Taikai convention from 1983. It was made by a bunch of art students who would go on to form the anime studio Gainax, and later Trigger, including *Evangelion* creator Hidekai Anno. This short feature sees a girl in a bunny suit fighting amongst others Darth Vader and the xenomorph from *Alien*, and also travelling on a sword like a floating skateboard. The character would be referenced in Gainax's OVA *Otaku no Video*. According to Kimi Rito's book *The History of Hentai Manga* (first published by Ohta in 2017, released in English by FAKKU in 2021), *Daicon IV* was for a long time accepted as

the first anime to depict the movement of breasts, in a sexy way at least, but as Rito writes (p76-77), "If the question turns to simply being about breasts moving in anime, period, there have been multiple reports of works before *Daicon IV* that depict just that."

7 – To be fair to Miyuki, that is a niche fetish. I write about an industry that has a reputation for weird porn. I call myself 'Wolf' because I am also in the furry fandom, the fandom of anthropomorphic animals, which has an even bigger reputation for porn – so much so I wouldn't be surprised if at least one reader burned this book in disgust right now because they're wrongly thinking I'm into beastality. So far, I've not come across any chess-based hentai or yiff, although I'm positive that you will be able to find an artist that could create something. All I'm saying is that I've never heard of anyone being turned on by a rook, but I have heard that some people like to bash the bishop, and I am happy to admit there are people who are into pawn. Look, this is a comedy book and it would be remiss of me not to have done that pun.

8 – Despite the fact that this should technically be a succubus.

9 – I can sympathise, because I too have been the victim of untoward sexual behaviour. I was looking at my phone while waiting to cross the road, when suddenly I felt someone grab my buttocks. I have been groped. When it happened, my mind was a blur. I was thinking things faster than I could write or say them. I knew there was a police station nearby, so I could run to there and report what happened, but first I needed to get a look at my attacker. I turned my head round to see my attacker's face, and discovered that I was being groped by a certain someone I knew, who was groping me as a practical joke! You know, that

classic gag of committing sexual assault on someone you know! In comedy, the other area of work I'm in, there is debate about whether you should tell rape jokes. I think most rape jokes should not be told, partly because they are offensive, but mainly because most of them are just shit, and no comedian should go on stage with such material unless they are capable of dealing with the repercussions.

10 – And yes, I did have to look up what 'nadir' means. I'll save you the trouble by telling you that it is defined as: 'The lowest or most unsuccessful point in a situation.'

11 – A system of rating that I hate, mainly out of my time during the Fringe review collecting. If you are going to give a star rating, stick to whole numbers out of ten, or whole and half numbers out of five. I've seen websites give reviews of acts to two decimal places, as if 0.05 of a mark out of ten makes any difference at all.

12 – Or indeed Osamu Tezuka's own erotic mouse drawings. In 2014, his daughter Rumiko managed to open a locked drawer of her late father's desk, unopened since his death in 1989. In it was some half-eaten chocolate, an essay about *Akira* creator Katsuhiro Otomo in which he praised his work as both a director and an animator, and lots of sketches, including ones featuring sexy female mice and other anthropomorphic animals. Tezuka created several adult works including the anime feature films *One Thousand and One Nights* (1969) and *Cleopatra* (1970), both of which predate the more respected American adult animated film *Fritz the Cat* (1972). Given all this, on behalf of my fellow furries, can I just say: "Let us be. If yiff was good enough for Tezuka, it's good enough for us."

13 – I know that other songs like 'The One I Love' by R.E.M. might be more suitable, but given that is a manga by women and about women's romance, Twain seems more appropriate. For other anime and manga that also make me think of songs, see the Elvis Presley-inducing yaoi manga *Don't Be Cruel*, the Blur-inducing pop idol franchise *Love Live!* ('Parklife'), the Guns 'n' Roses-inducing dancing anime and manga *Welcome to the Ballroom* ('Welcome to the Jungle') and CLAMP's *Gate 7*, which has a character in it that makes me think of one particular song, but let's wait until we get to the chapter covering it.

14 – A chapter which also involves the women trying to find a Sonic the Hedgehog doll, which will be of interest to all fans of the fast blue one.

CHAPTER 6

Driven by Will, Named after Nissan – *Magic Knight Rayearth* (1993-1996)

This series, the first mainstream success for CLAMP, might be their most familiar work to some British readers, as the TV anime was released in the UK on Blu-Ray in two collections while I was in the middle of writing this book. The *Magic Knight Rayearth* anime was the first TV adaptation of CLAMP's work debuting in 1994 (the TV version of *CLAMP School Detectives* didn't debut until 1997, *X* didn't arrive until 2001 and all the previous anime had been either films or straight-to-video OVA releases). This series also had an OVA release available in the UK on DVD as well, which came out in 1997.

The actual manga version of *Magic Knight Rayearth* debuted in 1993 in Kodansha's *Nakayoshi* magazine, the same magazine that released the massively popular magical girl series *Sailor Moon*, and whose editors were looking for a new title to appeal to a slightly older readership. CLAMP were surprised to get the job, as their most well-known series at the time – *RG Veda*, *Tokyo Babylon* and *X* – were far from the cuter kind of works the magazine normally published. What resulted was the first CLAMP series to be completely original, with none of the characters having previously appeared in their earlier doujinshi.

The series was split over two parts, the first written between 1993 and 1995, and the second between 1995 and 1996, each part consisting of three volumes each. This one series has been translated in English by three different publishers. *Rayearth* was originally released by TokyoPop in its individual tankobon, then two larger editions by Dark Horse, and most recently in a pair of 25th anniversary boxset collections by the English-language arm of Kodansha – and if there is one thing we anime and manga fans love, it's a good boxset.[1] *Rayearth* is one of several titles published by both TokyoPop and Dark Horse, which has now been brought out in special hardback versions by Kodansha. In this book I am using the complete Dark Horse versions, except in *Clover*'s case in which I can use the Kodansha version. After completing the original draft of this book however, the second half of Kodansha's *Rayearth* collection came out, so while the Dark Horse version is the main basis for this chapter, I will go over the new version too.

Looking back, *Rayearth* is perhaps now considered to be an early example of the 'isekai' genre of manga, anime, computer games and, in particular, light novels. As mentioned in the introduction, isekai are series where one or more characters find themselves transported to another world. Methods of travel between worlds differ series to series, and include magical spells, problematic technology, or reincarnation after death. The most common method of death seems to be being run-over by a truck, to the point that now there is a meme of 'Truck-kun', the idea that the truck that kills all of these characters is the same truck appearing in lots of different series. I've even heard *CLAMPcast in Wonderland* talk about characters being, "isekaied by the truck."

Today, isekai is one of the most commonplace genres, and they cover all sorts of worlds from fantasy settings like *Rayearth*'s Cefiro, to the virtual worlds in series like *Sword Art Online* (probably the first series to be listed in the genre as it was being written, rather than retrospectively) and *Log Horizon*, as mentioned in this book's introduction. There is one anime series, *Isekai Quartet*, that cross-references mainly from four different isekai light novels – *Overlord*, *The Saga of Tanya the Evil*, *Re:Zero – Starting Life in Another World* and *KonoSuba: God's Blessing on this Wonderful World* – but it also features appearances from other titles too.

The four series that make up the *Isekai Quartet* are also some of the more sensibly named of the light novels. Many light novels, especially isekai and fantasy works, have bizarrely long and/or odd titles. Genuine isekai light novel titles, when translated into English, include *I've Been Killing Slimes for 300 Years and Maxed Out My Level*, *The World's Finest Assassin Gets Reincarnated in a Different World as an Aristocrat*, *Do You Love Your Mom and Her Two-Hit Multi-Target Attacks?*, and the record-breaking *Killing the People Reincarnated into the Other World: Cheat Slayer*. The record it broke was 'fastest cancellation of an officially published manga', running for just a single chapter in *Monthly Dragon Age* magazine on 9th June, 2021. It was intended to be a regular series, but it got pulled when people spotted that many of the villains in it were very similar to the leads in other isekai, where those characters were not villains, and some of the original authors did not take too kindly to the parody.

It should be stressed that *Rayearth* was not the first manga to be regarded as fitting the isekai mould, but it was one of the early ones. *Rayearth* and another series from the same period, *The Vision of Escaflowne*, which began as a manga a year after *Rayearth* and had an anime TV series in 1996, helped to create this genre, with some critics and reviewers labelling them as part of the 'first wave of isekai', while more modern series are the 'second wave'. Both *Rayearth* and *Escaflowne* also happened to be involved in another anime-centric genre: mecha. This is the genre featuring humanoid robotic tanks. Mecha had been around since the 1970s at least, and both of these titles featured these machines. One of the reasons behind *Rayearth*'s appeal was that it was one of the few series at the time in which girls fought in the mecha rather than the boys.

There is however a key difference between *Rayearth* and *Escaflowne*: *Rayearth* is regarded as a shojo girls manga, whereas *Escaflowne* originally started as a shonen boys series and even ran in a magazine called *Shonen Ace*, although it later had shojo spin-offs. This is worthy of note as both mecha and isekai are normally seen as rather male-dominated genres, but CLAMP tried to appeal to both male and female readers. Most of the first wave isekai were also shojo series, with 'shojo isekai' also being used as a term for series of the period, whereas today isekai are dominated by male protagonists, with some exceptions.

Due to *Rayearth* trying to appeal to both boys and girls, one of the odder aspects of the story is that nearly everything and everyone in the fantasy land that *Rayearth* is set in is named after a car. In the *CLAMP no Kiseki* interviews Ohkawa talks about how she couldn't remember the names of characters from fantasy stories, and thought that a way to help younger readers remember them would be to give them a theme. She said: "Car names are well designed/researched, so there's a lot of cool, easy to remember names. I thought this would help the readers connect with the characters." One of the few things that is not named after a car in the story is the Rayearth of the title, although they asked a friend, illustrator Takeshi Okazaki (creator of manga *Eleamentalors* and *Explorer Woman Ray*), to come up with a name that sounded like a car, and 'Rayearth' was his suggestion.[2] As a result, when writing about the plot, I will put the car details of each place/character in square brackets, although you can see a more detailed list in the appendixes. Please also keep in mind that as the story is told in two parts, obviously I need to give away a fair amount of information in the first part in order for the second part to make sense.

Magic Knight Rayearth (1993-1995)

The first part of *Rayearth* debuted in Japan in 1993, and would go on to form the basis of CLAMP's first TV series, as well as the first video game based on their works.

•

The story begins with a young girl. She is being held captive and is praying for a group of 'Magic Knights' to help save her and her world. From this prayer, a massive beam of light erupts, that will soon land on Tokyo Tower in our year 1993. In the tower are several school trip parties, and three girls in particular: Hikaru Shidou (dressed in red), a short, fiery child whose family runs a kendo dojo; Umi Ryuuzaki (in blue), a cool kid who is a member of her school's fencing team; and Fuu Hououji (in green), an intelligent and polite girl who is in her school's archery team. The beam of light shines upon them as the trio hear the girl's prayer, at which point the floor seems to turn into liquid and they sink down into it. When they come to, they find themselves high in the sky above a totally different land.

Before the three plummet to their deaths, they are rescued by a gigantic flying fish named Fyula, which belongs to the Guru Clef [named after the Mazda Clef]. Clef, who looks younger than the girls but is actually 745 years old, tells the girls where they are and why they are here.

The three have been transported to the land of Cefiro [sometimes spelt Cephiro, named after the Nissan Cefiro]. Cefiro is a world that is driven by the will of the people who live there. The ruler had been the Princess Emeraude [Mitsubishi Emeraude], who is the land's 'Pillar'. It is the prayers of the Pillar that help maintain the land. However, Emeraude has been abducted by Zagato [the name of an Italian coachbuilding company], who is the high priest of the land. With Emeraude locked away, Cefiro is becoming a dark, more hostile world. Monsters attacking innocent people are starting to appear. The only people capable of saving both Emeraude and Cefiro are the Magic Knights who come from another world, i.e. ours. These Magic Knights are Hikaru, Umi and Fuu, and they can only return to Tokyo once they complete the mission they have been summoned for. In order to do that, they must awaken the 'Mashin', three elemental, magical beings (also known as 'Rune-Gods' in some translations, including the Kodansha manga).[3]

At first Umi and Fuu are against this, while Hikaru is just really excited about the whole situation. Eventually the threesome agree to do the task that has been set out for them. Clef gives them armour and grants them the ability to use magic, but only Hikaru is given the full ability to use it before they are all attacked by one of Zagato's minions, the sorceress Alcyone [Subaru Alcyone], who was once Clef's student. The Magic Knights are able to escape using one of Clef's other magical beasts as he fights off Alcyone, with help from Hikaru's newly gained magic that allows her to control fire.

Upon Clef's instruction, they first go to see Presea [Nissan Presea], Cefiro's master artisan and blacksmith, who can provide them with weapons. Clef also tells them to look for Mokona (not named after a car, but after the CLAMP member Mokona). When they arrive at Presea's house, they find Mokona, who it turns out is a strange, small, white blobbish creature with rabbit ears and a magical red jewel in its forehead.[4] Mokona is making a mess of Presea's house, and upon meeting Mokona the Magic Knights find themselves trapped in a cage that Presea set up to catch Mokona, although Presea soon realises her mistake.

Before going on however, it should be mentioned that this scene in which Presea tries to trap Mokona contains what is seemingly the most politically incorrect moment in all of CLAMP's work. When Presea thinks she has trapped Mokona, she begins to ask herself how she will punish it: "Shall I see how wide I can stretch your ears? Hmmm… or hang you by your feet and dance about?" then laughs to herself. However, in the panel where she talks about hanging Mokona, it shows Presea dressed in a Native American headdress whooping. While it is possible that CLAMP and the Japanese in general did not realise that in the USA this is a rather offensive stereotype, and thus arguably excuse their ignorance, this is still not the worst stereotyping in the comic.

When Presea discovers she has actually trapped the girls, she ponders how to punish them for trespassing her house, saying: "Shall I see how wide I can stretch your mouth? Or should I dump all three of ya in a big pot and boil you?!" and once again we see her in the Native American headdress whooping. Not only do they use the stereotype again, but they add a second one of boiling people in a big pot which – and do correct me if I'm wrong – isn't a Native American stereotype. That's a stereotype you associate more with racist depictions of cannibalistic jungle tribes. Thus, not only are CLAMP using dodgy racist stereotyping, they are using inaccurate dodgy racist stereotyping. Fortunately, this is an isolated incident in their work, unless you count that whitewashing/Nipponwashing in *RG Veda* and some of the more fascistic illustrations in *CLAMP School Detectives*, but it is still uncomfortable to read. Looking at it, I feel compelled to make the remark that all white English people make when they see something racist, but think there is nothing that they can do to sort it out: "… *sigh*, *shake head*, *tut, tut, tut*."[5]

Anyway, the story…

Presea eventually realises that the Magic Knights were able to enter her house due to the power of Clef, and thus agrees to help them. She starts by loaning them weapons, but what the trio really need are custom-made weapons. For this, they need the raw material 'escudo' [Suzuki Escudo], which is found in the floating Spring of Eterna [Mitsubishi Eterna]. Escudo has the power to make weapons and armour evolve as the user becomes stronger. The three set off, guided by Mokona, and meet another ally along the way: the green-haired and scarred swordsman Ferio [named after CLAMP's own green, scratched Honda Civic Ferio]. Together they also fight Alcyone again and defeat her, thanks to Mokona using its power to send messages from Clef that allow him to give Umi and Fuu the full ability to use magic, Umi's powers being based on water, and Fuu's on wind. In anger, Zagato kills Alcyone for her failure.

The Magic Knights are able to reach and dive into the Spring and recover the escudo, which Presea is able to convert into three magical swords for the girls, using her special weapon-making method… the medium of dance. With these weapons and more magical assistance from Mokona, the girls travel across Cefiro to meet and revive the three Mashin – Ceres [also known as Selece, named after the Toyota Corolla Ceres], who becomes controlled by Umi; Windom [or Windam, named after the Toyota Windom], used by Fuu; and Rayearth (which as discussed earlier was a name that was made up that sounded like a car) for Hikaru.

This next section gives away the end of the first part of the story, but I need to mention it so we can discuss part two, so once again this will be in mirror writing.

As they meet the Mashin, Zagato sends even more of his minions to fight them, namely the child-like beast summoner Ascot [Honda Ascot], the illusionist Caldina [Toyota Caldina] and the swordsman Rafaga [aka Lafarga, named after the Honda Rafaga]. However, all three of these people eventually swap sides

There is much to discuss about *Rayearth*, although some of it is best brought up after we have examined Part 2 of the story.

One thing that we can look at is the artwork, which according to CLAMP themselves was hard work, as highlighted in this exchange in the *CLAMP no Kiseki* interviews when asked: "Were there any difficulties?"

Nekoi: *Drawing Rayearth required a lot of time and effort. There were the clothes, the hair, the robots [mecha], and the style of screen* *tone we chose was so intense we nearly died. *laughs* It was hard once we finished penning, we'd have to go straight to sticking on the screen tone.*

Igarashi: *Even Mokona's body needed tone.*

The 25th anniversary collection includes an illustration collection which describes the full process of creating one of their colour images. It took over 13 hours to complete, using, among other materials, mechanical pencils, charcoal paint, nibbed pens, Copic markers and an airbrush.

It was certainly worth the effort though. The world of Cefiro is a spectacular one, with floating islands, magical creatures, hideous monsters, and wonderful characters – most of whom having a particularly odd bunch of names, admittedly. The one bit that is lacking is the design of the mecha, aka the transformed Mashin. In the same interviews, Ohkawa said that they didn't draw a design for a cockpit because they wanted to show the expressions of the heroes more. I think this was a mistake. In mecha series, some of the best scenes are in the claustrophobic confines of the cockpits, with their monitors and panels dimly lit. In comparison, *Escaflowne*, *Rayearth*'s contemporary, has a better design for their mecha, while at the same time giving it a suitable fantasy setting, with their mecha being operated by pulleys and cogs, almost giving them a steampunk quality. If mecha interests you more than the fantasy, you may want to sample *Escaflowne* instead.[6]

While Ohkawa said in the interviews that one of the reasons for the car theme was because she could never remember the character names from fantasy stories and thus decided to go with a car theme, I have come across some other theories. The most believable is that if she could not remember the names, children would also have trouble too. One article I came across from the website *Anime Theorist,* entitled: 'How Deep Is the

Car Connection in *Magic Knight Rayearth*?' puts forward two theories:

1) To attract more male fans, because of concerns that the series was too focused on elements that girls would like to read but not boys. The author of the article however dismissed this idea on the grounds that other series aimed at girls still attracted large male readerships.
2) For more exotic sounding names, which is closer to what Ohkawa said in her interview about car names being well-designed and researched.

Personally however, I think these two theories are doubtful. As for Hikaru, Umi and Fuu, their names have meaning too, relating to their magical powers. 'Hikaru' is the verb 'to shine' and contains the Japanese character for 'light', while her dog Hikari uses the noun version of 'Hikaru'. Umi's name has the character meaning 'ocean'. Fuu's name has the character for 'wind' or 'air'.[7]

For those who may have watched the anime version, you may be surprised by the number of differences between it and the manga original. The anime tends to follow a 'monster of the week' trope, with the Magic Knights having to slay a monster in order to survive, help locals or continue on their mission. In one of these fights, Presea is even killed while she is perfectly okay in the manga. Zagato meanwhile does not kill Alcyone and he also has loyal sidekick called Inouva [Honda Ascot Innova] who never appears in the manga. Also, the alternative spellings mentioned earlier all appear in the subtitled version of the anime, whereas the Dark Horse manga version uses the spellings used by the actual car manufacturers to make the references clearer.

However, the anime does help shine a light on some of the issues regarding translation. Having read the Kodansha version after completing this chapter, there are some issues regarding the Melissa Tanaka translation. One of these is when Hikaru is casting her fire magic. In the Dark Horse version, the spell is 'Flame Arrow', while in the Kodansha version it is 'Arrow of Flame'. Which term is the most accurate? Well, if you listen to the anime in the original Japanese dub, the answer is clearly 'Flame Arrow'. How can someone, even a non-Japanese speaker like me, know this to be the case? Simple: because Hikaru casts the spell in bloody English! There's no need for translating that, surely? Having said that however, there are other bits of Tanaka's translation I do like, but we'll get to that later.

Rayearth was also the first of CLAMP's works to be adapted for video games. These included games on the Nintendo Game Boy, the Super Nintendo, and the Sega Game Gear, but these never got outside of Japan. One *Rayearth* game did make the transition abroad though. This was the *Magic Knight Rayearth* game for the Sega Saturn, which was based on just the first part of the story. One of the first Saturn games announced, it was released in Japan in 1995. However, the American game publisher Working Designs had problems with localising the game, translating the written text, the audio and the dubbing. They planned to release the game in 1996 but it did not come out until 30th November 1998, which meant that *Magic Knight Rayearth* became the last ever video game to be released on the Sega Saturn in North America. The game never even made it to Europe.

Magic Knight Rayearth 2 (1995-1996)

The second half of the series was again released in three volumes, between 1995 and 1996.

•

Hikaru, Umi and Fuu have been feeling rather forlorn since returning to Tokyo. The trio agree to meet up at Tokyo Tower once again, where Hikaru expresses her wish to return to Cefiro. It appears that her will is powerful enough to allow her to summon the light and for them to make the trip to the fantastical land, where, much like last time, they end up in the middle of the sky, only to be rescued again by Clef's flying fish, Fylua.

The girls soon discover the Cefiro has changed dramatically. Following the death of Princess Emeraude, the land has deteriorated because there is now no Pillar praying to maintain it. The one stronghold is a castle which Fylua takes them to. Upon arrival they are greeted by Presea, who in turn leads them to Clef and to the Prince of Cefiro. The Magic Knights were unaware there was a prince but they have met them, for the prince is Ferio, who it is revealed is the younger brother of Emeraude.

Clef tells the Magic Knights of the current situation. Cefiro is in a dire state. As the land is slowly being destroyed by the lack of a new Pillar, invaders from three other worlds are coming, each with someone planning on making themselves the Pillar.

The first of these invaders is the technologically advanced but polluted world of Autozam [a former branch of Mazda]. From this land comes Eagle Vision [named after the… err… Eagle Vision, which in Europe became the Chrysler Vision], the sickly son of Autozam's president who wants to be in an eternal sleep in Cefiro. He travels on the battleship *NSX* [Honda NSX], armed with its Laguna Cannons [Renault Laguna, or possibly the Laguna Seca racetrack] with his second in command Geo Metro [named after the… err… Geo Metro], and both of them operate their own mecha, the FTO and GTO respectively (both named after cars by Mitsubishi). Keeping the mecha in check is their mechanic Zaz Torque [aka Zazu Torque, named after the ZAZ car makers of Ukraine].

The second is the Indian/Middle Eastern influenced Cizeta [aka Chizeta, named after an Italian car maker]. From here come twin sister princesses Tata and Tatra [aka Tarta and Tatra, named after India's Tata Motors and Czechia's Tatra car maker] on board their fortress *Bravada* [Oldsmobile Bravada]. Their reason for invading Cefiro is to colonise it. Cizeta is too small to support their population and they want to turn Cefiro into a colony for their people. Tata and Tatra fight by summoning a pair of giant djinn. Cizeta is also revealed to be the homeworld of Caldina.

The third is the Chinese/Far Eastern influenced Fahren [named after a German car part manufacturer]. From their fortress (*Dreamchild* in the Dark Horse version, *Daydream* in Kodansha), rules the brat-like crown princess Aska [Isuzu Aska], who wants to turn Cefiro into a land which caters for her every whim and pleasure. She is able to use magic to draw creatures and turn them into giants to attack the enemy. Aska is assisted by her servant and friend Ssangyong [aka Sang Yung, named after the South Korean car maker Ssangyong] as well as minister and regent Chang'an [aka Chang Ang, named after the Chinese Chang'an car makers].

The Magic Knights again agree to help protect Cefiro, donning their weapons and armour, and once more controlling the Mashin. The three are also helped out by Mokona, Zagato's former allies who are now supporting their cause – namely Rafarga, Caldina and a now grown-up Ascot – and one new person. This is Lantis [Mazda Lantis], Cefiro's only magical swordsman. He also happens to be the younger brother of Zagato. Lantis never appeared to the Magic Knights before because he was not in Cefiro, but in Autozam, and was friends with Eagle. Lantis's wish is to destroy the Pillar system as he considers it unfair for one person to sacrifice all of their happiness for the sake of everyone else in the world. Lantis is also assisted by a fairy named Primera [Nissan Primera], who he saved from an attack by a monster.

Primera not only has her own magic, but she is also massively jealous of any woman who she thinks might be trying to get between her and Lantis.

As the story progresses, the forces of Autozam, Cizeta and Fahren all fight the Magic Knights and each other in order to try and secure rule over it, but things become even more complicated when they encounter the being that is not just responsible for creating the Pillar system, but all the worlds in the story, including Earth. It is safe to say, it is not the person you are expecting. What we do know is that there is a final battle between one of the Magic Knights and one of the invaders to secure the Pillar.

•

Pretty much what was discussed in the first part applies to the second, although part two is darker in tone what with Cefiro being threatened by both destruction and invasion. As Ohkawa says in the *CLAMP no Kiseki* interviews: "Writing the script to part two was difficult. Due to the evolution of the story, I couldn't put in many happy scenes. *laughs*" If it is humour you are looking for, most of it comes from Mokona and Primera. In a different interview given in January 1996 for their 'Materials Collection' of the series that marked the final chapter, Ohkawa says: "That perfection has no justice," regarding what she wanted readers to feel through the story. "There are always other people around you who are not yourself, and each one has a different way of thinking. That's why I want people to understand and interact with each other."

We should also discuss the anime version of the series. The anime series was already in full swing by the time the second part of *Rayearth* began. The anime ran from 17th October 1994 to 27th November 1995. It was directed by Toshihiro Hirano, who had past work on previous mecha series like the original *Mobile Suit Gundam*, where Hirano was an animator for one of the episodes. The series helped to establish CLAMP's reputation and even won an award: at the first Animation Kobe awards in 1996, the show's theme tune, *Yuzurenai Negai*, sung by Naomi Tamura, won 'Best Theme Song'. In Brazil, the first edition of anime magazine *Animax* had the *Rayearth* anime as the debut cover feature in May 1996, although in Brazil that series was retitled *Reiarte*.

The final chapter of the manga was published in January 1996, meaning the anime adaptation ended before the original manga comic. There are many differences between the two versions of the story. For example, as already mentioned, in the anime Presea is killed, but in the manga she is alive. To account for the fact that in the manga she reappears – in fact she is the first person the Magic Knights meet again upon returning to Cefiro – in the anime she appears to have returned from the dead. Clef claims the Princess Emeraude wished for all those who died while she was imprisoned to be brought back to life. This is actually a lie to keep the girls happy, with this 'Presea' actually being her identical twin sister Sierra [Ford Sierra].

Another difference is that in the anime Alcyone is not only alive in the second half, but she has also been brainwashed and is supporting another invading force that only appears in the anime, in the form of the evil Debonair [Mitsubishi Debonair]. Debonair is also helped by her daughter Nova [Chevrolet Nova], who fights with her own Mashin called Regalia (which is not a real car, but it did later appear as the name of a flying car in the *Final Fantasy* series of video games). This is where we return to the Kodansha manga and to one element of Tanaka's translation I do like. In her version, Tanaka adds some extra words when spells are being cast. In the finale of the first half of the story, one spell cast uses the word 'Debonair', which I assume is a nice reference back to the anime. Although there are some Americanisms in the second collection that do stick out. In one scene, in which Geo tells Eagle that he has noticed something strange, the Dark Horse version has Geo say: "Over the road… there's something strange." In the Kodansha version he says: "We've got some bogeys ahead on the road." To my ear it doesn't sit right, but that's just my personal taste.

Along with the TV anime, there was also the three-part OVA series that was released in 1997. For those who think that the changes made in the second-half of the TV anime may have gone too far, the OVA takes the deviation to a new level. Directed by Toshiki Hirano and Keitaro Motonaga, the OVA, simply called *Rayearth*, is totally different from the original. Hikaru, Umi and Fuu are not strangers, but are already friends going to the same school, and rather than travelling to Cefiro, they are fighting to save the Earth from being invaded by Cefiro instead, with Clef helping the girls to become the Magic Knights. Thus, the OVA version of *Rayearth* is a 'reverse isekai' – one where characters from a different world visit ours. Therefore, *Rayearth* is one of the few series that is both a standard isekai and a reverse isekai. However, it is not alone for doing this, with another series which formed part of isekai's first wave, 1991-1996's *Fushigi Yugi* by the non-binary artist Yuu Watase, also mixing both styles. For a long time, the Manga Entertainment DVD release of these episodes was the only anime version of *Rayearth* in the UK. These episodes are there for people who want something a bit different, and were re-released in the second UK Blu-Ray collection of the TV show.

Both the anime and manga versions of the story have their own merits, but there is one strange aspect about the very final moments in the manga that is worth highlighting, and which again will be in mirror writing.

•

Rayearth would go on to become a popular series, both as a manga and an anime. While *X* would eventually become a big hit, it was thanks to *Rayearth* that CLAMP would gain their first big audience, and thus attract an increasingly larger readership to their other titles, including the continuing *X*. If you are interested in learning more about *Rayearth*, I would direct you in the direction of the blogger ShidouHikaru15, who has created a blog devoted to the series.

As both *Rayearth* and *X* progressed, yet another new series began. It would see CLAMP going back to religion once again, Christianity being the basis of their work this time. However, it is hard to imagine the characters in this title being welcomed into the Church.

---

1 – In terms of boxsets in the UK, the distributor All The Anime (aka Anime Ltd.) offer some of the most grandest and most expensive of the lot, in particular their 'Ultimate Editions'. These have included a 20th anniversary boxset of the sci-fi anime *Cowboy Bebop* which came in an individually numbered themed vinyl flight cases (full RRP £299.99) and a special release of the *Fullmetal Alchemist* in a specially made resin Blu-Ray case. I witnessed a talk given by one of the company's executives who described the resin case as being so heavy that it is possibly the only boxset you could use to bludgeon someone to death with.

2 – Regarding the car naming idea, one thing that I came across during the *Cheat Slayer* scandal, was some people commenting that the best name parody in the series was a character who referenced the lead in *Re:Zero*, called Subaru, who in *Cheat Slayer* becomes someone named Honda. CLAMP, however, were doing car references in isekai back in the 1990s. I'm not saying the creators were also ripping off CLAMP, I'm just saying that even the car gag wasn't original.

3 – 'Mashin' is made up of the characters 'ma', meaning 'demon' but it can also refer to 'magic', and 'shin', meaning 'god'. To the Japanese, it thus reads something like 'magical god'. It is also a pun on the English word 'machine'. Most English translations however go with 'rune god' instead, making the Dark Horse version rather different to the other English versions.

4 – 'It' is the choice of pronoun used in this manga. Mokona's gender is never identified.

5 – Having pointed this out however, I do expect a bit of a backlash. Things like racial discrimination are often not talked about in Japan. In December 2020, Nike faced a backlash after releasing an advert highlighting racial discrimination in the country. While some back the ad for highlighting these issues, there is also a view that people outside the country should not be telling the Japanese to change their ways. See also: just about every EU member state telling the UK that Brexit is a bad idea, and then the UK voting for Brexit nevertheless.

6 – It should be noted that outside of their manga, CLAMP also worked on the mecha anime series *Code Geass*, but only as character designers, thus the mecha were once again not a concern to them. For more on *Code Geass*, see the epilogue.

7 – This information comes from the useful translation notes in the 25th anniversary boxset version of the manga, although weirdly it does not mention anything about the cars.

8 – Of course, if this naming thing happened now the new name would be decided via an online poll and it would probably end up being called Landy McLandface.

CHAPTER 7

Must Be Talking to an Angel – *Wish* (1995-1998)

Compared to the dramatic goings on in both *X* and *Rayearth*, the relatively short fantasy romcom *Wish* is a much more light-hearted affair, although the series does take some darker turns, especially near the end.

Originally released by *Mystery DX* magazine, published by Kadokawa Shoten, *Wish* came out in November 1995. The series would go on to be translated by TokyoPop, then became an online-only release with Viz Media, and in 2019 Dark Horse brought the series back into print, with all four volumes released in a single omnibus edition over 800 pages in length.

The series is partly notable for being the first lengthy work in which Nekoi was the principal artist, as illustrated in this exchange from the *CLAMP no Kiseki* interviews.

This was Nekoi's first long serialization, wasn't it?

Nekoi: *I thought I'd never make the deadlines. *laughs* While planning out the storyboard I'd be thinking, "I'll never make it!", as I drew I'd be thinking, "I'll never make it!" …I was constantly hurrying. *laughs**

Igarashi: *It wasn't just that it was your first long series, but also the fact that we didn't know how many pages we'd have to draw in a certain period. One time it would be twenty pages in five days, but that wouldn't necessarily be the case next time. It changed every time.*

Nekoi: *Then I'd panic when I had to draw difficult background scenery, or a particularly elaborate scene. *laughs* Looking back, I can't believe how much time I'd spend on planning the storyboard and with the drawing. However, I was happy that I was the first one to read Ohkawa's scripts. *laughs**

<u>*Wish* (1995-1998)</u>

Most of the characters in *Wish* are angels and demons. With Japan not being a country with Christianity as the principal faith, the series features elements that you suspect might raise a few eyebrows elsewhere in the world, particularly when you see the kinds of relationship the two lead characters have.

•

Set in an undisclosed place, the story begins with 28-year-old Dr Shuichiro Kudo walking back from work at his local hospital one night. However, as he walks along, he spots what at first appears to be a baby stuck in a tree, but he notices that the head is too big for this creature to be a baby. A crow then suddenly comes to attack this… whatever it is, and as a result whatever it is falls out of the tree. However, Shuichiro catches this being and saves them. It is then Shuichiro spots that this creature has a tiny pair of wings coming out of their back.

The creature, who is named Kohaku, says that they are an angel, albeit in training,[1] and wants to repay Shuichiro's kindness for his rescue. Shuichiro however is not at all interested. At first he believes that all of this cannot be real, but Kohaku eventually proves their divine abilities. Kohaku follows Shuichiro to his house, sleeps in the garden, and in the morning Kohaku is able to fully transform into a fully-formed angel, in a much more normal humanoid body – if you ignore the huge wings.

Kohaku informs Shuichiro that the difference between the fully-formed and smaller bodies[2] is caused by the time of day. Angels do not eat as it is forbidden for them to take away life, even from plants. The only human food they can consume is milk and honey, and the angels get most of their energy from the sun and fresh air. As a result, at night Kohaku shifts into a smaller, energy-saving form. Meanwhile, demons get energy from the moon and human souls, and thus are in a full-body form at night and a smaller form during the day. Plus, in both Heaven and Hell there is no gender. Kohaku later states that neither 'man' or 'woman' are accurate terms, but in the English manga Kohaku is normally referred to using male pronouns.

With Kohaku insisting on granting a wish, Shuichiro agrees to let Kohaku stay in his house until he can think of one. Until then, Kohaku does various chores around the house, like watering plants and delivering things. Soon however, things become more complicated for the duo. For starters, Kohaku bumps into Koryu, a demon-in-training who is constantly bullying Kohaku. Helping Koryu are a pair of twins, Hari and Ruri, who transform into a pair of cats and are constantly involved in Koryu's schemes.[3]

Another problem that arises is in the form of another angel called Hisui. The reason why Kohaku is on Earth in the first place is because Hisui, one of the four most powerful angels in Heaven that represent the four elements (wind in Hisui's case) has been missing, having gone down to Earth. Kohaku has been on a mission from God to track Hisui down and make the angel return, with messages being sent to Kohaku by a silent messenger named Ushagi (also spelt Usagi or Usyagi), who takes the form of a white rabbit and sends messages using magic flowers. Shuichiro agrees to help Kohaku, but the plan is interrupted by Koryu, who learns what is going on, thanks to Haru and Ruri overhearing the whole things.

Just as things are about to get ugly however, Hisui appears to stop the fighting, and says to Kohaku that they will not return to Heaven. The reason for this comes soon enough, for as Koryu is about to attack once more, Koryu is stopped by another demon by the name of Kokuyo. In the same way Hisui is high-up in Heaven, Kokuyo is high-up (or should that be low-up, or low-down?) in Hell, being the son of Satan.[4] Hisui and Kokuyo reveal that they are a couple, and have even made love. Thus, both of them abandoned Heaven and Hell respectively and have decided to live on Earth. Kokuyo even removed part of one of his eyes, using its power to protect Hisui – again a reoccurrence of the CLAMP trope of characters losing one eye. Eventually the couple ends up living in Shuichiro's house with Kohaku.

Later chapters see Kohaku meeting Shuichiro's grandfather Shinichiro, who reveals details about Shuichiro's childhood, including the deaths of his parents, although Kohaku later learns that Shuichiro's mother was a different kind of supernatural being altogether. Kohaku also has to continue lying to God about Hisui's whereabouts, and for a time he is forced to go back to Heaven to do his normal day-job, giving birth to new angels by singing, which makes them hatch out of eggs. Kohaku does make it back to Earth however, and as the story progresses, Kohaku and Shuichiro do become increasingly close, with them eventually expressing their love for each other. However, the ending of *Wish* is ultimately both tragic and joyful, taking place 100 years in the future.[5]

•

Wish is a series that perhaps illustrates some of the positive sides of being what is an obscure art movement as far as the West is concerned, because you get the impression that if manga was more popular over here, this series would attract some controversy from the more evangelical, conservative religious groups. Having said that, the fact that most of the characters in the story have no gender and are thus arguably transgender is enough to be controversial now in some quarters.[6]

Given that in the story Kohaku is genderless but still normally referred to in English using male pronouns, the fact that he loves Shuichiro appears to indicate at least some kind of LGBTQ+ relationship that would certainly anger some conservative Christian readers. Not only that, but the relationship between Hisui and Kokuyo is of two genderless characters, one from Heaven and one from Hell, making things even more troublesome. It might have got more problematic if CLAMP had stuck with their original plans. The *CLAMP no Kiseki* interviews reveal that originally the series was not going to be set on Earth, but in either Heaven, Hell, or some other world. Also, Kohaku was only going to be a side character. Hisui and Kokuyo were going to be the main stars in what was going to be a story mainly aimed at adults. In the end, they went with a cuter story.

This is not the only element of the story that might have got CLAMP into trouble. At one point, Kokuyo reveals that it is not the fate of humans to go to either Heaven or Hell. Instead, they reincarnate. This is something that would go against most of what is taught about the afterlife in Christianity, but this is a view that they will repeat in their later work *Gate 7*.

In my opinion, it would be wrong to say that *Wish* is blasphemous. It is not trying to be anti-Christian or be insulting about Christianity. You might argue that it is heretical, given that it goes against most standard teachings of the afterlife, but that feels to be a very heavy handed way of looking at what is just a romcom with fantasy elements. It's certainly nowhere near as problematic as *Monty Python's Life of Brian* was when that came out. It's not mocking any important figures from the Bible in any cruel way. The only Biblical figures mentioned in *Wish* are God and Satan, and neither of them actually appear in the story. The closest that any of them makes to an appearance is when God sends messages using Ushagi. When it comes to this, the major thing that God does that causes an upset is when God learns where Hisui is, and comes to punish both Hisui and Kohaku, with Kohaku's punishment coming across as being very harsh. However, as the story comes to its conclusion, we see that God does show compassion to Kohaku.

The series does have some similarities to other CLAMP works, in that there is once again the use of themed names. While *Rayearth* used cars, in *Wish* the angels and demons are named after gemstones. For example, Kohaku is named after amber, Koryu after garnet, Hisui after jade and Kokuyo after obsidian.[7]

•

While *Wish* is frequently described as a romcom, the ending of the story is full of drama, and overall it feels like the story is more rooted in drama than comedy. The comedy mainly comes from Kohaku and Koryu's squabbles, which are made more amusing when the characters are in their shrunken forms. The ending of *Wish* is one of CLAMP's better finales, and is worth the read.

As CLAMP worked on this, as well as ending *Rayearth* and continuing *X*, yet another series would emerge. This series would go on to be what is seen as their most loved work. It is the series that would become big globally, even getting that rare honour of being broadcast on terrestrial British television. It would also see the debut of CLAMP's most famous character. For those of you who are new to CLAMP, or indeed anime and manga in general, I would like to introduce you to a young girl… meet Sakura Kinomoto.

1 – Or should that be: "Kohaku Odbody: Angel, second class"?

2 – What is known as a 'chibi' or 'super-deformed' style in manga.

3 – Various sources claim that Hari and Ruri appear in *Miyuki-chan in Wonderland.* I believe they are the twins Cho Lee and To Lee, seemingly representing Tweedledum and Tweedledee.

4 – Although given that Hell's demons supposedly have no gender in the story, I'm not sure if 'son' is the right word. That's what the English-language manga goes with however, so let's stick to it.

5 – Which should give us perhaps more clues to a more upbeat ending to the unfinished *X.*

6 – It should be said that CLAMP are not alone in writing stories with angels and demons of ambiguous gender. In January 2022, Neil Gaiman was asked about the genders of the angel Aziraphale and the demon Crowley in *Good Omens*, which he co-wrote with Terry Pratchett. His response suggested that they were neither male or female, with Neil himself posting on Twitter that: "Crowley's Gender is Fallen Angel" and Aziraphale's gender was: "Angel (retired)."

7 – 'Kohaku' however differs from 'Kōhaku', while the former means 'amber', the latter can mean either 'red or white' or 'gold and silver' depending on the Japanese Kanji characters used. Kōhaku is a variety of koi, while *Kōhaku Uta Gassen*, the *Red and White Song Battle*, is an annual TV show in Japan. Akin to a Japanese-only version of the Eurovision Song Contest and airing every New Year, it pits a team of women in red against a team of men in white (what non-binary contestants do I don't know). It is one of Japan's big TV highlights every year.

CHAPTER 8

The Clow Card That I Need is... – *Cardcaptor Sakura* (1996-2000) and *Cardcaptor Sakura: Clear Card* (2016-Present)

Cardcaptor Sakura is the best known and most loved of all of CLAMP's works. Perhaps the biggest indicator of this from a British perspective is that the anime version of it is one of the few anime series to be shown on a mainstream TV channel. The anime aired on CITV, back in the days when it was a segment on the main ITV channel. The first series was once made available to stream on Channel 4's online service All4, and in July 2021, the anime streaming website Funimation made the entire series available to stream in the UK and Ireland legally. A 'Collector's Edition' Blu-Ray box set was scheduled for release on Valentine's Day 2022 by All The Anime, but it got delayed to 28th March and then again to 23rd May, then once more to the 4th July, and then again to the 25th July.

This entertainment was rare then and rare now. However, when I say that it aired on CITV, that is not the entire truth. It is more accurate to say that a particular version of *Cardcaptor Sakura* was broadcast. This was called *Cardcaptors*, and this translation by the Canadian company Nelvana is one of the most notorious reworks of any anime known. Not only was the title changed, but so were the names of the characters and locations to make them more English-sounding, and elements of the story considered unsuitable to children, such as gay romance, were removed, despite children being the target audience for the series back in Japan. Jake L. Godek from the website *T.H.E.M.*

Anime described *Cardcaptors* as: "The worst thing that has ever happened to anime that had a good Japanese name." It was one of the worst rebrandings ever.[1] The original dub is one of the reasons why many anime fans, myself included, automatically distrust just about any English-language dubbed anime, and why even more distrust Hollywood adaptations of manga.

Because of the whole *Cardcaptors* thing, when people eventually came to read the original manga, fans came to realise just how different it was, including the scenes in which there was genuine love between male characters. Not surprisingly, the manga is one of CLAMP's biggest sellers, with over 17 million copies in print.

Before we go into the manga however, first we need to look at something that is very particular to this artform.

A brief history of the 'Magical Girl' genre

Cardcaptor Sakura is an example of 'magical girl' manga, a branch of fiction that only really appears in Japan and in media such as manga and anime. Thus, for those unfamiliar with it, here is a brief guide to this field.

The basics of the genre are pretty simple. Magical girl stories are fantasy works in which one or more girls (although it is not just limited to female-identifying characters) gain magical powers, and use them to right wrongs, help friends and/or defeat evil forces.

There is argument as to where the genre starts. Some claim that Osamu Tezuka started it with *Princess Knight*, a manga from the 1950s following Princess Sapphire, a girl born with a boy's heart who has to pretend to be a prince as only men can rule her land. However, given the setting, it is more akin to a classic fairy tale, whereas magical girl stories tend to be set in the present day. I personally would not count *Princess Knight* as a magical girl story.

Series normally considered to be the first magical girl series proper include 1960s series *Sally the Witch* aka *Little Witch Sally*, and *Himitsu no Akko-chan*. In *Sally the Witch*, the title character travels from a magical kingdom to Earth – arguably making it an early example of reverse isekai – and becomes friendly with humans. The title character was originally called Sunny rather than Sally, but according to *The Anime Encyclopedia*, the name had to be changed in order to avoid protests from Nissan.[2] The series ran for over 100 episodes between 1966 and 1968, and was remade for another TV series and a film between 1989 and 1991. Sadly however, despite being an important series in the development of magical girls, *Sally the Witch* has never been released in English. These early magical girls fit into what is called the 'little witch' or *majokko* style of magical girl, which arguably *Cardcaptor Sakura* fits (even Sakura's magic staff is capable of flight like a witch's broomstick).

Another series to mention is Go Nagai's *Cutie Honey*, the original manga of which ran in *Weekly Shonen Jump* between 1973 and 1974. Given Nagai had in the past worked in erotica, with the sex comedy *Harenchi Gakuen*, it should come as no surprise that Nagai's magical girl, the android Honey Kisaragi, always loses her clothes when she transforms into her magical self.

Many manga and anime of magical girl genre came and went, but in 1991 the most famous magical girl series was released. Like *Magic Knight Rayearth* and *Cardcaptor Sakura*, it was published in *Nakayoshi* magazine, and while *Sakura* is one of the few series that can rival it, it does feel that the Queen of the Magical Girls is Usagi Tsukino, or, as she is better known, *Sailor Moon*.

The story sees Usagi being transformed into a soldier who will fight to save the Earth from evil. The 'Sailor' part of her name comes from her outfit, based on the traditional Japanese schoolgirls' uniform that is in turn based on the naval uniform.

She fights with the help of other 'Sailor Soldiers', whose names come from other bodies in the solar system, each having their own magical powers. *Sailor Moon* was not only popular when it was made, running to 18 volumes (not including the earlier series *Codename: Sailor V* to which *Sailor Moon* was a sequel), but is still one of the most loved anime and manga today. It has been adapted into two anime series, several films, and has been the subject of many other adaptations in other media.

More magical girl series sprang up, one of the most famous being the *Pretty Cure* franchise, which began in 2004 and is still going today. The next really big magical girl series however went in a starkly different direction, in the form of the 2011 anime *Puella Magi Madoka Magica*.[3] While all other magical girls previously had been fun, happy and full of light despite the fact they were fighting shady forces, *Madoka Magica* turned things on its head by being a tragedy. The title character, Madoka Kaname, spends the entire series wondering if she should become a magical girl when she comes to realise the high price that magical girls have to pay for gaining their powers. It became one of the most critically acclaimed anime of the entire 2010s.

Due to my love of comedy, it would also be remiss of me not to mention one other series that I have a fondness for that fits the genre. The 2015 anime series *Cute High Earth Defense Club LOVE!*[4] and its sequels wonderfully parody the genre and its tropes, whether it be the outfits, dialogue or characters. There is also one other way it parodies magical girls – in that the series is actually one starring magical boys. The sight of guys having to act out and do all the same cutesy stuff the girls do in these series is just funny, plus it also deals with some of the more problematic elements of the genre. For example, in most magical girl series, including the ones all previously described, the girls don't wear disguises to hide their identities. *Cute High Earth Defense Club LOVE!* does however have a form of disguise – because when the guys transform, their faces are pixelated to everyone else in the show.

There are some other series that are not normally considered magical girl shows but arguably have some of the tropes. The light novel series *Haruhi Suzumiya*, for example, features as its title character a girl who is unaware of the fact she has magical powers that allow her to alter reality. For example, the fact that she believes that aliens, time travellers and espers exist means that these beings exist right under her nose. However, everyone is doing their best to prevent Suzumiya from knowing about her powers, because there is the danger that if she knew what she was capable of she could potentially destroy the world.[5] Another possible example is *Kill la Kill*, an anime created by the same people responsible for my personal favourite anime of all time *Gurren Lagann*. *Kill la Kill*'s central figure, Ryuko Matoi, has no magical powers herself, but she gains them by wearing an intelligent schoolgirl sailor uniform, which gives her powers for a period of time when it absorbs Ryuko's blood. She is also armed with a scissor blade – i.e. one half of a massive pair of scissors that is more like a sword.

There are many recurring tropes in magical girl stories. One is the transformations. Often the main character will say a certain sequence of words to activate their transformation into the magical girl, which is often about 5-10 seconds long and involving changes in costume or accessories that might be used as tools. This sequence is called the 'henshin'. These lead to the creation of some anime catchphrases. For example, after reciting her spell, Sakura in *Cardcaptor Sakura* completes it by shouting: "Release!" In other anime, Usagi in *Sailor Moon* exclaims: "In the name of the Moon, I will punish you!" Regarding costume changes, in *Cute High Earth Defense Club LOVE!* the magical boys find themselves being forced to say bizarre lines before transforming and find themselves in rather fluffy white outfits.

Ryuko's sailor uniform in *Kill la Kill* doesn't leave much to the imagination when it transforms. Not only does she end up in a microskirt, but the only things covering her nipples are buckles on her braces, and those braces are the only things covering her torso. Look it up if you don't believe me.[6] Then you have Honey in *Cutie Honey* where she always ends up naked.

The second main trope is the mascots. The magical girl will often be assisted by a cute creature with powers of their own. Sakura is helped by Kero, who looks like a winged lion cub; *Sailor Moon*'s girls are helped by three talking cats named Luna, Artemis and Diana; *Madoka Magica* has Kyubey, who appears as a rather attractive white alien but is in reality the primary antagonist to the entire story; the boys in *Cute High Earth Defense Club LOVE!* are also helped by an alien, in the guise of a pink wombat.

Cardcaptor Sakura (1996-2000)

The original incarnation of the series ran across 12 volumes, and has been translated by various companies into English – first by TokyoPop, then by Dark Horse, and has recently been given hardback releases by Kodansha, similar to the situation with *Rayearth*. While at first glance it seems the entire story is split into two parts, with the second half being the *Clear Card* stories that began in 2016, the original *Cardcaptor Sakura* was itself a two-part story, so it is more accurate to say that the series is in three parts.

Cardcaptor Sakura stands out rather drastically from the other stories CLAMP were working on at the time, like *X* and *Rayearth*. It is closer in tone to the CLAMP School stories in terms of lightheartedness, but there is still an element of danger to them. One thing that Ohkawa made clear in the *CLAMP no Kiseki* interviews is that they wanted the story to be cute, and that no one would be killed. When it comes to death in the story, there are characters who are dead before the story begins, but no one actually dies during it. Ohkawa also said that originally Sakura was going to be a witch, but they later decided to come up with something unique with regards to her magic. Interestingly, none of CLAMP members claim to have paid attention to magical girl series before making the series, and this may explain why it feels different in some respects to other series of the same genre.

•

Sakura Kinomoto is a 4th grade elementary school student (making her aged 9-10). She lives in the fictional city of Tomoeda, near Tokyo. Her family (all of whom share their names with flowers) consists of her archaeology professor father Fujitaka and her older brother Toya, with whom she regularly gets into rows.[7] Sakura's mother, Nadeshiko, died aged 27, when Sakura was just three. When Nadeshiko and Fujitaka married, she was 16 and he was 25 – the exact same ages Subaru and Seishiro are when we first meet them in *Tokyo Babylon*, although disturbingly even this is not the most disconcerting age gap in the series.

Sakura goes to school, via rollerblading,[8] meeting up with Toya's classmate Yukito Tsukishiro, who she is also in love with. However, as we readers come to discover, Yukito is actually in love with Toya. The boys are also workmates in many part-time jobs, as well as lovers. At school, Sakura mostly excels at sports, and she is a member of the school's cheerleading team. Her friends and classmates include a fellow cheerleader Chiharu Mihara, who is in a relationship with another classmate, Takashi Yamazaki, a boy who keeps telling tall tales on every subject that are totally false. There is also Naoko Yanagisawa, another cheerleader and lover of books, whose passion for scary stories disturbs Sakura who hates ghosts; and Rika Sasaki, who Sakura knows is in love but she does not know with whom. We readers discover that she is actually already engaged to be married… to the class's homeroom teacher Yoshiyuki Terada.[9]

Sakura's best friend however is Tomoyo Daidouji. Her mother, Sonomi, runs a large toy company and was cousin to Nadeshiko (Sonomi has never forgiven Fujitaka for taking Nadeshiko away from her), making Tomoyo Sakura's second cousin. As well as being a talented singer in the school's choir, Tomoyo is also very close to Sakura and appears to love her. This love normally takes the form of getting Sakura to dress up in a range of different outfits and filming her for her own entertainment. Sakura herself says that: "She's a good friend, but just a liiiiiittle… weird."

While in her father's study, Sakura bumps into and opens a book which contains lots of cards. These cards turn out to be magical, and by opening the book Sakura has let them loose around the town. Opening the book also releases the guardian of the cards, a magical being called Cerberus, who despite being named after a three-headed dog, actually takes the form of a cuddly toy, looking a bit like a winged lion cub. Cerberus, or, as Sakura decides to call him, Kero, tells her that the cards were created by a long-dead Anglo-Chinese sorcerer named Clow Reed. With the cards loose in the world, they do as they please and thus need to be captured and returned to the book. By opening the book in the first place, this demonstrates that Sakura has some form of magic power within her, and thus Kero makes Sakura the 'Cardcaptor'. He gives her the key to the book, which Sakura can transform into a magic staff that she can use to get the cards back. Every time Sakura captures a card, she writes her name upon it to make the card hers, and then she can use its magical properties. The Clow Cards themselves include: The Fly, The Jump, The Windy and The Sword.

Sakura and Kero thus try to find all the Clow Cards and secure all this magic, although when with others Kero normally has to pretend to be a cuddly toy to avoid arousing suspicion. Apart from themselves, only Tomoyo knows about Sakura and Kero's predicament, Tomoyo becoming Lois Lane to Sakura's Superman. This is good news for Tomoyo, as every new card gives her the chance to dress Sakura up in a new outfit and another chance to film her. However, it should be said that unknown to her, Toya also knows that something is going on, as he has some magic powers of his own, but he does not exactly know the full details of Sakura's task.

Shortly after capturing some of the cards however, a new student joins Sakura's class. His name is Syaoran Li (known in some versions of the story as Xiaolang Li), a student originally from Hong Kong. He is also a distant relative of Clow Reed. At first, Syaoran tries to take Sakura's cards off her and attempts to collect all the cards himself, but as the story progresses it is Sakura who becomes the collector of the cards. He too also begins to fall for Yukito, but we later learn that this attraction is because Yukito also has a magical power inside him that he is totally unaware of – this power being the sexless spirit Yue, the other guardian of the Clow Cards, whose job it is to test anyone who tries to become their new owner, i.e. Sakura. Syaoran, meanwhile, eventually moves on from Yukito, and begins to realise that Sakura is the one he truly loves.

Syaoran is not the only newbie to join Sakura's class. She also gets a new substitute teacher, Kaho Mizuki, whom we later see works as miko (shrine maiden) at Tomoeda's Tsukimine Shrine. Using a moon-shaped bell, we learn that she too has her own magical powers and connection with the cards.

While the first half of the story sees Sakura trying to find all of the Clow Cards, the second half sees her trying to make the cards her own. Beginning 5th grade at school, she has to use more magic to change the Clow Cards into her own 'Sakura Cards', with their own design. This leads to another transfer student joining the class, a boy from England named Eriol Hiiragizawa, whom the readers soon come to realise is the reincarnation of Clow Reed, come to test Sakura and her powers. He, like Sakura, also has his own helpers: Spinel Sun, who is akin to Kero; and Nakuru Akizuki, who is like Yukito in that she too has another identity as a sexless spirit, Ruby Moon. Nakuru transfers to Toya and Yukito's school and often annoys Toya.

•

There is a fair amount to discuss with this series, some positive, some negative, and some ideas that I have that make the story a bit weird.

As for the positives, one of these is the look. CLAMP's art again is shown off brilliantly in this work, especially when it comes to the character design. One of the things that put off some people from magical girl series, or at least the anime versions of them, is the length of the henshin transformations. In comparison, *Cardcaptor Sakura* transformations feel shorter than those in *Sailor Moon*, and also while in *Sailor Moon* it is the heroes that transform, in *Cardcaptor Sakura* it is Sakura's key that transforms into her staff instead. An even bigger difference though is in the costumes. Most magical girls/boys just have the one costume and wear that for all of their missions. Thanks to the extensive wardrobe supplied by Tomoyo, Sakura has a diverse range of looks on offer. She stands out from the other magical characters because she is not limited to a single look. The Japanese word 'kawaii', meaning something or someone being cute, or making something cuter, fits Sakura Kinomoto more than any other of CLAMP's characters and possibly explains why she and the series is the most popular in the CLAMPverse. Having said that, defining 'kawaii' in English is difficult. It is like trying to translate the German word 'gemutlichkeit', which generally means cosiness, but of a particular kind.

We also see some connections with the rest of the CLAMPverse too, with Sakura owning stuff from the shop Piffle Princess, which appears in *X*. However, despite the series ending in the year 2000, no time is given as to when the story is set. Nothing from *X* appears in *Cardcaptor Sakura* apart from Piffle Princess and Tokyo Tower, so it would appear that Sakura escapes any apocalyptic fighting.

In terms of production, one thing you will notice when reading the manga is the appearance of column-like side-panels which feature profiles of the characters. There is a reason for these beyond explaining the characters, which is that when the chapters were originally published these spots were taken up by adverts. This is common in various shojo manga magazines, and when the tankobon comes out they are replaced with these little side-panels. While character description is common, more often it just features the writer or artist just talking about their life.

The anime version of the series is also the largest of all their adaptations. Not including the later *Clear Card* series, the anime TV show had 70 episodes, airing between 1998 and 2000, and two feature length films – *Cardcaptor Sakura: The Movie* from 1999 and *Cardcaptor Sakura Movie 2: The Sealed Card* from 2000. All of these were directed by first-time director Morio Asaka, who would also direct the *Clear Card* anime and another CLAMP anime adaptation, *Chobits*. Both films would win the Theatrical Film Award in the Animation Kobe awards in 1999 and 2000 respectively.

The fact that the TV series is so long however does mean a lot of episodes feature totally original plots that don't appear in the manga. In the manga, there are just 19 Clow Cards. The TV anime has a full deck of 52 cards, with a 53rd appearing in *The Sealed Card* film. The anime also features some totally original characters that never appear in the manga. The most notable of these is another transfer student. Meiling Li is the cousin of

Syaoran, she claims to be Syaoran's fiancé, and thus she is very jealous of Sakura and anyone else she thinks might split them up. Unlike Syaoran, she has no magical power, but makes up for it by being a skilled fighter. She often joins in the hunt for the cards.

However, there are issues with the story. The whole 10-year-old-engaged-to-her-teacher thing is rather disturbing, although not exactly new either – remember that in *Man of Many Faces*, Utako has already been rejected in love by her teacher before meeting Akira. The engagement is never mentioned in the anime, although Rika is still shown to love Mr Terada. There are oddities as well, in particular when it comes to translating between the manga and anime. For example, a scene in the manga where Sakura confesses her love to Yukito where she says: "I love you," appears in English subtitled versions of the anime as: "I like you." The changing of Far-East to Western units of measurement is also a challenge. 1,000 Ri, the Ri being a Chinese version of a mile, is translated as: 2,440 miles, which is understandable. 100 tatami, this being a type of mat that is used to measure floor space, becomes: 1,776 square feet, which is a push, but it is still something you can go along with. However, the scene in which Sakura's cookery class needs to cook croquettes at 170 degrees Celsius does not need translating. Only the Americans would feel the need to translate a nice round 170 degrees Celsius, a unit that almost every other country in the world is happy to go along with, into 338 degrees Fahrenheit. It's the fact they went with the exact conversion that sticks out so much. Even a rounded-up 340 degrees would be permissible, but they had to be so exact about a scale of temperature that just about no other country uses.

Despite all this, the thing that still angers most fans, not just of *Cardcaptor Sakura* but anime fans in general, is the *Cardcaptors* adaptation. Created by the Canadian studio Nelvana, a lot was changed: the title for starters. Sakura's name was removed in an attempt to make the series appeal to boys more by trying to remove the fact that a girl was the lead character. Of the 70 episodes, only 39 made it into *Cardcaptors*, with the first episode actually being the eighth in the original version. That first episode happened to be the one that introduced Syaoran, the male lead, into the story. Then again, that itself is not entirely accurate as most of the character names were anglicised. Syaoran Li became Li Showron, Sakura Kinomoto turned into Sakura Avalon, and Tomoyo Daidouji somehow was renamed Madison Taylor. The location was also altered, changing from Tomodea to Readington.

Another major change was to the relationships with the characters. Rika and Terada's love was just the most obvious one to change given how inappropriate it is. However, the gay relationship between Toya and Yukito, Syaoran's feelings for Yukito, Tomoyo's great passion for Sakura, and even straight relationships such as Syaoran's later romance for Sakura, all fail to appear in the show, all being considered inappropriate to show to Western kids.[10] As a result of this, many viewers of *Cardcaptors* got a surprise when they were finally able to read the original manga. Shamus Kelley wrote a piece for *Den of Geek* in June 2020 entitled 'How *Cardcaptor Sakura's* Queerness Broke Through Censorship'. He said despite the censorship, he was still able to pick up things, but not directly:

"I was nine years old and still hadn't had my first crush yet. But even with all the edits in the show, I could feel there was something more going on between the characters. The most obvious was Sakura and Syaoran's relationship which, for as many rewrites as they tried to shove in, couldn't be hidden. Syaoran's crush on Yukito, rewritten to be Syaoran simply being afraid of him, still shone through. They weren't able to change the animation and despite what the characters said I could see Syaoran blushing when Yukito appeared. That boy was not straight."

The *Cardcaptors* ended in December 2001. Kelley then found the original manga in 2004. He continues:

"Boy, let me tell you, if I didn't realize I liked men… this manga did it. The fourth volume includes the scene where Yukito admitted his feelings for Toya without any censorship. My mind couldn't process what I was seeing. This was a guy who liked guys… and everyone supported him in it! It was treated as a normal thing, with Sakura proudly proclaiming she'd punish Toya if he picked on Yukito. It was not only charming and adorable, it was the first time I'd ever seen an openly queer character. Because of Toya and Yukito, I was able to figure out my sexuality in a safe way. I wasn't afraid of the slow realization that I liked women and men; I knew it was okay because Cardcaptor Sakura *showed it was okay."*

It should be mentioned that Kelley does not cover the relationship between Sakura and Tomoyo in depth in his article, because he was uncomfortable writing about it due to them being cousins. However, the fact that they are second cousins still does not make it the weirdest relationship in the series for me. Sakura herself says in the story that Tomoyo is a little weird, but, having read the story, I think Tomoyo goes beyond that. With all these costumes and constantly filming her all the time, I think Tomoyo comes across as a bit of a creepy stalker, filming the girl she likes for her own pleasure, in bizarre costumes that she herself made. In the *Cardcaptors* version, this never comes across as weird as Tomoyo is just obsessed with filming things.

For me, this is made evident in one of the anime episodes. One of the cards Sakura has to capture is The Thunder. In both the anime and the manga, Sakura hunts the card down in the middle of the night wearing a catgirl/maid outfit. Catgirls are common stock characters in anime and manga, and there is even another magical girl series, *Tokyo Mew Mew*, in which the main heroine turns into a magical catgirl. The *Cardcaptor Sakura* anime has a latter episode in which Sakura is magically sucked into a copy of *Alice in Wonderland*, an idea CLAMP had already kind of done with *Miyuki-chan in Wonderland*, and that features Eriol as a Cheshire catboy. In the *Carcaptor Sakura* manga, Sakura captures the card quickly, the whole thing is just a few pages long. In the anime, it forms the basis of an entire episode, namely the eighth episode, which would become the first episode of *Cardcaptors*. Sakura struggles to capture the card because of the thunder it produces, so to help, Tomoyo provides Sakura with this maid outfit. She says it is made out of rubber to protect her from shocks. When Sakura asks why part of the outfit consists of cat ears, Tomoyo says that: "It looks cute."

In order to illustrate the problem with this scene, I believe it is best displayed as a Venn diagram.

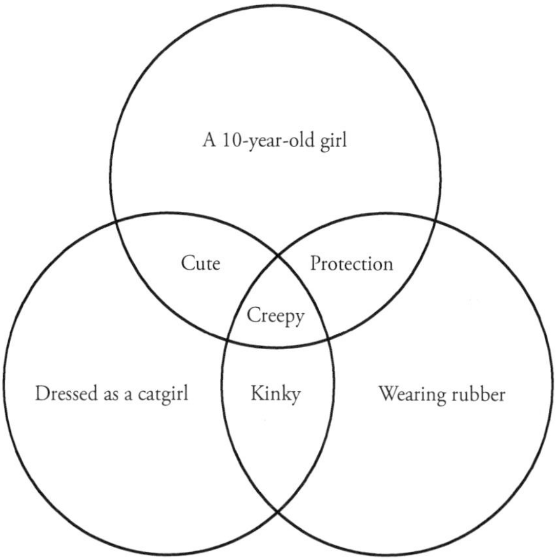

Each of the three things on their own or even as a pair are not really a problem. A 10-year-old girl, which is what Sakura is, dressing as a catgirl is not bad. It is rather a cute thing to see. A girl wearing cat ears and a tail, perhaps with some face-paint for whiskers, is a cute image, and there is nothing wrong with that. A 10-year-old girl wearing rubber makes sense if you want to protect the girl. Sakura is wearing rubber to prevent herself from being electrocuted. If it is raining, you might put a young child in wellies and a rubber mackintosh to protect the girl from getting wet. That too makes sense. Dressing as a catgirl wearing rubber is quite the kinky, sexy image ('nudge nudge'). It might not be for everyone, but the idea is not too weird. It's on the lighter side of kinky. A 10-year-old girl dressed as a catgirl wearing rubber, however, does come across as decidedly creepy. If you spotted a real-life 10-year-old girl dressed like that, eyebrows would be raised, and I suspect a few phone calls might be made to the appropriate authorities.

The thing is that, in my head, after having read *Miyuki-chan in Wonderland* and seeing all the stuff Miyuki goes through which she does not consent to, what Tomoyo makes Sakura wear and films her doing at her age feels somehow weirder. I know that Tomoyo is only ten, but, if anything, that makes it creepier, especially when you remember that she and Sakura are cousins as well. You know what, forget comparing her to Lois Lane. Tomoyo comes across more like the 13th Duke of Wybourne from *The Fast Show*. I'm half expecting her to make an aside to camera, and then both sneakily and lasciviously say: "Me? Tomoyo Daidouji, here, in Tomoeda's Penguin Park, dressing a 10-year-old girl in a rubber catgirl costume, while armed with a camcorder, at three o'clock in the morning, with my reputation? Poor little thing's never even heard of upskirting!"[11]

This girl must be stopped! Instead, Tomoyo, Sakura, Syaoran and Kero all came back 16 years later.

<u>*Cardcaptor Sakura: Clear Card* (2016-Present)</u>

CLAMP eventually decided to return to their most popular series. The series is notable immediately in one aspect, in that this is currently the one and only manga that CLAMP currently make, after years of doing multiple projects at the same time. As such, this is obviously a series that is rather hard to sum up as it is a work in progress. It also contains spoilers to the end of the original *Cardcaptor Sakura*, so spoilers are clearly going to come up. If you want to avoid those, you might want to skip ahead of this bit.

•

Clear Card sees Sakura now starting middle school (7th grade), meaning she is aged around 12-13. Moving to a new school has clearly seen some changes, mainly in the way her friends are split. She is still in the same class as Tomoyo and Chiharu, while Takashi and Naoko are in the class next door, and Rika is in an entirely different school and as such has only appeared occasionally throughout the series.[12] As for Syaoran – and this is a spoiler for the end of the original manga series – he left for Hong Kong at the end of the series, but Sakura gave him a teddy bear as a present as a sign of their love. The very end sees them uniting again a few years later. This manga begins with that meeting, as Syaoran has now moved back to Tomoeda and is living in Japan permanently. It is a moment that sparks great joy in Sakura because of their love, and great joy in Tomoyo who is sneakily recording the whole thing on her camcorder. Syaoran ends up in Takashi and Naoko's class, where he finds himself the victim of Takashi's lying.

As for everyone else, Sakura is still living at home with her father Fujitaka and brother Toya. Toya and Yukito are still very close, Yukito is aware of Yue being inside him, Kero is spending his time mainly playing computer games, and Eriol is continuing to monitor everything back in England in the company of Mizuki, Spinel and Nakuru.

One night, Sakura has a strange dream. All of the Sakura Cards have become totally blank and transparent, and there is someone wearing a strange hooded robe acting in a most sinister way. When Sakura wakes up, she finds to her horror that her cards really have turned completely blank and have no magical power. Her key that transforms into her magical staff still works however. But then the following night she has another dream. The hooded figure is now riding a dragon and has transformed Sakura's key, giving it a new look. Waking up, again Sakura sees that the key has changed to look like the one in her dream.

Walking to school that morning, Sakura and Kero are attacked by a strange wind. She takes out her new key which upon her command of "Release!" transforms into a new staff. She finds in herself a new magical command to capture this wind, which turns into a new partly transparent card: Gale.

Soon Sakura finds herself capturing more of these 'Clear Cards', with the help of Kero and Syaoran, while Tomoyo once more supplies more strange costumes and records on camera as much as she can. During this time, Sakura keeps having more dreams involving the hooded figure. Meanwhile, some of the Clear Cards take on familiar appearances. Not only do they appear to have similar powers to the Sakura Cards, but the people shown on the Clear Cards begin to look like Sakura's friends and family.

Later, Sakura's class gets a new transfer student. You will have now realised that any person being a new introduction to the class will be significant to the story, as evidenced by the inclusions of Syaoran, Mizuki and Eriol. This student is Akiho Shinomoto, a girl who has lived in many different countries: Hong Kong, England, France, Germany and Italy among them. Sakura and her group all quickly become friends with Akiho. Among the things regarding Akiho that interest Sakura are her love of books and a cuddly rabbit toy she carries with her that she calls Momo, which in turn leads to Akiho liking Kero, although as always he has to pretend to be a stuffed toy to avoid all sorts of problems arising regarding Sakura's magic. Regarding books, Akiho's favourite is one called *Alice in Clockland*, which was inspired by Lewis Carroll's novels but by a different author.

Things become more intriguing for Sakura when she finally gets to visit Akiho's house in the company of Tomoyo. Akiho happens to be living in the same place Eriol lived in when he was in town. Her parents died when she was young, so she is looked after by a single guardian named Yuna D. Kaito, who works as Akiho's valet.[13] When news of this reaches Eriol's ears, we learn that the 'D.' in Katio's name is actually a title given by a group of powerful magicians in England to the most powerful of all magic users. We the reader come to discover that Kaito is indeed a hugely powerful user of magic, and can use the strongest kind of magic of all – the ability to stop and even reverse time. However, reversing time drains the user of their life force. Momo turns out to be a magical being like Kero and Spinel who works with Kaito, but Akiho is unaware of what either of them are up to. It appears that Kaito wants to gain control of the Clear Cards in order to make his magic even more powerful.

•

Obviously much of what can be mentioned in discussing *Clear Card* has already been covered in the original series, and much of what can be said may be altered by the time the series eventually ends. During the 16 years the series had been away, CLAMP made some wise changes, particularly when it comes to moving troublesome Rika to the sidelines, but most of what made the original series good is still there: the design of the characters, outfits, cards etc. still shine through. The plot is also nicely mystifying, and with modern technology we Western readers can now read the story at the same time as Japanese readers. The *Clear Card* manga is published in Japan by Kodansha, and the English version is also published by them. Thus, they can release English translations of new chapters abroad when these same passages become available in their native Japanese.

The manga has been partly adapted as an anime as well. In 2017, a one-off OVA episode entitled 'Sakura and the Two Bears' was listed as 'Episode 0' of the story, and adapts the end of the original *Cardcaptor Sakura* manga, as the anime version of the original series had a different ending. In 2018, a 22-episode long series was made. This featured the return of Meiling to the story who still doesn't appear in the manga, the use of modern technology to make the animation more crisp and of a higher quality, and best of all there is no dodgy *Cardcaptors*-like dub.

However, despite the fact that CLAMP are able to tell and illustrate such a wonderful story, there is one big issue about *Clear Card* that sticks out like a sore thumb. The original series ended in 2000 when Sakura was in junior school at 5th grade. This series, which CLAMP began in 2016, now sees Sakura and her friends now attending middle school in 7th grade. As a result, *Clear Card* should be set in between one or two years into the future relative to the original. Given this, how come Sakura and all of her friends are using technology from 2016?

I know that the Japanese are known for developing advanced technology that doesn't get adopted by the West until later, although having said that, Japan is also famous for being the country that still uses fax machines, but how the actual fuck are Sakura and her friends able to use smartphones, remote-controlled drones, online gaming and social media, when in the opening chapter of the original manga, Sakura is seen returning a VHS tape to Tomoyo, and in the original anime series Tomoyo is seen having to work with a minidisc player?

In one of the anime episodes, Kero says he is worried that an incident with one of the cards is going to cause a lot of discussion on social media. I don't think he needs to worry. Japan's most popular social network, Line, wasn't released until 2012. Instagram didn't come about until 2010, Twitter in 2006, Facebook in 2004, and MySpace in 2003. Even if the series ended in our real-life 2000, social media would be so insignificant that it would be no cause for alarm.[14]

When it comes to the phones, somehow in Sakura's world they have jumped from the Nokia 3310 to the iPhone 7 in an instant, and as for the use of drones that can be flown by smartphones, I think we can all guess what one girl is secretly suggesting: "Me? Tomoyo Daidouji, here, dressing my best friend in a new outfit, while I operate a remote-controlled camera drone, in the middle of my massive garden, with my reputation? Those drones blades really are helping with that skirt, aren't they?"

•

When it comes to sales of magical girl manga, *Sailor Moon's* sales of 35 million make it the stand-out favourite. However, one aspect where *Cardcaptor Sakura* and its sequel come out on top is the success of the writer. CLAMP have produced so many different works, while *Sailor Moon* is sometimes dubbed as manga's greatest one-hit wonder. A 2014 article from *Anime News Network* listing '7 Things You Probably Didn't Know About Sailor Moon' by Lynzee Loveridge states that author Naoko Takeuchi, "...hasn't produced another popular series in almost 20 years since the manga ended in 1997." Takeuchi still hasn't created anything as remotely as successful as *Sailor Moon*. *Sakura* meanwhile is probably CLAMP's most beloved title, and it isn't even their biggest-selling series.

Not only that, but when you combine the total number of tankobon collected volumes of *Sailor Moon* and its fellow series *Codename: Sailor V*, it comes up to 21 volumes. Add up all the volumes of *Cardcaptor Sakura* and *Cardcaptor Sakura: Clear Card*, you also come to 21, with 12 in the original series, and 12 volumes of *Clear Card* released in Japan so far, making it the longer-running series. In January 2022, Ohkawa confirmed during a Twitter space that *Clear Card* was entering the final stage of the story.

Love for *Cardcaptor Sakura* takes on many forms. Fan art, cosplaying, fan fiction, or in my case writing a book in which you accuse one character of being a pervert. Possibly the most impressive demonstration was by Matthew Emblidge of Columbia, Maryland, USA, who set the Guinness World Record for the largest collection of *Cardcaptor Sakura* memorabilia. As of 2nd January 2021, he collected 4,873 items, breaking the previous record held by Sofia Pichihua of Peru whose collection consisted of 1,086 items. According to the Guinness World Record website, Emblidge attempted the record to mark the 25th anniversary of the series.[15] Emblidge can be followed on social media, mainly on Tumblr at 'The Cardcaptor Museum' as that website is more photo-based, although he is also on Twitter on @CCM_Yamato.

Cardcaptor Sakura is a series which has its flaws, some by CLAMP themselves, some by outside forces, but it remains to this day not just their stand-out work, but one of the most loved manga series by fans, in Japan and abroad. Also, let's not forget that CLAMP were still working on other stuff at the time. Not only was *X* still being written, but so was *Wish* too. There would also be another series emerging, but one that had a darker tone to it.

1 – Having said this, some anime and manga rebrands have had a more positive effect. One recent example was the yaoi manga *The 8 Warriors* by Reibun Ike, which debuted in 2019. The series is set in a remote archipelago where the selected champions fight sexualised battles called 'The Great Wyrm Tournament' to become king. In 2021 SuBLime, the Boys' Love imprint of Viz Media, released the series in English, but did so with a new title: *Dick Fight Island*. Most likely as a result of this change, the series ended up topping both the 'Romance Manga' and 'Yaoi Manga' Amazon bestseller lists in both the UK and USA, as well as the 'Action & Adventure Manga' list in the UK (second in the US). If you want my personal review, it would be: "You come for the cock, but you stay for the arse." Also, one minor point of criticism: as someone with a comedy background, it does annoy me that there was an open goal of a punning title SuBLime totally missed. Surely *Cockfight Island* would have been better?

2 – A company that must have changed its tune back in the 1990s seeing as how CLAMP were able to name so many characters after cars in *Magic Knight Rayearth*.

3 – By the way, I can't do the accent so I've never tried it out, but to me *Puella Magic Madoka Magica* does come across as a title that sounds more entertaining if you say it in a Mexican accent. If you can do the accent, try it and see if it works.

4 – Note the use of the American spelling of 'defense' with an 's' rather than a 'c'.

5 – The series is also famous for having a bizarre impact on the world of mathematics. The first season of the anime adaptation of the series, *The Melancholy of Haruhi Suzumiya* ran for 14

episodes, but the episodes had two different orders: the broadcast order and the plot's chronological order. Thus a question on website 4chan asked: "If you wanted to watch the 14 episodes of the first season in every possible order, what would be the shortest string of episodes you need to watch?" This became known as the 'Haruhi problem', and ended up helping to solve a question regarding the lower bounds in superpermutations, the answer to the problem being a lower bound of 93,884,313,611 episodes that you would need to watch, and an upper bound of 93,924,230,411 episodes.

6 – And after seeing her in those braces, feel free to imagine her recreating a routine by the comedians Cannon and Ball. Rock on, Matoi!

7 – Also, while he is technically the older sibling, he is also in a way the younger sibling as his birthday is on 29th February. Sakura's birthday is 1st April, a key day in the world of CLAMP as we will discuss in the epilogue.

8 – It was the nineties.

9 – I assume it's some kind of arranged marriage, but the age gap definitely still makes me feel uncomfortable.

10 – It should be said that *Cardcaptor Sakura* is not the only magical girl anime to have experienced problems with translation and attitudes towards gender and sexuality in other nations. In *Sailor Moon*, there are three characters called the 'Sailor Starlights'. In the original manga, they are women disguised as men. In the anime, there are men who transform into women when fighting. Different countries dealt with these characters in different ways, with some keeping the original plot, other

countries saying the characters were always boys or always girls, but the oddest version was the Italian dub. In this version, the boys summoned their twin sisters, and thus claimed there were six characters rather than three.

11 – If you are interested in a much more innocent series involving magical girls with cat-like features, try *Tokyo Mew Mew*, originally a manga written by Reiko Yoshida and illustrated by Mia Ikumi between 2000 and 2003. It was published in English by Kodansha, and the subject of two anime adaptations: one in 2002 which was the subject of some *Cardcaptors*-like reworkings when it was translated into English, and another commissioned for 2022 started. In this series, the magical girls are infused with the DNA of endangered animals, central character Ichigo Momomiya having the DNA of an Iriomote Wild Cat. The other magical girls in series have the DNA of a lorikeet, a porpoise, a tamarin, and, happily for me, a wolf.

12 – You suspect that this is a wise move on CLAMP's part, get rid of what is on the surface the most uncomfortable character in the story, given her relationship with her teacher. That teacher, Mr Terada, only appears briefly in conversation, but it is known that he is still working at Sakura's old school.

13 – Some translations describe Kaito as a butler, but this strictly speaking wrong. A butler is in charge of all the other domestic servants in a household, and so has other people like maids, footmen, cooks etc. below them. A valet is a lone personal attendant, and as Kaito is the only servant in the entire house that makes him a valet.

14 – It is a pity that MySpace wasn't around then. I like the idea that the first 'Friend Space' section may have consisted solely of

Tom and people from Tomoeda, making the whole thing look like some weird marketing gimmick.

15 – For a video showing the collection at the time of the record, visit https://youtu.be/JvRTwsUHLrE

CHAPTER 9

Das Kraftwerk – *Clover* (1997-1999)

Looking at the way CLAMP is structured and the simple fact that they are a team rather one lone creator or a pair, which is how most manga are produced along with the help of extra assistants, CLAMP have been compared to other groups in different art forms.

It's downright predictable to compare the CLAMP foursome to a pop band, and as CLAMP are the most famous manga group, it is equally predictable that they often get compared to the most famous pop band of all. In *The Rough Guide to Manga* (2009), Jason S. Yadao claims that: "Fans rattle off their [CLAMP's] names as easily as an earlier generation would those of John, Paul, George and Ringo."

I'm not so keen on this Beatles comparison, partly because there is an issue with rattling off the names of CLAMP's members, what with them changing their names to mark the group's 15th anniversary. Also, let's be honest, to English ears at least: "John, Paul, George and Ringo" scans better than: "Ohkawa, Mokona, Nekoi and Igarashi". The larger number of syllables doesn't really help the ladies.[1]

While it might act as a useful analogous shorthand to say: "A is the B of C",[2] it doesn't really say that much about what the original subject is like. You could go around saying: "CLAMP are the Hitler of manga" and crowbar in any evidence remotely connected to fascism to support such a nonsense claim, like the Imperial Japan and fascistic outfits displayed in promotional art for *CLAMP School Detectives*. This whole formula has as much critical credibility as a Norwich radio DJ describing Lexus as: "the Japanese Mercedes".

Yes, you can say: "CLAMP are The Beatles of manga", but you can just as easily say: "CLAMP are the Kraftwerk of manga." In fact, that is what I'm going to do in this chapter. I'm going to argue that CLAMP are more like Kraftwerk than The Beatles, for no other reason than the fact that anyone can sound intellectual if they just stick to such a simplistic method of description. For this purpose, I will be covering CLAMP's most typical sci-fi-like manga. Although it is not the only time technology becomes a theme in their work, as it is also being covered in *Chobits*, a series that's very much the *Computer World* of CLAMP's canon, the cyberpunk setting of *Clover* feels more adept when dealing with technological themes.

Also, there is the relationship with *Clover*'s title. A clover is a type of plant, and in the story, people with great power formed part of a 'Clover Project'. This powerful clover is thus a 'power plant', and in German the word for a power plant is 'Kraftwerk'.

Clover (1997-1999)

Beginning in 1997, *Clover* is another of CLAMP's works with Kodansha, it being published in a magazine called *Amie*. In English, the series would be first released by TokyoPop, then Dark Horse as a single omnibus, and most recently as a hardback collector's edition by Kodansha themselves.

Ohkawa says in the *CLAMP no Kiseki* interviews that the title of the series came from the fact that the story was to be told in four parts. Indeed, the series consisted of four collected tankobon volumes.

It should also be mentioned that the CLAMP sci-fi manga *Clover* should not be confused with Toriko Chiya's romance manga *Clover*, although Chiya's work has not been released in

English, or indeed with Yuki Tabata's *Weekly Shonen Jump* fantasy anime and manga *Black Clover*, which is available in English.

•

Set in an unknown country and unspecified time, the world of *Clover* is a militaristic one. The land is ruled by five generals who are also known as 'wizards'. One of these generals, Ko, gives orders to an ex-soldier named Kazuhiko Fay Ryu to deliver a particular package. However, when Kazuhiko comes to collect the package, he discovers it is a young girl named Su – her name coming from 'sì' the Chinese word for four.

Kazuhiko tries to deliver Su to her destination with the help of his former ward Ran, and Gingetsu, a friend who is still in the military. They are helped partly by the use of technology, including teleportation devices and a weapon that Kazuhiko has implanted in his artificial right hand, and partly by providing extra muscle in battle in Gingetsu's case, with Ran never going outside. However, Kazuhiko and Su constantly find themselves under attack from various groups of people, inside and outside their native land. While Kazuhiko's past military skills often get them out of trouble, sometimes it is Su who comes to rescue, as she is able to summon up great magical powers of her own.

It is later made clear that Su is part of the government's Clover Leaf Project. This was a ten-year-long project to find children who were capable of using these magic powers. Children in this scheme were given a ranking based on the clover plant. Su is the only '4-leaf Clover' known in existence, and is thus the most powerful of all, hence why so many people are after her. Ran meanwhile is a slightly less powerful '3-leaf' and Gingetsu a '2-leaf'. The powerful clovers were kept imprisoned because their powers might be dangerous.

During their journey, Kazuhiko learns that Su actually has

a personal connection to him. Su has an affinity with a dead singer called Ora. Actually, it is more than affinity. They worked together on a song called *Clover*, which Ora performed. Ora also happened to be Kazuhiko's lover.

The travels of Kazuhiko and Su form the first part of the *Clover* manga. Parts two and three are both flashbacks. Part two tells the story of Kazuhiko and Ora's love for each other, and how Ora and Su came to create their song. Part three focuses on Ran, how he grew up as a 3-leaf Clover with others of similar power, how he escaped his confinement and was helped by Gingetsu. Part four meanwhile, never got made. Like *The Legend of Chun Hyang*, the magazine that published the comic shut down, and thus the fourth part never got started. It was planned to be two-volumes long, bringing all of *Clover* to six volumes in total, the same length as *Rayearth*, but to this day the series remains unfinished.

The "CLAMP is the Kraftwerk of Manga" 'argument'

To put forward my 'case' for this viewpoint, I will simply write a bulletpoint list of arguments, some of which are admittedly flimsy, to justify this claim that the Japanese manga group are akin to the German electronic music pioneers.

- **Retro-futuristic technology**: *Clover* is the most typically sci-fi like of all their stories, being set in a near-future with advanced technology. Although other works by CLAMP have other such elements, such as computers in *Chobits*, parallel worlds in *Tsubasa*, the Beast computer in *X* and the end of *Wish* being 100 years in the future, *Clover* is one that purely by the nature of its setting feels most like your typical science fiction story. However, like Kraftwerk, while there is a love of technology and the new, it also looks back to the past as well. One look at any of the colour illustrations that they used to promote the story will show you that most of the technological gubbins that appear in the story appear brass-like and rather old fashioned. The aesthetic feels more like Victorian-looking steampunk than cyberpunk. A look at the front cover of Kodansha's 'Collector's Edition' English release seems to demonstrate this, showing Su in an outfit consisting of mechanised, Icarus-like wings, as well as a waist cincher/corset garment.

- **Minimalism**: Kraftwerk are known for a minimalist approach, from the recently redesigned album covers which often consist of just a symbol and two or three different colours, to their live performances which sees the group simply standing behind podiums containing their instruments. While CLAMP are known for many lavish pictures, *Clover* is certainly their most minimalist work. Often pages consist of just a white or black plain background rather than a vast picture like most of their canon. If it is the case that a page is mostly plain, then it might also consist of just a small drawing and a lone speech bubble. One nice highlight of the recent Kodansha release is the different style of lettering in comparison to all of other CLAMP's English releases. While almost all CLAMP's work in English is released in the normal comic sans, including past releases of *Clover*, the typeface here, chosen by Scott O. Brown, uses a more simplistic, straightforward typeface called CC Credit Crunch Soft.[3]

- **Interconnectiveness**: While writing this book, I listened to the audiobook *Kraftwerk: Future Music from Germany* by Uwe Schütte, which documents the history of the band and talks about the concept of it. For the group, Kraftwerk is not just about the music, but the art and modern life, similar to how the Bauhaus art movement thought of art as part of the way we live. I would argue that CLAMP also have a similar interconnectiveness, combining their storytelling and art from so many different series to create a single world, their CLAMPverse.

- **Reclusiveness**: Kraftwerk are famous for rarely giving interviews and for using their robot dummies in photo-shoots. As mentioned previously, CLAMP don't give out interviews often. They don't have robot versions of themselves, but many of their titles end with a small bonus chapter featuring chibi versions of themselves.

- **Museums**: CLAMP's artwork has appeared in museums, including the British Museum (see *Miyuki-chan in Wonderland*), as has Kraftwerk's creations and indeed Kraftwerk themselves, who have performed in museums.

- **The number four**: Kraftwerk and CLAMP both have four members, *Clover* was intended to be told in four parts, but in the end was stopped after four volumes. Kraftwerk's song *Numbers*, the lyrics of which consist of numbers being read out in foreign languages, consists of the numbers one to four being read in Japanese, CLAMP's native language: "Ichi, ni, san, shi". Indeed, if for some reason I was lucky enough to get this book adapted into a film documentary, I would talk about *Clover* over the tune of *Numbers*. I would mention the number of members in each group: "Ichi, ni, san, shi". I would say how many volumes *Clover* had: "Ichi, ni, san, shi". I would say how many parts *Clover* was meant to have: "Ichi, ni, san, shi", then point out that after three, the magazine shut and the series was pulled, and symbolically, I would remove the plug and stop the electronic song. As this is the ninth of 18 chapters and thus half-way, it would also be time to have a break or interval.[4] However, we would stick to some of the themes discussed in the next chapter, as it too has some technological, robotic themes to it, albeit in a more light-hearted setting.

1 – It also feels a bit unfair on Tamayo Akiyama, as it would make her the Pete Best of CLAMP, which definitely doesn't feel like a comparison that you want. For that matter, do all of the other early CLAMP members want be referred to as the Quarrymen of CLAMP?

2 – Indeed, you could fit anything into that formula and sound clever, but pompous, and at the same time have no real meaning. Try it. "Manchester United is the AK47 of football teams", "Donald Trump is the gangrene of US Presidents", "Elizabeth II is the Stalin of monarchs". Quite fun this. I think you can turn this into an improv game. Get people to draw out things out of a hat to fit "A is the B of C" and the winner is the person who best argues for that statement.

3 – Why would you want to name a font after a financial crisis? Is there also a font called Great Depression?

4 – The history of CLAMP is a long one, and if I did adapt this book into a film documentary, I would need an interval, and thus other people would too, to reference Ohkawa's attitude to fantasy character names as discussed in *Rayearth*.

CHAPTER 10

Deuses, Stand By. 3, 2, 1, Activate! – *Angelic Layer* (1999-2001)

When I reviewed the Blu-Ray anime adaptation of *Angelic Layer* for *Anime UK News* on 29th September 2018, I began the review with a quote from another review of the series.

This misguided review of the US DVD release of the series for *Anime News Network* was written back in 2003 by Zac Bertschy, a man who I should point out a) sadly died in May 2020 while I was writing this book, and b) was well respected among English-speaking anime fans. He wrote:

"The problem with Angelic Layer *is it apes the formula found in these other series [i.e. game-based stories] to a tee, but you can't actually play the* Angelic Layer *game, so what's the point? It's as if the director [Hiroshi Nishikiori] saw these other shows and didn't understand that the story was written in order to sell collectable game cards. Essentially, you have something that's written and designed like a marketing gimmick, without the product to back it up."*

I thus went on to tackle this complaint. Bertschy may have argued that there is no point to a game series that doesn't plug the game, but personally I think the series is better for it. *Angelic Layer* is not about trying to plug a product; it's about a girl who falls in love with a particular game.

A few things came to mind when writing about this work. Firstly, games-based manga is a mixed bag. Personally speaking, the best series of this kind are stories that adapt the plots of actual games, the best examples being series that adapt video games. The sheer success of *Pokemon* demonstrates this. Below this are series that spawned games themselves. The most famous example is *Yu-Gi-Oh!*, a manga originally about all kinds of games that ended up spawning the world's biggest trading card game, and as a result the game is now much bigger than the original manga. Some might argue that *Yu-Gi-Oh!* has sold out because of it, and indeed the later works are all about the card game, but the original series is still worth a read.[1] The worst are series that from day one are just plugging a commercial product – e.g. *Cardfight!! Vanguard*, a manga plugging the trading card game of the same name, is one of the worst manga I have ever reviewed. I totally and utterly hate it. All this series is about is selling this stupid game, pure and simple… which is why my heart sank when in January 2021, a new *Cardfight!! Vanguard* anime series was announced called *Vanguard overDress*, in which character designs were to be done by CLAMP. REALLY?! At least it looks like CLAMP are making some improvements to the series in terms of diversity, in that the main character in *overDress* is genderfluid.

Secondly, as a fan of British comedy, I am all in favour of games that you cannot actually play in real-life. I've never played Mornington Crescent or Guyball, but they are both fun and silly. They prove that you can make something entertaining that you cannot actually do.[2] The game of 'Angelic Layer' is certainly one that you cannot play, but it is still entertaining. In fact, I believe that the anime has some claim to being the best adaptation of a CLAMP manga.

Angelic Layer (1999-2001)

There is one stand-out feature regarding the publication of this manga. It was released in a Kadokawa Shoten magazine called *Shonen Ace*. Whereas just about all their other series have been aimed at what is regarded as the girl-focused 'shojo' genre of manga, including their more violent series like *X*, *Angelic Layer* debuted in a boy-focused 'shonen' comic. This is kind of understandable as the series features fighting as part of the game, but at the same time it is fighting with dolls, the traditional toy for girls, and nearly all of the players of the game are female.

However, this all adds up to the diversity of CLAMP's work. While they aim the work at as many people as they can, they are still able to go into different areas they want to cover.

Originally released by TokyoPop in five individual volumes, it was later re-released by Dark Horse in two separate books.

•

Misaki Suzuhara is a girl who has moved from the city of Wakayama to Tokyo.[3] She is about to start seventh grade and is going to live with her news reporter aunt Shouko – not that she likes being called an 'aunt' as it makes her feel old. What Misaki doesn't like is people thinking that she is younger than she actually is. She is so small that people think she is still in elementary school rather than middle school. After emerging from the train station, she spots TV coverage for the game 'Angelic Layer'.

The game works like this: two players, each called a 'Deus', create their own 'Angel'. These Angels are special dolls which are hatched from liquid-filled plastic eggs. If you are thinking: 'Angels hatched from eggs? Like in *Wish*?' that is well remembered and congratulations to you. The Deus uses various advanced forms of technology to create their Angel to their own particular style. Each game involves the Deus throwing their Angel into the field of play, the 'Layer'. Using a special pair of goggles, the Deus controls their Angel with their mind where they engage in martial arts-style combat. The winner is the one who knocks the opposing Angel down until the opponent's health bar goes to zero; whichever Angel still has the most health after a certain time limit; or the Angel that is able to knock the opponent out of the Layer first.

Misaki becomes engaged in the match she sees, mainly because the winner, an Angel called Athena, is the lightweight in the battle. Being small herself, she backs the smaller fighter. Soon however, she encounters a rather suspicious man. Calling himself Icchan, this gentleman in glasses and a white lab coat claims to know everything about 'Angelic Layer' and encourages Misaki to buy all the stuff needed to play the game from a nearby shop: Piffle Princess. If you are thinking: 'Piffle Princess? The shop mentioned in *X*?', you are on a roll.[4] The shifty Icchan is taken away by store guards leaving Misaki on her own, and having to make a long trek to her aunt's flat after spending all her money on 'Angelic Layer' equipment. However, Icchan constantly crops up to help Misaki in learning the game, even if everyone else thinks he is odd. As Icchan exclaims on p71 of Book One of the Dark Horse version: "Why does everyone think wearing a white lab coat and glasses and screaming automatically makes you some kind of mad scientist?!" Is it: "Because you are a mad scientist, mate?" In fact, I don't think you even need to shout. Just walk around in the street in a lab coat and people will think you are odd.[5]

In her first evening at her new home, Misaki creates her own Angel. She makes it short, like herself, and designs it to be a fast, lightweight fighter. She also gives the Angel short, red hair, and names it after the heroine of a manga she was reading on the train to Tokyo. Her Angel's name is one that it is familiar to you: Hikaru. That's right, Misaki names her Angel after the central figure in *Magic Knight Rayearth*, a fact made explicit in the blurb on Book One of the Dark Horse re-release. This does make things slightly confusing in that this means that the characters in CLAMP read the work of their creators. Does this mean that the characters in *Rayearth* are fictional characters within the CLAMPverse? Is it a manga within a manga? It's all getting rather confusing. Anyway, the story…

The following day, Misaki starts her first day at her new school, Eriol Academy. This is probably another CLAMP cross-reference, linking to *Cardcaptor Sakura*. The cross-referencing doesn't stop there, as the academy contains in it the first example of the Duklyon fast food shop, referencing *Duklyon: CLAMP School Defenders*.

On the way to class, she makes three new friends: Hatoko Kobayashi, a kindergartner who turns out to be a brilliant Angelic Layer player; her older brother Kotaro, who is in the same class as Misaki; and Tamayo Kizaki, a female classmate whose main hobby is practising almost lethal martial arts moves on Kotaro. These three all help in their own way, with Misaki learning more about the game from Hatoko, and Tamayo's martial arts moves on Kotaro helping her to come up with moves for Hikaru. As the manga progresses, romantic feelings between certain characters also develop.

Misaki, due to some 'tutorage' from Icchan, ends ups being entered into a professional Angelic Layer contest. Amazingly she wins plenty of matches, and ends up being nicknamed the 'Miracle Rookie'. She also ends up playing against Hatoko, while Kotaro and Tamayo support both of them from the vast stadium crowds. As Misaki progresses however, we learn more about the world that surrounds the game. It turns out that Icchan, whose full name is Ichiro Mihara, is actually the president of Piffle Company, which creates 'Angelic Layer'. He is closely watching Misaki as she climbs up the ranks and takes part in bigger contests, in the hope that she will finally get a chance for Hikaru to take on Athena. Athena is the Angel belonging to the Angelic Layer national champion: Shuko Suzuhara – Misaki's mother, who Misaki has not seen in years, believing she has been away working.

•

Angelic Layer has things for and against it. In the negative side of the scale, I would argue that the kids in *Angelic Layer* have the worst school uniforms of any of CLAMP's characters. For starters, I know that the traditional Japanese school uniforms are based on military designs, but the ones used in Eriol Academy are way too militaristic, what with them including medals and armbands. I can sort of understand why CLAMP went for this look, given that the series is about a fighting game, but it still feels off. Also, the main colour of the uniform is white. Are you seriously expecting school children to keep white jackets, skirts and trousers looking pristine? They are going to get dirty almost instantly. Despite this, not only do the main characters wear the uniforms at school, they wear them during the 'Angelic Layer' tournaments. I can kind of understand Misaki and Hatoko wearing them while playing because they want to look their best in front of a paying crowd, but Kotaro and Tamayo are just in the audience. Why do those two need to wear them? In a bizarre way it feels like the costume budget for the manga had been wiped out by *Cardcaptor Sakura* and they couldn't afford as many costumes,[6] except that this is clearly bollocks, because it is comic book, and CLAMP could have drawn the characters wearing anything. Still, could be worse. One of the other players in the competition, Sai 'The Ice Machine' Jounouchi, wears a uniform which is even more militaristic. It's even olive green in colour.

Also, while this is a futuristic game, there are certain aspects of 'Angelic Layer' that feel dated, the main one being the use of ring girls during the official tournaments. That's an aspect that hasn't aged too well.

However, there are plenty of positives to the story too. One is the comedy. This comes from the slapstick antics of Kotaro and Tamayo, as well as Icchan. There is not just his odd behaviour, there is also his relationship with his staff. One of the side characters in the story is Masaharu Ogata, a man who works behind the scenes on the game, but his job mainly involves trying to get Icchan to do his job. Ogata normally comes the worse off, with Icchan often 'penalising' him for just about anything, and forcing him to do all kinds of disgusting or embarrassing things.

Speaking of side characters, another person yet to be mentioned is Ohjiro Mihara, who is the younger brother of Icchan. As well as being related to the main person behind the game, Ohjiro stands out by being one of the few male characters who plays 'Angelic Layer'. In the manga, Ohjiro is the only guy Misaki faces in a competitive fight. Other side characters to bring up include Misaki's other competitors. Aside from Sai, she also takes on the intelligent Kaede Saito whose parents are divorced, pop idol Ringo Seto, Kung Fu practitioner Madoka Fujisaki and her Angel-creating sister Arisu.

But the main appeal of *Angelic Layer* is the game itself and how it is played. Misaki becomes deeply involved in not just what is going on, but caring for Hikaru. She is desperate not only to win, but to care for the Angel she has created. Things become more passionate as the battles become harder.

The anime version of *Angelic Layer* was made by the studio Bones in 2001, which had only released its debut series, a historical mecha show called *Hiwou War Chronicles* the previous year. Running for 26 episodes, *Angelic Layer* was the second TV series made by Bones, but they have since become one of the bigger studios around, also creating anime versions of *Fullmetal Alchemist*, *Ouran High School Host Club* and *My Hero Academia*. *Angelic Layer* was directed by Hiroshi Nishikiori, who also directed the comedy anime *Azumanga Daioh* and the sci-fi action anime *A Certain Magical Index*, which are also well worth watching.

There are differences between the manga and anime, but personally speaking I think many of these changes were for the better. Interestingly CLAMP said that they were not involved in the anime version. Igarashi stated in the *CLAMP no Kiseki* interviews: "In the TV series, even the romantic element is a lot more serious. Although they're saying the same lines as the manga, it's got a totally different feel. That was cool."

Sadly, Clements and McCarthy don't have much to say about the series in *The Anime Encyclopedia*, again summing up the series by saying it is a gaming anime with no real-life game to tie to. However, as said earlier in this chapter, I think that this is one of the best anime adaptations of one of CLAMP's works. The fact it won the 2001 Animation Kobe Television Award is surely evidence of this.

One of the differences is the romantic relationships between characters, as referenced by Igarashi. At the end of both versions, certain characters end up dating each other, but they differ between the two productions. I won't give away who is going out with who as that is a bit of a spoiler, but it is interesting to see the differences, and overall it doesn't impact too much on which version you prefer.

Personally speaking however, the big difference for me is the way that Misaki's mother Shuko is depicted. In both versions of the story, the reason Shuko has been away for so long is due to medical reasons, but the manga and anime versions differ as to how this is done. In CLAMP's original manga, Shuko has an extreme form of anxiety that prevents her from being able to talk to Misaki. As someone who has anxiety, this is something I can kind of relate to, although my anxiety, even when combined with my Asperger's, is nowhere near as severe as what Shuko has. In the anime however, her condition is physical. Shuko has an illness called degenerative neural syndrome. Shuko primarily gets around using a wheelchair, and often has poor spells of health resulting in her having to remain in bed. As for how Shuko copes with her illness after the series ends, we don't know. However, later CLAMP manga show that other characters in *Angelic Layer* have unfortunate ends.

In both cases however, it is Icchan who comes to her aid. It is he who uses 'Angelic Layer' to help Shuko rehabilitate and recover from the conditions in both versions of the story. While Icchan supplies most of the comedy in the story and does often comes across as creepy, he is actually a real hero in his attempt to help both Shuko and Misaki become close.

One other area worth highlighting is that *Angelic Layer* is a story that explores new genres. Yes, it covers gaming series, but there is also another genre of work that it is a prime example of: the plucky underdog. Misaki is someone who comes to the game a complete newbie and ends up reaching for the top. As for the very top? Well, you have to actually read or see the series, although I should say that again there are some differences in the endings.

When it comes to problems with the anime however, probably the main one is with the English dub. In the series, there is a host who acts as the MC for all the matches in the main competition. In the dub, the man who voices the host is someone called Vic Mignogna, who has starred in many anime including *Dragon Ball, Naruto, Bleach, Ouran High School Host Club*, and was also the voice of Fai D. Flowright, one of major characters in another CLAMP series, *Tsubasa.*

Now, I have to be careful about talking about him in a legal sense. What I will therefore write here is all factual rather than opinion, and let you draw your own conclusions, so here we go.

In 2019, allegations of sexual assault, some dating back to 1989 and involving people underage, were brought up against

Mignogna. In January that year, Sony Pictures ended their contract with Mignogna, and in February the production company Rooster Teeth ended their relationship with him. Several anime conventions cancelled appearances he was going to make, but Mignogna denied all claims against him. In February 2019, Mignogna filed a lawsuit against distributor and streaming service Funimation, voice actors Monica Rial and Jamie Marchi, and Rial's fiancé Ron Toye for defamation and tortuous interference. In June, Mignogna was deposed, and then in July Funimation, Rial, Marchi, Toye and others filed 12 motions to dismiss Mignogna's lawsuit. Mignogna's team failed to file a response by 27 minutes, citing technical issues. In September, Mignogna failed to turn up to court in case regarding these motions. By October, all the cases ended up being dismissed, and Judge John Chupp ordered Mignogna to pay defendants' attorney fees totalling just over $223,000. The entire thing is thus seen by many as being anime's #MeToo moment.

•

Angelic Layer is a series that sees CLAMP continuing to cross-reference their other work, and indeed this series would see characters crop up in later titles. It is a fun, entertaining show. Admittedly, some elements of the story might put people off. While it is a series which sees fighting action figures, it is arguably also a series about children, mainly girls, playing with dolls, which could be seen as reinforcing gender stereotypes.

Having said this however, when this series was being made between 1999 and 2001, and with the anime also being released in that year, there were other TV programmes that were on that might have appealed to a similar audience. Let's distill what the game of 'Angelic Layer' is. The game involves people creating advanced dolls which they can control remotely. Arguably these dolls are more machine-like than the dolls you normally play with. Then they are put into a field of play and fight each other while people watch in the arena or from the comfort of their own homes.

Have you got it yet? No? Let's try it a different way. Let's say that 'Angelic Layer' the game really existed, and did so in the years the manga and anime were made. What if the TV stars that Misaki and Shuko Suzuhara would surely be were invited to perform an exhibition match for a UK audience? How would have UK audiences have watched such a fight? You should know by now. I mean, you should have realised what the comparison would be from the name of this chapter.

"Roboteers, stand by."

There is young Misaki Suzuhara there, wearing the goggles that allow her to control Hikaru, and on the other side her mother Shuko, controlling Athena.

"3, 2, 1, activate!"

And off we go in this special exhibition match featuring these two lightweight walking machines, as Hikaru runs to Athena, but Athena backs away. Walking robots are normally slow, and are allowed to be twice as heavy as rollers, but in the Japanese games they seem to prefer the more nimble machines, and Athena comes on the attack, trying to land punches on Hikaru which she blocks. Hikaru ducks, swings her legs to try and trip Athena up, but Athena jumps out of the way there! We haven't had a jumping robot on Robot Wars in the UK, so it will be interesting to see if the British Roboteers can learn something from this battle.

Athena moves towards the edge of the arena, Hikaru comes on the charge, and Athena jumps up and on to Hikaru which is dangerous!

Hikaru has run straight into the CPZ, the Corner Patrol Zone, which means the House Robots can come and attack and... oh nearly! Hikaru just manages to escape from the axe of Shunt, and gets out of the CPZ. But that was bad control from Misaki Suzuhara, who is controlling Hikaru using these strange goggles. Remember, if it goes to the judges they will be looking at style, control, damage and aggression.

Hikaru is now in the middle of the arena and it is now Athena on the charge. She tries to launch a blow on Hikaru... but Hikaru grabs Athena by the shoulders and tosses her over her shoulder! Athena lands in another CPZ and, oh my word! Dead Metal tried to grab Athena with his pincers, but to no avail. These Japanese robots are so quick and nimble, she was able to escape with ease. Brilliant work from Shuko Suzuhara there. The mother is teaching her daughter who is boss, and she is now coming back with another charge, and this time Hikaru can't avoid it in time! Athena lands a mighty punch on Hikaru, a vicious uppercut. Now she has got her in a half-Nelson! For those who came to watch Robot Wars, looks like we've got wrestling instead.

And Athena is now lifting Hikaru onto her shoulders, and yes, I think she is about to throw Hikaru out of the arena... and she does! She flies... NO! Look at that! WHOA! As Hikaru flew through the air, almost out of the arena, Hikaru managed to grab the top of the arena wall and has avoided crashing onto the ground. But even more spectacular than that, she pushes herself off the outside wall of the arena, flips up into the air and lands back into the arena! We have never seen that in Robot Wars ever! No robot has ever managed to grab onto the walls and lever themselves back into the arena. Hikaru may be the underdog in this fight, but that will be a lot of points for style if this goes to the judges, which I suspect it will.

Athena prepares herself as Hikaru now comes in on the attack. There's a fierce trade of blows there, punch after punch, and now a kick from Hikaru knocks Athena back an- OH NO! As Athena was knocked back, she tumbled into another CPZ, and fell straight into the flywheel of Matilda, and one of Athena's legs has come clean off! That is the problem with these lightweight robots, they are nippy and agile, but don't have the protective armour that stand up to attack from the House Robots, even when it is accidental. But Hikaru managed to knock Athena into that CPZ, and now that she only has one leg to stand on, that is Athena immobilised and Hikaru will win this Japanese exhibition match.

And now the House Robots can have their fun. Matilda tossing Athena's severed limb into the air with her tusks, as Sir Killalot comes in and oh my word! Sir Killalot just rolls over Athena, and his mighty treads and turns Athena's head into pulp. How dare you, Sir! That is no way to treat a lady, Killalot! You scoundrel! I think Hikaru might actually be coming in to try and help Athena from being damaged further. Remember our Roboteers are mother and daughter, but Shunt and Dead Metal are keeping her at bay. Sir Killalot meanwhile has got himself into position and has picked what remains of Athena in his mighty claw. That claw is based on the jaws of life used by the emergency service to free people from wrecked cars, but these are very much jaws of death. Now, where shall we take Athena? Ah, the flame pit, and Sir Killalot shuts his claw completely, splitting the torso of Athena in two, and what remains of the corpse is left burning on the flames, the plastic melting. It's a shame to see these highly developed machines being trashed so easily by our House Robots, isn't it? No, not really. This is Robot Wars! We want violence, and mayhem, and destruction! You may like to make your robots look cute and fancy, but we like to take that and… err… mash it all up.

"Cease!"

That's it, Hikaru wins. Young Misaki Suzuhara beats her mother. Don't expect any pocket money to come your way anytime soon, Misaki.

See Bertschy, Clements, McCarthy, there was a game like 'Angelic Layer' after all, and we Brits had it all the time on BBC Two, at the same time CLAMP were making their own, more technologically advanced version.

---

1 – The anime adaptation is also available on DVD to UK viewers, but be aware of the fact that you can only get it in an English dub. For more, see my reviews of the series which are also on Anime UK News.

2 – For anime examples of games and contests that are very difficult to do in real-life, see The Great Wyrm Tournament from *Dick Fight Island.*

3 – Wakayama is around 600km West of Tokyo.

4 – Although admittedly, given that this manga began in 1999, the year *X* is set, Tokyo seems to be standing up very well to the forthcoming apocalypse.

5 – My brother wears glasses, and for his work wears a lab coat. I've seen photos of him at work, and there he looks normal, but if you took him out of the lab and just put him on the street in the exact same clothes, even I would find it a bit weird, despite the fact I've known my brother all my life. Having said that, my brother lives in Harrogate, Yorkshire, and on the surface it doesn't seem to take much for people to think you might be weird. Harrogate comes across as a place where people think you

are weird for owning a car that's less than £100,000, not voting for the Conservative Party, or not thinking the prices in Bettys Tea Rooms might be too expensive, and before anyone complains 'Bettys' is spelt without the apostrophe.

6 – Damn you, Tomoyo Daidouji!

CHAPTER 11

I Will Always Like You – *Suki: A Like Story* (1999-2000)

Again, we see more changes of direction in this short series. While it is rightly described as a romance, which is something CLAMP have covered several times, the drama in *Suki* feels like the main attraction. It also differs in terms of appearance. Another series in which Nekoi provided much of the art, it looks so much different from their other work.

As you see in the *CLAMP no Kiseki* interviews, Ohkawa made explicit the fact she wanted *Suki* be different in terms of drawings and story. She said: "We wanted fans who'd been reading our works for a long time to shake their heads and wonder, did CLAMP really make this? The drawings are not as sharp as usual, the character's eyes are small."

The less-sharp art seemed to help the team. Nekoi said in the interviews that: "The drawing process was quick. I'd draw out ten pages in one day and then I'd ink them in. After having worked so hard on *Wish* I couldn't believe it how quick it was. *laughs* It's because the way I drew out the rough sketches is so different."

When reading this series, a lot of peculiar thoughts go through your head. At first, the romance comes to the front, but then you sometimes feel like it might be a social commentary piece, and at times the story does feel genuinely creepy. If you were to compare this story to something Western, then this manga feels most like a stand-alone play. The series length would actually make it rather appropriate to adapt as a film, animated or live-action.

Suki: A Like Story (1999-2000)

The three volumes of *Suki* were published in Kadokawa Shoten's *Mystery DX* magazine, where they had just finished *Wish* a year earlier and where they were still creating *X*. It was once again published by TokyoPop, with this series now only available as an e-book from Viz Media. Personally speaking, I think it is strange that other publishers like Dark Horse have not tried to re-release the series in an omnibus or collector's edition version, as three volumes would easily fit into a single collection. A missed opportunity, I think.

While *Suki: A Like Story* is the title of the series in English, the original Japanese title feels the better version. This is *Suki. Dakara Suki*, meaning *I Like You, That's Why I Like You*.

•

16-year-old Hinata 'Hina' Asahi is a student at Outo Private High School for Girls. She lives on her own in a large house, paid for by her wealthy but busy father, Hina's mother having died five years earlier. Her father, who never appears in the manga, also happens to be the chairman of Outo School. Hina spends most of her time playing with her teddy bears Waka and Tono, reading picture books by an author called Tomo, and singing rather unusual songs to herself.

One snowy night, Hina learns that someone has moved into the empty house next door, a man named Shiro Asou. Shiro is somewhat standoffish, but he is nice enough. Hina however begins to fall for Shiro almost immediately, despite the fact he is much older than her, aged 32. The following day, when Hina is at school, she learns that her homeroom teacher is away on maternity leave and thus she is getting a substitute to take over the class. This substitute is – you've guessed it – Shiro Asou.

Living so close together, Hina and Shiro walk to and from school together, during which Hina becomes ever more smitten with her teacher. This worries Hina's classmates, Touko Shinohara and Emi Kishitani. The two worry for Hina, partly because Shiro is so much older, and partly because Hina is totally naive in her belief in the goodness in all people. She repeatedly says that she believes that no one in the world is *truly* bad. Touko and Emi thus go out of their way to try and protect Hina and to investigate Shiro, worried that he might have some dark desire for her. Despite all this, Hina continues to be increasingly friendly and falls even more in love with her teacher, even inviting him round to her house for meals.

More suspicions arise when Hina encounters a man named Tomoaki Namiya. Coming across him in a bookshop when he is in conversation with Shiro, we learn that Tomoaki is an author. The first works we see from him are erotic, but we later learn he writes children's books.[1] Indeed, as you may have guessed from the name, we later learn he is Tomo, the writer of Hina's favourite series of books. Shiro seems to have a troubled past with him and someone else close to Tomo, a man named Masaya Kizu. Indeed, in private we learn from them that Shiro is keeping a deliberate close eye on Hina, Tomo describing Hina as "Shiro's target".

As the manga progresses, the story becomes increasingly dark. While Hina is still happily in love with Shiro, Shiro is still trying to keep back, on the surface at least. However, *Suki* is a series that has twists and turns which are dramatic shocks. These appear to relate to a more tragic backstory for Hina, as we learn that due to her father's wealth she has been the subject of kidnapping. To be exact, she has been kidnapped nine times, with her father always paying the kidnappers off, but somehow Hina always remains positive and firm in her belief that people are always fundamentally good. *Suki: A Like Story* tells the story of Hina's tenth kidnapping.

•

Suki is a strange story, given that it contains so many conflicting elements to it. A lot of the time the story is very light-hearted, with Hina being such a nice, fun character. Perhaps the stand-out feature of Hina is her rather strange songs. Here are a few examples. This first one comes from p54 of the first volume:

Yippee-skippy!
School is nifty!
Skipping to school
In the nice, bright sun!
Let's hope something
Good happens to me.
I just can't wait to see everyone!

Then there is this one from p125 of the same volume. Note that in Japanese the word for 'bear' is 'kuma':

Kuma-san,
The little black bear
Is best friends
With brown Kuma-san.
There he goes
To the baker in the woods
And buys some baumkuchen[2]
So good!
"Keep the change,"
He tells the baker…

However, these happy songs are balanced out by the darkness of the story. I said that this feels like an episode from an anthology series, and the twists in the plot might make someone think of

Inside No. 9 when reading this.[3] I would argue that there are two major twists to the story. Obviously they would be bad form for me to give them away, but I will say that they are in there and they will shock you when you come across them. It is because of this that I think that *Suki* would be a good series to adapt for the screen.

There is another element that deserves highlighting in this work, which is the role of Tomoaki. The stories he creates as Tomo not only give joy to Hina, but also allow CLAMP to add another trope to their canon – the story within a story. We see Tomo's written and illustrated short children's books, which as they progress echo the plot of the series. [4] Interestingly, the main series of books we see from Tomo is also called *Suki*, with the two main characters, an old black bear accused of doing something wrong, and a younger white bear who refuses to believe the rumours and thinks the black bear is good, echoing Shiro and Hina respectively.

•

Suki is a short but thrilling tale. The artwork makes it stand out from the rest of the CLAMP canon, but the story is what makes it interesting for me. You see other connections to the rest of the CLAMPverse in this series too, with Hina wearing items from the shop Piffle Princess.

Suki also marks a turning point as it was the last of CLAMP's works to debut in the 20th century. Entering into the next millennium, post 1999, while *X* was still being written despite passing the year it was set in, the group would next create another series with an element of mystery and romance to it, albeit gay romance and supernatural mystery.

1 – Work on both kids' stuff and porn, Tomoaki is a bit like CLAMP in that respect.

2 – Baumkuchen is a festive German cake, helpfully explained in a brief note in the manga. I suspect that there will be quite a lot of people in Britain who actually know what baumkuchen is, but this manga was translated into English in 2004, and I have never watched *The Great British Bake Off*.

3 – The numbers of Hina and Shiro's houses are never given, so one of them could be No. 9. I didn't see any statues of silver hares however.

4 – Not the porn mercifully, apart from one tiny extract that Hina spots when she sees Tomoaki's laptop when they first meet.

CHAPTER 12

Unusual Side-Effects and Side-Characters – *Legal Drug* (2000-2003) and *Drug & Drop* (2011-2013)

The first CLAMP work to debut in the new millennium came out at a peculiar time for the women creating it. For starters, *X* was now set in the past, and the world had not fallen into ruin – good news for the Dragons of Heaven. *Cardcaptor Sakura* was also over (for now), and this next work was again a departure.

Risqué *Legal Drug* and its sequel *Drug & Drop* had darker sources of inspiration. Ohkawa revealed in the *CLAMP no Kiseki* interviews that: "At the time, a major thing we were really into was underground stuff. Things like bondage, seedy environments, tattoos… so, pulled towards that kind of gimmick, the series took on that influence."

You can see all three in the series. Much of the promotional artwork features bondage-like scenarios between the two main characters; some of the settings are particularly unusual, such as a school with a bizarre element to its annual festival; and one of the main characters has a tattoo, which in Japan is a big deal. Tattoos are often related to the yakuza, and certain establishments such as public bathhouses ban people who have tattoos because of the associations with the organised criminal gangs.[1]

Another source for where the series began is with another of their doujinshi, a web-based product based on the supernatural adventure *JoJo's Bizarre Adventure*. Created in 1987 by Hirohiko

Araki and still going today, the manga follows multiple generations of the Joestar family, beginning in Victorian England. The most famous part of the story is *Stardust Crusaders* (1989-1992), in which juvenile delinquent Jotaro 'JoJo' Kujo and his friends must travel across Asia to Egypt in order to save his mother's life, using fighting spirits called 'Stands'. It is the characters from this section which would go on to influence *Legal Drug*.

Across both series, CLAMP would continue to cross-reference with their earlier works, and, in the case of *Drug & Drop,* some series we have yet to cover in this book. If you want to skip ahead and stick with the chronological order of when each series was published, feel free to do so, but I will continue to group these two series in this chapter, given that the latter is a direct continuation of the former.

Legal Drug (2000-2003)

Another of CLAMP's series published in Kadokawa Shoten and originally in the magazine *Mystery DX*, the three-volume long *Legal Drug*, or *Gouhou Drug* in Japanese, was first released in English by TokyoPop and then by Dark Horse as a single omnibus.

It has several elements that make it stand out from the rest of the CLAMP catalogue. The first of these is the title of the manga as well as certain design elements. Regarding the design, one of the first things you spot when you look at the cover of the manga is a drawing of a cannabis leaf. This is strange given the manga's English title, as cannabis is actually illegal in Japan and has been since 1948. The title also gave rise to some problems with CLAMP and their editors. When asked in the *CLAMP no Kiseki* interviews as to how the title came about, this was the reply:

Ohkawa: *At the time, I wanted to do something very naughty. *laughs* Our editor was quite against the title 'Gouhou Drug'. The correct English translation of the title would be 'Legal Drug', but to emphasize the 'justice' nuance, we made it 'Lawful Drug', but the title has nothing to do with medicine. *laughs**

Igarashi: *I think he didn't notice the significance of the leaf in the logo.*

Strangely however, the drawings of leaves are the only reference to cannabis CLAMP make through the entire series, and indeed throughout the course of their work. There are several characters in the CLAMPverse who smoke, including ones in *Legal Drug*, but it's all tobacco rather than cannabis.

Another thing that makes *Legal Drug* stand apart from CLAMP's previous output is the lack of female characters. All four central characters in the story identify, on the surface at least, as male. This appears to have been a wish from Nekoi, who was the central artist on this series, with Ohkawa commenting in the *CLAMP no Kiseki* interviews: "Up until now all the series Nekoi worked on had girls or angels as the main characters, really fluffy material, so she wanted to try out something more dark. With that in mind, I tried to put in as many males as possible. It's kind of like the opposite of *Miyuki-chan in Wonderland.* *laughs*"

It is particularly interesting to mention *Miyuki-chan*, because again there are elements of connection between it and *Legal Drug*, in that non-consensual sex pops up its ugly head once more, so readers will want to proceed carefully.

•

The series follows the staff and associates of Green Drugstore. The main characters are employees Kazahaya Kudo and Rikuo

Himura. Around Christmas, Kazahaya was lying in the snow on the verge of death and desperately not wanting to die. He is saved by Rikuo (the one with the tattoo), already an employee at Green Drugstore, and is brought into the staff with both men living above the shop – to their regret, as it soon becomes apparent that neither of them like each other.

The shop itself is owned by a gentleman named Kakei, while the most frequent visitor to the shop is a man named Saiga, a smoker normally dressed in black and who never takes off his shades. As well as getting Kazahaya and Rikuo to do jobs around the shop, Kakei also gets the two of them to do some extra jobs for a bit more cash. These jobs always tend to have a supernatural quality, which is good because we learn that both Kazahaya and Rikuo have supernatural powers themselves. Kazahaya has the power to read the 'memory' of a person or object that he touches, as well as absorbing emotions from these memories. Rikuo's powers are more telekinetic, allowing him to break objects. Saiga sometimes helps out the duo in their tasks as well.

Most of the stories in the manga are rather self-contained, lasting only a few chapters in length. They include encountering the spirit within a fig tree, capturing invisible fireflies by the light of the moon, an encounter with a cat which can show to people the thing that they most want to see. In the case of Kazahaya and Rikuo, the people they most want to meet is the central motivation for both guys in the story. For Kazahaya, he most wants to meet his twin sister Kei, the woman that Kazahaya wanted to meet so much that he vowed he would not die in the snow that Christmas when Rikuo encountered him. Rikuo meanwhile most wants to meet his missing elder sister Tsukiko. The unwilling duo thus continue to carry out Kakei's tasks in the hope they will solve the mystery regarding the missing women in their lives.

•

The most interesting element for *Legal Drug* for me is that in comparison to the longer tales CLAMP have created, the stories in this series are mostly short tales, with the exception coming in the third volume in the series which lasts the entire volume.

Out of these stories, the best involves more of CLAMP's cross-referencing and encounters with their past characters. One job involves Kazahaya having to investigate a time pocket by walking in between the space of a lamppost and a fence, but in order to do so he needs to wear the right clothes. Unfortunately, the clothes he has to wear is a school uniform. A girl's school uniform to be exact and, to make things worse, he can't just go out and buy one, he has to go up to a girl wearing a uniform and ask to borrow it. Thus, this very dodgy scenario sees Kazahaya having to hang outside the gates of a school on graduation day and having to eventually ask a girl if they wouldn't mind loaning their uniform.

Luckily for him, the school he is standing outside happens to be Outo Private High School for Girls, and the girl he asks just happens to be Hinata 'Hina' Asahi from *Suki: A Like Story*, the single most trusting/naive person in the entire world. She is more than happy to let a total stranger take away her school uniform, with Kazahaya giving her some fresh clothes from Piffle Princess. Afterwards, she meets up with Shiro Asou, who is rightly angry at her, assuming that she has given her uniform to a crossdressing pervert.[2]

Bizarrely, this is not the only time crossdressing appears in *Legal Drug*. The story in the third volume sees Kazahaya and Rikuo going undercover to try and locate a ring at a private school for boys. This ring only comes out for special occasions, one of which is the fast-approaching school festival, which holds a 'marriage ceremony' contest where the school's most attractive boy is elected to act as a bride. Kazahaya ends up in the running for the contest. Also at the school and indeed in the competition is a boy called Satoru Nayuki. Kazahaya shares a class and dorm with Nayuki, who among other things tells him that the school once had a separate bathhouse, but no one uses it anymore, partly because of an incident where someone tried to rape him. Kazahaya is clearly horrified when Nayuki mentions this, but Nayuki is uncomfortably cheerful about the whole thing.

As for what happened after the incident at the all boys' school, we would have to wait another eight years to find out what Kazahaya and Rikuo did next. Once again, the magazine that published the work closed down while CLAMP were still working on the series. In fact, it changed several times. In 2001, *Legal Drug* moved to another magazine called *Shojo Teikoku* for a few months, then in 2002 it went to *Monthly Asuka*. In September 2003, the series went on hiatus, and when it returned for the fourth time, the manga had changed names.

Drug & Drop (2011-2013)

CLAMP were eventually able to return to the series in 2011, with the re-titled *Drug & Drop* being published in another Kadokawa Shoten magazine, *Young Ace*, and with these two volumes being released in English by Dark Horse.

That year marked a key event for CLAMP. In December 2011, it was reported that one of the members got a serious injury. We don't know which one, but one of CLAMP was diagnosed with a lumbar compressed fracture, a back problem caused by having to sit down for long periods of time. A 2019 article from *Anime Feminist*, 'What We Owe to Creators: Burnout in manga artists and how to prevent it' by Priya Sridhar, said that the injured member worked, "…for nineteen hours a day for weeks on end." Doctors ordered the person in question to undergo a period of rest and recuperation for six months, otherwise they may be subject to continued pain and a shortened career. As a result of this, there would be lower page counts in this and their other work at the time, *Gate 7*, while in 2012 both series had to go on hiatus after one of the members had a sudden illness.

Sadly, these conditions are rather commonplace in the manga industry. Long hours for even the most highly regarded artists are the norm, and obviously things are worse for most lone manga creators. Eiichiro Oda, creator of the best-selling *One Piece*, has claimed that he only gets three hours sleep a night. Another series, *Hunter x Hunter* by Yoshihiro Togashi (husband of *Sailor Moon* creator Naoko Takeuchi), began around the same time as *One Piece* and is also hugely popular, but it has become infamous for going on multiple hiatuses, one lasting four years. As a result, it has had 36 printed tankobon volumes, while *One Piece* has over 100.

As for CLAMP, other series had been made and published between *Legal Drug* and *Drug & Drop*, and thus manga are referenced in this section that we have yet to cover in this book, namely *xxxHOLiC*. Kazahaya and Rikuo both made appearances in the *xxxHOLiC* manga and anime TV series. If you want to skip forward to that chapter before reading this part, feel free to do so.

•

Drug & Drop appears to carry on pretty much from where *Legal Drug* ended. Kazahaya and Rikuo are continuing to carry out jobs for Kakei. Their first sees them being given a job by *xxxHOLiC* lead Kimihiro Watanuki, which involves going to a nearby house to deal with some kind of alcoholic spirit, by which I mean a spirit who drinks a lot, although the ghostly figure in question does appear to drink spirits.

Another job sees Kazahaya Kudo visiting the house which belonged to a different Kudo. It is a familiar-looking house, because when he touches one of the trees in the garden, he is visited by a rather small angel who is in the middle of a 100 year sleep. Yes, Kohaku from *Wish* makes an appearance in the story. Indeed, Kohaku is not the only character from that series to appear in *Drug & Drop*. When Kazahaya and Rikuo are away, with Kakei and Saiga on their own, we learn that they set up Green Drugstore because they knew that fate would bring Kazahaya and Rikuo to them. Something big is going to happen to the two employees, and they know because of their otherworldly qualities. By removing his shades, we see Saiga is missing an eye, and eventually we come to learn that in reality Kakei and Saiga are actually the angelic and demonic lovers, Hisui and Kokuyo.

We also learn more about the past of both Kazahaya and Rikuo, and in particular their relation to the missing women in the past, Kei and Tsukiko. Tsukiko has been kidnapped and Rikuo is trying to find her. Kei, who like Kazahaya has some supernatural abilities, namely seeing the future of something when she touches it rather than the past, loves her twin brother Kazahaya so much that she was seemingly happy to resort to extreme violence to stop anyone else from getting close to him.

After that, we have no idea what happens because, guess what, the series went on hiatus again, and has been on hiatus ever since.

•

If you include the sequel, *Legal Drug* is the only one of CLAMP's works to have been stopped completely in its tracks twice. We know that CLAMP wanted to go on for longer. Ohkawa said in the *CLAMP no Kiseki* interviews, after *Legal Drug* had ended that: "We've only told 1/5 of the planned story." That would imply that the series was intended to last 15 volumes. With three volumes written then and another two with *Drug & Drop*, a third of the story has thus now been told. With so many of their series ending early, part of me is wondering if this is some kind of unconscious reference to *The Tale of Genji* and their plan to deliberately end their works mid-sentence, leaving everyone hanging on to find out what was meant to happen next.

As for *Drug & Drop*, something crops up here in CLAMP's work for the first time that we have mentioned earlier in this book. Some schoolgirls come to Green Drugstore and take photos of Kazahaya and Rikuo. Kakei, keen to protect them from being spotted by more sinister forces, kindly asks the girls to delete the photos they have taken… on their smartphones. It would appear that the massive technology discrepancy that appeared between *Cardcaptor Sakura* and *Cardcaptor Sakura: Clear Card* can be traced back to here. Our two leads have only known each other for a year, and yet smartphones managed to become a thing in 2003. In the English translation, Kazahaya overhears one of the girls saying about the photos they just took: "I gotta post it… …I'll be all over Snapchat with this…" Snapchat was not released until 2011, the year *Drug & Drop* began publication. The tech gap is not as bad as the one in *Sakura*, and it could just be a case of a rather poor translation by William Flanagan, but it is still an annoyance.

•

It is hard to feel overly positive about either of the two series covered in this chapter, given that they have both been halted. Whether CLAMP would return to them for a third time remains to be seen, but you get the feeling that we will forever be denied the right to know what will happen next. I hope I'm proven wrong.

1 – This tattoo issue proved problematic during the Rugby World Cup, which was held in Japan in 2019. A quick search online about the issue reveals several news reports about tattooed rugby players being told to cover up their tattoos, which was something of an issue given that tattoos are a big part of the culture of many Pacific Island nations, including New Zealand.

2 – By the way, just how gullible is Hina? With this trusting nature it's no wonder she has been kidnapped ten times. She must be the easiest person in the world to mug. Just go up to her, ask if you could borrow ¥1,000 to buy petrol because your van has run out and she would probably reply: "Sure no problem, I'll just wait here. You're not sure that's enough. Oh well, here's another 1,000. Yes, it's probably easier if you took all the cash. Your van needs repairs too. Yeah, you can use my credit card. I don't mind, my father is quite wealthy. Oh yes, I'd love to see your van. #Oh Kuma-san, Kuma-san, he drives a white van. Listen to the wheels, he turns the steering, he taking the berries to the market. Oh Kuma-san, Kuma-san...# Oh, well I like singing that song, but if you want me to stop, then okay. Oh, that is a nice van. Yes, I'd love to look inside. Yes, very spacious. Oh, if you are offering then yes I'd like to go inside. Yes, it's very ni… oh, you've seemed to have shut the doors… and you've locked them as well. Ah, have I been kidnapped again? *sighs* Oh well, sensei will be here soon enough."

CHAPTER 13

You Don't Have to be Beautiful to Turn Me On – *Chobits* (2000-2002)

Having already discussed technology in CLAMP's work in *Clover*, as well as 'arguing' about their similarity to Kraftwerk, this series takes us into the realm of 'Computer Love'.

However, it should be noted that while on the surface, someone who has never read *Chobits* may think of it as a story about robots, it is very specifically a story about computers that look like people. It is also a successful story. Republished editions of the story describe *Chobits* as CLAMP's best-selling manga in the USA. It is a story that contains not just technology, but also comedy, tragedy and beauty.

It is also a manga that you should not read on a bus, which is what I did when I first read *Chobits*. To explain, at the time I had what the Japanese call a 'tsundoku' – a pile of books that were going unread. One year I had such a backlog of manga that I promised myself as my New Year's resolution to read one print volume of manga a day until I got through the entire lot. It took me the entire year but I did it. One of the books in my backlog was *Chobits*, which I started reading on a bus from Stockton-on-Tees to Newcastle-upon-Tyne, where I was going to stay for a few days as I was attending the SunnyCon Anime Expo.[1] I hadn't read the manga before so I wasn't sure what to expect, which is why it was problematic when I suddenly came across scenes of the female-looking lead character topless. Take this as a word of caution.

Chobits (2000-2002)

This was another of Kodansha's titles, originally published in *Weekly Young Magazine*, a magazine that had already made its name publishing two series that spawned a pair of the most famous anime films known: *Akira* and *Ghost in the Shell.* This was another development for CLAMP as the magazine was catered towards the young adult men, making it an example of what is called a 'seinen' manga.

Released in eight volumes, *Chobits* was again originally released in English by TokyoPop in 2002, although in terms of our chronology it would be the last CLAMP title TokyoPop would bring out. In 2009, Dark Horse took the title over, bringing it out in two omnibus editions, each containing four standard tankobon volumes each. In August 2020, Kodansha's English language arm began another collector's edition release of another CLAMP title, this time to mark the 20th anniversary of the debut of *Chobits*. An anime version of the series was released in 2002, and was released by MVM Films on DVD in 2011 and on Blu-Ray in 2016.

The *CLAMP no Kiseki* interviews reveal that the origin of the series was an idea of having computers that could actually talk to you, rather than how they actually respond in real life. Igarashi commented: "The only thing our computer at the time would say was 'Error, Error'. It never told us, or gave the slightest clue, as to what was the matter."

Robots in manga are nothing new. Probably the most revered manga ever is Osamu Tezuka's *Astro Boy*, whose title character is a robot. This is part of the reason CLAMP decided to go a different route and instead have a walking, talking, humanoid computer as the central figure. Ohkawa said: "The Japanese have a tendency to accept robots being personified, which makes it easy to empathise with them, doesn't it? But computers have a stronger association of being just an electronic appliance. We decided to use computers to stress the fact that they weren't living beings." Perhaps the fact that computers are not associated with the human form made it easier for CLAMP to depict these machines as being more scantily clad when they needed to be, and sometimes when they didn't need to be.

•

Set some time in the near future but with no specific date given, *Chobits* begins with a slightly more grown-up character, compared to most of CLAMP's works. Hideki Motosuwa is a 19-year-old man (although the anime says he's 18), originally from the countryside, who wants to go to university in Tokyo. However, he failed the entrance exam. He has still travelled to the city, but is now studying at Seki Cram School.[2] Hideki's parents, who never appear in the story, have also cut off his allowance, meaning that while Hideki is studying in the day, in the evening he also has a job serving in a local pub called Club Pleasure (known as My Pleasure in the English translation of the anime).

Like any man his age (whether it be 18 or 19), Hideki also wants the latest tech, including a computer. To be exact, a very special type of computer: a 'persocom' ('personal computer'). These are computers that are designed to look and act like human beings. The major difference in terms of appearance between the two is that persocoms have large robotic ears, inside of which contain leads that you can use to connect them to the mains to charge them, or into other devices such as televisions or games consoles. Hideki really wants one, so that he can do what any young adult male would do with a computer – look at online porn. Yes, he can also go on the internet, use it in his studies, but it is made clear that porn is what he is after. There is just one problem: persocoms are incredibly expensive and there is no way he can afford one.

Hideki however is in luck. Walking home to his flat one night, Hideki comes across an abandoned persocom, shaped like a young girl with floor-length blonde hair, covered in bandages, in a pile of rubbish ready to be taken away. As no one clearly wants this persocom, Hideki decides to take the machine away for himself – failing to notice that a computer disc containing the software needed to work the device is on the ground. As to what Hideki says as he takes it away, that depends on the translation that you use. In the new Kodansha version Hideki says: "No one would care if I took her home with me, right…?! Right?!" This is probably more accurate than the Dark Horse version, where the translator must have been watching *The Lord of the Rings* films at the time, as in this version Hideki instead says: "We *wants* it, yes we does, precious!" Given that the films had yet to come out by the time the opening chapter debuted, that CLAMP were probably too busy to read the original three-volume novel, and on top of that Ohkawa probably would have had trouble remembering the names of the characters in a fantasy novel, my guess is that this isn't what CLAMP wrote in the original Japanese.[3] Anyway, the story…

Hideki gets the persocom back to his place and after much struggling finally finds the on switch, which is located in the worst possible place – the computer's groin. I know, it's creepy, but there is a reason for it, as we will later discover. The persocom finally awakens and says their first word: "Chi…" Indeed, this is also the only thing the persocom can say, and thus Hideki names the persocom Chi. At first, he tries to avoid treating Chi like an actual woman and more like a computer, which is difficult for a young man who is also a virgin, talking to what looks like a beautiful girl. He says to himself (p37 of Book One in the Dark

Horse version), "Not she, it! It!" which these days looks a bit linehan, but eventually he starts referring to Chi using female pronouns.

Unable to figure out how Chi can work when all she can do is say one word, he gets help from his friend Hiromu Shinbo, who lives in the same building as him and also sits next to him at school. Shinbo uses his little mobile persocom Sumomo, akin to our laptops, to examine Chi, but Sumomo crashes, leading Shinbo to conclude that Chi must be custom-built. Shinbo thus advises Hideki to see a persocom expert. This expert turns out to be a wealthy 12-year-old boy and son of divorced parents, Minoru Kokubunji, a lad with multiple persocoms, most of whom are dressed as sexy maids. Only one, his most prized persocom, Yuzuki, dresses in a more refined maid outfit. We later learn that this more modest look stems from the fact Yuzuki is meant to resemble Minoru's late sister. Tragically for fans of *Angelic Layer*, we learn that Minoru's sister is Kaede Saito. During the latter half of the series, we see a flashback with the backs of Misaki Suzuhara and other 'Angelic Layer' players turned away from a dying/dead Kaede in mourning.

During their research, Minoru and Yuzuki also fail to fully analyse Chi. Minoru puts forward a theory that she might be an example of a 'Chobit'. Chobits are allegedly specially designed persocoms that have an advanced artificial intelligence, allowing them to think for themselves. However, Minoru does not believe it himself. Minoru later asks Hideki for his phone number, and when he does, they discover that Chi is able to learn it, and can thus say something other than her name. As a result of this, Hideki begins to educate Chi in the basics of everyday life.

Much of the series is about Hideki trying to raise Chi, teaching her the most simple of things and in particular the correct way to behave around others, given that she lacks any form of common sense. Chi meanwhile slowly begins to develop and learn.

She is able to get a job at a place where Hideki used to work, Patisserie Chiroru (called Patisserie Triol in the anime),[4] a place where Hideki used to work, and she is able to get enjoyment by reading books. Her favourite is a series of picture books called *A City with No People*, written by an anonymous author and another example of CLAMP using the 'story-within-a-story' trope. When reading it, Chi is able to access what appears to be another version of herself within her memory that she can talk to in her head.

As the story progresses, Minoru uncovers strange images online that appear to be of Chi with the word 'Chobits' written on her. Other strange occurrences happen with Chi. At times, she is able to gain a mysterious power that makes other persocoms and different forms of technology cease to function properly. Evidence begins to build that Chi really is a Chobit. Chi meanwhile learns more about emotions such as love. Reading *A City with No People*, Chi begins to look for someone to love, or as she puts it, thanks to the book: "the person just for me."

We learn that many people and indeed other persocoms are after Chi due to the possibility of her being a Chobit. At one point, Chi is even kidnapped by a man named Yoshiyuki 'Dragonfly' Kojima, a morally dubious custom persocom designer, leading to Hideki and friends to mount a daring rescue. Kojima also has his own laptop-like persocom named Kotoko, who we see in other CLAMP works. Elsewhere, there is a pair of government-owned super persocoms, Dita and Zima, monitoring Chi due to fears that she might be so powerful that all other persocoms might be destroyed by her. Then there is also the issue of *A City with No People*, as Hideki and Chi come to realise that the story closely resembles the relationship between the two. We the reader know first, but more photographic evidence from Minoru reveals the author of the stories. The author is a woman named Chitose Hibiya. She used to work for Piffle Princess on 'Angelic Layer', and later helped to develop persocoms with her late husband, a man who we have also come across before: 'Angelic Layer' inventor Ichiro 'Icchan' Mihara.[5] As well as working as an author, her main day job is as a landlady. The place that she owns just happens to be the flats where Hideki and Chi live, and in the basement of this flat is a massive bank of computers that Chitose is able to operate. The reason why Chitose is writing the stories is to encourage Chi to find her 'person just for me'.

The relationships between human and persocom is another recurring element in the story. As well as the ever increasing romance between Hideki and Chi, there is also the brotherly-sisterly relationship between Minoru and Yuzuki. There are also other people we meet in the story with their own troubled history with persocoms. Hideki and Shinbo's teacher at the cram school, Takako Shimizu, is discovered to be in an unhappy marriage because her husband has become more infatuated with a persocom than his own wife. This results in her having an affair with Shinbo and the pair eloping together, with Shinbo leaving Sumomo in Hideki's care. Then there is the sad tale of the owner of Patisserie Chiroru, Hiroyasu Ueda, who fell in love with and later unofficially married a persocom, only for his electronic bride to suffer what can only be described as a kind of computer dementia. There is also a young girl that previously worked for Hiroyasu, and, now at Club Pleasure, Yumi Omura, who has developed an inferiority complex, believing that persocoms are better than humans, and especially her.

Ultimately, we come to learn if Chi is a Chobit, if she can find the 'person just for me', and how Hideki relates to all of this.

•

There is a fair amount to unpack when it comes to dissecting *Chobits*. This is partly due to the length of the series, despite the short time it ran, relative to other works. The chapters are all rather small as they were released weekly rather than monthly, meaning that the series has one more tankobon volume than *Tokyo Babylon* despite being around for two years rather than *Tokyo Babylon*'s three years.

It should be mentioned that the idea of someone finding a piece of intelligent machinery which has forgotten its memory is not unique to *Chobits*. Another manga to feature a similar character is the early 1990s series *Battle Angel Alita* by Yukito Kishiro – although this is just the English-language title. In Japanese the series is called *Gunnm* ('gun dream') and the title character Alita is called 'Gally'. The series was later adapted by Hollywood as the film *Alita: Battle Angel*. In this cyberpunk series, Alita/Gally is a cyborg found among scrap who has no memory of her old life and tries to recover her memory.

One of the issues to bring up is the relationship between humans and technology, which in the world of *Chobits* takes on a romantic and sexual edge. In the manga, Chi is seen several times topless (she never appears like this in the anime), but this is mostly for comic effect. Much of the humour in the series is broad, as is evidenced by the scene where Hideki discovers that Chi has to be turned on via her groin. When you see this, you immediately worry, thinking: "Is that how ALL persocoms are turned on? What pervert designed these? And do male-looking persocoms turn on in the same way? Do I have to turn on a male persocom by giving them a handjob?" Fortunately, we later learn that Chi is an exception, and it is part of what makes Chi special. Hideki learns from Hiroyasu that most persocoms are turned on by a switch inside their distinctive ears. This special switch is actually key to understanding an important aspect of the relationship between Hideki and Chi: because of where the switch is, Hideki cannot make love to Chi, because it would mean turning Chi off and running the risk of her losing all her memory. Thus, the relationship between the two is actually a chaste one... if you ignore oral sex, and the possibility of anal sex, but we never learn if persocoms have something resembling an anus, and indeed there is no need for a persocom to have one. However, Hiroyasu does tell Hideki that some people are into persocom sex (Dark Horse version, Book 2, p162).

Bizarrely, Hiroyasu's marriage to a persocom would later have similarities to something that happened in real-life Japan. There is a singing voice synthesizer programme called Vocaloid, which advertises its products using fictional characters that are voices in the programme. The most famous of these is Hatsune Miku, a virtual pop idol who has performed in concerts all over the world. According to a 2018 story from the website *Techspot*, about 3,700 real people have claimed to have married Miku, and one man, 35-year-old school administrator Akihiko Kondo, even held his own wedding to Miku, in a ceremony costing ¥2million ($17,600). 40 people attended the wedding, but not Kondo's mother, who refused to do so and disapproved of her son marrying someone fictional.

While there is clearly ever growing love between Hideki and Chi, you could argue that while the relationship might be loving, it is not strictly speaking a romantic one. Given that Hideki is spending a lot of his time teaching Chi about everyday life, it is possible that the relationship between the two of them might be more akin of that between parent and child. You can see something similar in *RG Veda* in the relationship between Yasha and Ashura. Hideki is trying his best to be a father to the child-like Chi, educating her in the basics of modern life. This again may explain the chaste nature of the relationship, as you wouldn't want the parent to have sex with the child, obviously.

Another point about their relationship was brought up by Alexis Harper on *Anime Feminist* in March 2022. In her article: "Love, Agency, and Androids: A Chobits Retrospective", she mentions that while the series is written by women and has a large female cast, the series is aimed at men and the relationship, "…is told from the vantage point of an often titillating Male Gaze. This makes for a very complex viewing of a show rife with contradictions." She talks about the idea that in the media men look and women are looked at, with women being treated as an object, which seems especially relevant to persocom Chi, while we witness the story through Hideki's perspective rather than Chi's. Chi's childlike nature leads Harper to make comparisons to other adult-child relationships in CLAMP, like that between Rika and Terada in *Cardcaptor Sakura*. As Harper concludes: "*Chobits* is ultimately a love story with valuable lessons, but a flawed one nonetheless. Twenty years after the manga's completion, in an evolving landscape of narratives about AI and romance, it deserves revisiting."

One aspect of Chi that I find interesting is how she is being used to promote other people's products. For example, there is a US-based lingerie company called Moe Flavor who sell an item called the 'sweet talk heart ruffle lingerie'. Before it was launched, the company commissioned an artist known on Twitter as @ BOMHAT to make a drawing to promote it, and rather than draw an original character, they drew the outfit being worn by Chi. I don't know if they had or needed CLAMP's permission to use her, and Chi's not the only manga character they have used, but I can tell you that if you got to the customer reviews on the Moe Flavor website, several people who have posted photos of themselves wearing this lingerie have done so while also wearing Chi-like ears.

Given all of this, I would propose that if Sakura and Syaoran are CLAMP's go-to heroes, and if Seishiro is CLAMP's go-to villain, then Chi is CLAMP's go-to sex symbol. This does feel a bit weird given that it is *Miyuki-chan in Wonderland* that is CLAMP's out-and-out adult work, but while Miyuki-chan is a figure caught up in unwanted sexual escapades, Chi is more inviting, even if she doesn't know what it is she herself is inviting others to do. It's disturbing, yet compelling.

The series once again references other CLAMP works. *Angelic Layer* is the most obvious, although *Duklyon* appears as a restaurant once again. However, in terms of similarity between other works, possibly the one it has the most in common with is actually *Man of Many Faces*, in that it is a series that started off as a comedy but became more romantic and dramatic as time passed by. However, while *Man of Many Faces* is a children's story, *Chobits* has a more adult take. Ohkawa comments in the *CLAMP no Kiseki* interviews that readers became more confused as the story progressed saying: "I think there were people who just wanted to restrict the story to about Chi-chan's cute daily life."

In terms of the production, Mokona was the main artist for *Chobits*, and used ballpoint pens for the main drawings in the work, the reason being that Ohkawa wanted lines that looked like it was pencil-drawn. One particular aspect of the production is the different use of fonts. The original Japanese, and later foreign language versions, use different fonts to distinguish between humans and persocoms, as well as a third italic font that is used in *A City with No People* and within Chi's dreams as she reads it. In the Dark Horse release, a special segment explaining the fonts appears. While humans use the standard Comic Sans, the typeface used for the persocoms is an angular font called Andale Mono. The use of this font is not universal among the persocoms however. Sumomo, who as well as acting as a laptop also works as a mobile phone, reverts to the human Comic Sans when a phone call comes through to sound like the caller. Yuzuki meanwhile speaks in Comic Sans to reflect Minoru's desire to make Yuzuki resemble his late sister.

As mentioned, *Chobits* also received an anime adaptation, directed by the same man who did the *Cardcaptor Sakura* anime,

Morio Asaka. This consisted of 24 standard episodes, three recap episodes/clip shows (reportedly made because the show had a low budget), and a short OVA. There were several differences between the anime and manga. For example, Hideki is not already working at Club Pleasure/My Pleasure at the start of the story, but gets the job later. Hideki has also never worked at the patisserie. There are episodes in the anime that are entirely original too, with one episode seeing Hideki, Chi and their friends playing an online video game, while another sees practically all of the main cast visiting the beach together. Other than the anime, there were also two video games released based on the series, *Chobits: Atashi Dake no Hito* on the Nintendo Game Boy Advance, bundled with a special *Chobits*-themed console, and *Chobits: Chii Dake no Hito* for the PlayStation 2. Both were never released outside Japan.

While the series has been advertised as the best-selling CLAMP work in the USA, it has not met with universal approval from the critics. Reviews of it have been mixed, partly because so many of the persocoms are female, and these female characters are not only frequently servants of male masters, but are also literally objectified. However, Clements and McCarthy in *The Anime Encyclopedia* heap much praise on the series, writing that: "*Chobits* is one of the landmark shows of the early 21st century." On the issues just raised, they wrote: "Some viewers may discern an element of Lolita anime in the submissive vacancy of the persocoms, although… not all of them are 'female,' merely often made so by market forces. …*Chobits* acknowledges the pervasive nature of information technology while emphasising the need for real, individual emotional responses." Personally speaking, I prefer the *Angelic Layer* anime to the *Chobits* one, but I won't deny it is a good show. Chi in particular remains one of CLAMP's most popular characters.

•

With *Chobits* over and *Legal Drug* soon to be put on hiatus, in 2003 CLAMP began two new series, which would become their largest works to date, each spawning their own sequels and anime adaptations. However, before these series debuted, another manga by CLAMP made an all-too-brief appearance. This very short lived series, which ran in the same magazine as *Chobits*, is one that certainly still deserves its own chapter, although it is not without its problems. In fact, this series is arguably the most troublesome of all of CLAMP's work, not because of its content, but because of some troublesome legal issues.

---

1 – A quick explanation. SunnyCon gets its name from the fact it was originally held in Sunderland, but the convention became so big that there was nowhere in Sunderland large enough to host it, so it ended up moving to Sunderland's big rival city. In fact, not only is SunnyCon now in Newcastle, it's now held at St. James' Park, the home of Newcastle United F.C., much to the delight of this Teesside observer.

2 – The British equivalent would be going to a tutorial college.

3 – Of course this does raise the trivial question: "Which CLAMP characters would play which Tolkien character?" Would Misaki from *Angelic Layer* be Frodo, or Hikaru from *Rayearth*? With his white lab coat, would *Angelic Layer*'s Icchan become a creepy Gandalf? And with so many CLAMP characters only having one eye, which one would you cast as Sauron? Admittedly, antagonistic Seishiro from *Tokyo Babylon* and *X* would be the best bet, but can we be certain? If you have any better ideas, let me know.

4 –This is one of CLAMP's other recurring businesses. If you have been reading the manga in the order they are listed in this book, you will have already seen Toya and Yukito doing one of their many part-time jobs at this place in *Cardcaptor Sakura: Clear Card* Volume 2, although it is in *Chobits* where the business first appears.

5 – At which point, it is worth thinking about Misaki Suzuhara here. The poor girl has had to go through both Icchan and Kaede's deaths, and we don't hear her reaction to these tragedies. She is a girl who definitely needs a shoulder to cry on.

CHAPTER 14

The One That (has so far) Got Away - *Murikuri* (2002)

This is most certainly the most troublesome manga in the entire book for me to cover for one simple reason: *Murikuri* is most notable of being the only one of CLAMP's original published manga to have never been given an official English release.

This title is a 'yomikiri', a one-shot manga. It is a standalone series that only appeared once in the magazine publishing it. Because of this, it has never been given a proper release in English, although it has been released in French, France being the biggest consumers of manga outside of Japan. However, in this chapter I will argue that *Murikuri* does deserve to have a translation, and not just into English.

Murikuri (2002)

Murikuri came out on 20th December 2002, in a double-length issue of *Young Magazine*, published by Kodansha, the same magazine that published *Chobits*. Due to the series being so short-lived, information about the manga's production is lacking.

The series is a comedy, consisting of seven short stories. Including the cover, the entire series is just 17 pages long, which is probably among the reasons why the series has never been released individually.

While people have made photocopies of the comic and fans have tried to translate the works into English, it is obviously illegal to make such translations or indeed to distribute work in such a way as it breaks copyright, and the Japanese are very strict when it comes to copyright law, especially in manga. In January 2021, the country tightened their copyright laws even more. In Japan, you can now face legal charges for downloading illegally uploaded or pirated manga, magazines, anime, films, arts, scripts and visuals, amongst other things. You can also be charged for providing or pasting links to printed media, and operating 'leech sites and apps' that upload or distribute illegal and pirated media. If you are a repeat offender when it comes to illegal downloading, you can be jailed for two years or fined up to ¥2 million (about $18,250). Operating a leech site can get you five years in jail or fined up to ¥5 million (about $45,700). Given that, illegally downloading a manga, even one as small as *Murikuri*, is a definite no-no.

However, other people have been able to describe and critique *Murikuri*, and there is nothing wrong with using these descriptions to say what occurs in the comic.

•

Central figures are obviously thin on the ground in such a small work. Most of the characters don't even appear to be named. The main figures appear to be a boy and his friend, a talking pig. Most of the individual stories in *Murikuri* concern themselves with love and sex.

The stories include the pig receiving a love letter from a girl and his fondness for looking at girl's underwear, a man becoming pregnant, a housewife who is shocked by the cost of the damage caused when aliens crash into her roof, and Father Christmas arguing with his girlfriend because he has to spend Christmas working rather than being with her. I assume that the Father Christmas in *Murikuri* is not to be confused with Akira's father, who dresses up as Father Christmas in *Man of Many Faces*.

•

In terms of seeing *Murikuri*, the pig character is referenced in other CLAMP works such as *xxxHOLiC*, but in terms of reading the original manga it is hard to do so. Regarding what other people think, the Wikipedia article for the series links to one review of *Murikuri*, which is from the French-language website *Manga Sanctuary*, who rated it 5 out of 10.

The main purpose of this chapter however is to argue that it should be made available for people to buy and read legally. After all, if it is made more accessible, then people won't feel the need to pirate the series.

The main stumbling blocks towards releasing it are the obscurity of the comic and the length of it, or rather the lack of length. On the first point, yes, it is probably the least-known CLAMP manga, but then again it is still a CLAMP manga. The name of the writers is still a big enough draw to attract fans to buy it. There are completists like me out there who will buy it in a flash as soon as it becomes available. If people are going to compare CLAMP to music groups, think of it like this. Imagine if Kraftwerk, the Beatles or any other big band had a track that they forgot about, came across it again, and decided to release. People would go mad for it. They are so popular that sales should not be a problem.

Regarding the issue of length, the publishers Kodansha have themselves proven that this is not a problem, especially in today's age of e-books. Kodansha currently publish *Cardcaptor Sakura: Clear Card*, a new chapter of which comes out once a month, and these new chapters are translated into English on the day of release, and are available to buy legally via websites like Amazon. Some of the chapters, in particular individual bonus extra chapters, that they have translated into English and put on sale, are even shorter in length than *Murikuri* is. Some are in single-digit figures in terms of the number of pages. Kodansha have thus proven that even the shortest works can be put on sale, and be given a release, even if it is only digital.

Given that the series is available in French, there is no reason not to release *Murikuri* in other languages. We CLAMP fans should put pressure onto Kodansha to release *Murikuri*. Whatever language you speak, write letters, send emails, post messages on social media, saying that you want to read *Murikuri* and that you would be happy to buy it. If enough demand is generated, then Kodansha will realise the benefits of bringing out the title to the rest of the world.

There is one other issue that was highlighted to me by the people at the *Mangasplaining* podcast. They recently started releasing some obscure manga releases in English for the first time ever, and I suggested *Murikuri* as one to publish. One of the podcast hosts, Christopher Butcher, said that while the title was interesting, one problem with releasing it is the front cover. The cover features someone dressed in a Native American headdress while holding the pig, who is wearing a cowboy hat. Butcher said to me: "Given the cover image featuring a Native American headdress, I can see why it hasn't been published in English." What with nearly all English-language manga publishers being based in North America, and the sensitivity around this as mentioned in the *Magic Knight Rayearth* chapter, that would seem to put a kaibosh on any release.

Before moving on, it is worth expanding on this issue to talk not just about the problems of licensing manga to be released in English, but the licensing of anime too, because we in Britain often get overlooked when it comes to distribution.

It is partly because of the hostility towards anime and manga in the early years, with the general view among those in the public who had heard of it, that the medium contained mostly adult material. Because anime and manga has got this mostly unfair reputation, often when a new anime is announced, sometimes we Brits are not included in any distribution. While a lot of anime is translated and sometimes dubbed in English, often it is just for North Americans. Sometimes the Australasian nations might get it too, but often the British Isles is left out of the deal. When anime and manga arrive to Britain, we thus have to jump through more than one cultural lens – we get an American translation of Japanese culture, rather than something more direct.

The two main anime streaming services in English are the websites Crunchyroll and Funimation. Today they offer most of their stuff to Britain, as well as the other English-speaking nations, but in the bad old days Funimation did not stream to English-speakers outside of North America. If Funimation got hold of a new licence, it often meant that you had to wait until it was released on DVD before you could watch it… legally. Of course, lots of people just pirated. They straightahead illegally downloaded episodes themselves, or waited for someone to post videos up on streaming websites like YouTube and watch those. The latter of those two is something that I am prepared to admit that I have done. I know everyone says you should not pirate, but if you have no other option, you will fucking pirate, and I for one would consider it hypocritical of me to tell other people not to do it when I did it.

Things have since improved as Funimation does stream stuff in Britain today, with Funimation, now controlled by Sony, normally concentrating on dubbing titles. Meanwhile the AT&T-owned Crunchyroll normally does a lot of subbing. However, things changed in December 2020, with the news that Sony would buy Crunchyroll in a deal worth $1.175billion, a deal that was finally completed in August 2021. This news means that Sony pretty much now has an anime streaming monopoly, which is too niche for monopoly commissions to be interested in. Objections have already been expressed, partly due to the concern of job losses, which did transpire in April 2022, and also the continuing problem of UK distribution which is such a limited market, of both physical and digital releases. Funimation also took over Manga Entertainment, one of the UK's oldest anime distributors, in May 2019. In April 2021, the Manga Entertainment brand ended and the company became Funimation UK, then in March 2022 it was announced that the Crunchyroll brand would be taking over the Funimation brand. One of the first things they announced was a stop to offering advertising-supported free streams on the service which were used to encourage fans new to anime to sample shows, meaning that in order to watch an entire show you now have to subscribe. The signs are not good, but there is still some competition from other specialist services like HIDIVE, which streams, amongst other series, *Angelic Layer*.

Licensing is also a problem still for other websites. RetroCrush is a streaming website specialising in classic anime, but none of it is available to UK viewers. We are now being denied vintage shows, which include the first *Cardcaptor Sakura* film. Netflix also streams anime too but has its own problems, namely the fact they don't release any of the series episode-by-episode. If Netflix licences a brand new anime, you have to wait for the entire season to be aired in Japan before you can get the chance to see it in English. Amazon Prime also streams anime, but with Amazon the main problem is how much that company is coming to dominate just about everything there is already, and their unwillingness to pay tax.

Luckily, British streaming services are improving. All4, Channel 4's streaming service, streams some anime and for a while streamed the first part of the TV version of *Cardcaptor Sakura*. The selection is limited, and you can only see the series dubbed into English, but it is better than nothing. Then in August 2021, the BBC began streaming old episodes of *Pokemon*. There is also a children's TV channel called POP which shows not only *Pokemon*, but also *Dragon Ball* and the joint Japanese-Canadian animation *Bakugan*. Hopefully more options and more series will become accessible, but the Funimation/Crunchyroll deal will no doubt cause more problems.

•

After *Murikuri*, there was a big change in CLAMP. In 2003, two of their works, *Legal Drug* and *X*, would go on hiatus. *Legal Drug* would return briefly as *Drug & Drop* in 2011, while *X* has sadly never been returned to. However, CLAMP would instead start work on their two longest-running manga, marking a new period in their career with a pair of stories totalling 54 tankobon volumes between them. These two works were deeply interconnected, and indeed one of them would connect almost everything in the entire CLAMPverse. However, it is best for us to examine the other of these two works first. It is fate that decides this.

CHAPTER 15

Kismet Watanuki – *xxxHOLiC* (2003-2010) and *xxxHOLiC: Rei* (2013-2016, Returning in 2023)

A few things worth discussing before we go into the series in depth. Firstly, I do know that Lord Nelson never said: "Kismet Hardy" when he was dying. Actually, "Kiss me Hardy" were not Nelson's last words either, they were just among the things he said when dying. The very last thing he said was: "Drink, drink, fan, fan, rub, rub", as he was requesting someone to ease the pain of his wounds with drink and to keep him cool.

Secondly, those reading my footnotes will have already spotted the fact that the 'xxx' in *xxxHOLiC* is silent and thus never pronounced.[1] In fact, they are not even letters. They are blank spaces, like how we in the West would use underscores. We might write it as ___*HOLiC*. What is actually used is the multiplication sign, these referencing the connections between the objects and the people in the story, as once again the notion of fate plays a central part in this CLAMP title. As for the 'Holic' part, Ohkawa explains in the *CLAMP no Kiseki* interviews: "At the beginning we thought something on the lines of 'Addicted', but the term is a bit general. However, 'holic' reminds [people] of 'workaholic' in English, which is more used and easier to interpret. This is why we named it *xxxHOLiC*. In *Tokyo Babylon* we treated the social pathologies and this time we wanted to give a more esoteric tone to it."

As for the actual series, *xxxHOLiC* and its sequel *xxxHOLiC: Rei*[2] mostly ran in Kodansha's *Weekly Young Magazine*, except for the latter parts of *xxxHOLiC*, where between 2009 and 2010 it ran in *Bessatsu Shonen Magazine*. Together, both series ran for 23 volumes: 19 in the original, and four in the sequel. It would have been more but, guess what, *xxxHOLiC: Rei* got put on hiatus. It was all going to be yet another frustration to be included in this book, but in April 2022, shortly before this book was sent to the publishers, CLAMP announced *xxxHOLiC: Rei* would be returning in Spring 2023! Miracles can happen!

There were also two anime TV series, four OVA releases, an anime film and an eight-part live action TV series. The first anime series, directed by Tsutomu Mizushima, whose other works include the horror series *Another* and the alternative history comedy *Girls und Panzer*, was released in the UK by Manga Entertainment. *xxxHOLiC* also happened to be my first encounter with the work of CLAMP.

As for the manga, it got released by several companies. *xxxHOLiC* and its sister title *Tsubasa* were the first CLAMP titles not to be released by TokyoPop. In fact, there was even a brief release by a separate UK publisher. A company called Tanoshimi, part of Random House Publishing, released *xxxHOLiC* and its sister series *Tsubasa* in the UK in 2006, but the company went defunct in 2009 and they only got as far as nine volumes of the former and 14 of the later. In the USA, the company Del Rey Manga managed to release the entire series, but as mentioned in the preface, this company was later taken over by the American branch of Kodansha. Now released under Kodansha Comics, *xxxHOLiC* is currently released under seven omnibus volumes, the first five containing three volumes each, while the rest are in a pair of two-volume editions. The four *xxxHOLiC: Rei* volumes were released individually.

The Kodansha releases differ rather considerably from several of the other publishers we have covered so far. They use accents on the names of characters, although as already mentioned I will be avoiding them in this book. Also, their manga often contain 'translation notes', which are segments at the end of each volume explaining certain aspects of Japanese culture to Westerners, which are very useful if you want to get a better understanding of certain aspects of Japanese society.

Responsibilities for the art were split, with Nekoi responsible for male characters and supernatural 'yoaki' creatures, while Mokona was responsible for the female characters. Ohkawa said in an interview with *The New York Times* in 2006 that the art was based on ukiyo-e wood prints, ukiyo-e being a type of art that flourished during the Tokugawa shogunate period between the 17th and 19th centuries, and included artists like Hokusai. The manga also avoids using tones and shading. It can be quite shocking to look at, especially when you look at the rest of CLAMP's work. At first you might consider it to be the least visually pleasing of their work, but over time you do get used to the style.

xxxHOLiC (2003-2010) and *xxxHOLic: Rei* (2013-2016, returning in 2023)

Normally I write about each series separately, but as the events in *Rei* are not in the exact same chronology as the original series, it feels okay to combine it with the original series.

•

We begin with Kimihiro Watanuki, a bespectacled, rather lanky high school student at Cross Private School. He is a troubled boy, partly due to the fact that both of his parents are dead and thus he lives on his own, looked after by the caretaker of the apartment where he lives. However, there is something else that plagues him. Watanuki is constantly followed by horrible spirits that haunt him. Not only that, but he is the only person that can see them, so as he runs away from them, everyone else looks at him as if he is a weirdo.

Watanuki manages to make some of these spirits go away when he touches a particular fence. Upon closer inspection, he sees that the fence surrounds an old-fashioned house, which is itself surrounded by three large tower blocks. A mysterious force drags him inside the place, where he encounters the owner, an elegantly-dressed woman who goes by the name of Yuko Ichihara. Yuko claims that the fact that Watanuki was magically drawn to it is 'Hitsuzen', a naturally foreordained event. Yuko regularly claims that there is: "No such thing as coincidence. Only hitsuzen."

Yuko reveals that the house is in fact a shop and obviously no ordinary one. It is a shop that grants wishes. Only those who have a wish can see it, and the fact that the forces dragged Watanuki inside mean that he clearly has a wish he wants fulfilled: namely to be rid of these spirits that plague him. Yuko agrees to help, but every wish has a price, and the price for Watanuki is that he has to work in the shop. He finds himself agreeing to the role. Yuko indeed helps Watanuki by getting rid of those spirits that haunt him, and in exchange Watanuki finds himself cleaning the shop and cooking food for Yuko and her two special helpers, Maru and Moro, two beings who help keep the shop in existence, but who cannot leave the shop themselves as they have no souls. Watanuki actually ends up making a lot of food for Yuko and providing a lot of drink: the woman is very fond of alcohol of all kinds, as well as being a keen pipe smoker.

Many of the stories involve customers, normally women, coming into the shop with a particular wish. Yuko will agree to help them, given the right price, but often the customers are the victim of some kind of supernatural occurrence and find themselves paying an even greater price than they bargained for. For example, a woman comes to the shop who says she cannot use her little finger. Yuko asks her if she has any bad habits to which the customer says no. Yuko then gives her a ring to wear on the finger as this finger is associated with keeping promises in Japan, as I'll discuss later. Due to his abilities, Watanuki can tell that the woman does have a bad habit: lying. Watanuki sees the woman being swarmed by a vile-smelling black miasma which gets bigger the more she lies which ultimately leads to her grisly fate.

Some of these stories will be familiar to Western readers. In another tale, the shop is having a clear out, and a student buys a sealed cylinder. Yuko agrees to give it to her on condition that she never opens it. However, the cylinder does get opened accidentally, and inside it is a monkey's paw – the kind that grants multiple wishes that always backfire on those who make them.

There are other recurring characters in the story: two of these are classmates at Watanuki's school. One is a girl, Himawari Kunogi, who is always cheerful and with whom Watanuki is completely in love. The other is a boy, Shizuka Domeki, who lives at a Shinto shrine that was previously maintained by his late grandfather Haruka, and while he cannot see spirits, he can exorcise them, thanks to his skill as an archer. He is also a boy that Watanuki violently hates for seemingly no good reason, although Himawari views the relationship between the two boys as being like a comedy act. Despite Watanuki hating Domeki, Yuko will often make the two work together in order to fulfil some of the more supernatural wishes she has been tasked to grant.

There are also several customers who repeatedly come to the shop. Many of them are supernatural beings. These include Ame-warashi, a rain spirit who dislikes humans; Zashiki-warashi, a genderless shy spirit who lives on a mountain and has a crush on Watanuki, and father-and-son foxes who run a street food cart selling udon noodles. There are also characters that appear to look like people we have met before. Because of this, we need to discuss why CLAMP created the character of Yuko. Yuko is someone who is aware of the entire CLAMPverse. If you go into the back of the shop, you will see in storage several items that you will have seen in other CLAMP titles: Sakura's staff from *Cardcaptor Sakura*, swords from *Magic Knight Rayearth*, and the pig from *Murikuri* are among many other objects which appear. We know that Yuko is familiar with both Clow Reed and Subaru Sumeragi.

We also know that there are people who refer to Yuko as the 'Space-Time Witch'. We first hear this when some customers from various parallel universes appear in the shop's garden. Among them are two people who look like people we know very well: Syaoran and Sakura. They are not the ones we know from *Cardcaptor Sakura* however, but different versions of them who are the main characters in *Tsubasa*. Yuko and Watanuki help all these travellers in their journeys, at the right price relative to their wishes, providing them with another familiar helper: Mokona from *Rayearth*. In fact, there are two creatures called Mokona Modoki. One is white (named Soel, but this tends not to come up much in the book) and travels with Syaoran and his gang, the other is black (named Larg, again rarely used) and lives in the shop. Together the two Mokona can cast a screen that allows the two sides to communicate with each other, or send things between worlds by getting one Mokona to swallow something while the other spits it out. Our black Mokona gets on very well with Yuko, sharing her fondness for eating and drinking.

Watanuki carries out his various tasks, from collecting water from a particular well and carrying it in magic bottles, to helping dead spirits complete their path to the afterlife. He also starts to see Sakura and Syaoran in his dreams. As *xxxHOLiC* progresses, Watanuki's involvement with the supernatural comes with greater costs. When he and Domeki clean Domeki's shrine and disturb a spider's web, Domeki is cursed with a grudge when a spider sews a web over his right eye. To cure him, Watanuki sacrifices his own eyesight. Eventually Watanuki's eye is eaten by a prostitute-spider spirit called the Joro-Gumo, and his right eye is lost. Domeki thus donates half the sight in his right eye to help Watanuki see, and thus both boys are added to the list of CLAMP characters who lose an eye, or at least part of one.

Perhaps the most shocking moment in the entire story is when Watanuki makes a 'pinky promise', which involves crossing little fingers with someone else, with Himawari, promising not to overexert himself. When he does, Himawari the next day touches Watanuki on the shoulder. Watanuki then leans on a window with this shoulder, but the glass falls out, and Watanuki and the glass fall two storeys, with him crashing into the glass and onto the ground below. We learn that while Watanuki loves Himawari, Himawari is not good for him, as she is cursed to bring misfortune to everyone around her. Remember the monkey paw cylinder? It opened because she touched it. By touching Watanuki on the shoulder, she caused the boy's accidental defenestration.[3] Watanuki recovers, but the cost of the wish for him to heal is steep, with Domeki donating a large amount of his blood, and Himawari having to carry his scars on her back.

However, the biggest price for a wish is one for Yuko herself. It is a wish that will have implications on everyone around her, not just Watanuki and everyone else in the shop, but also the travellers in *Tsubasa* too. It is a wish that will see Watanuki's fate being tied to the shop for much longer than he would ever expect, and a wish which sees Yuko pay the ultimate price.

•

While the complete *xxxHOLiC* series is the second longest-running CLAMP title at the time of writing, in terms of describing the plot and themes, it seems to take less discussion. This is partly because *xxxHOLiC* follows a more episodic plot in comparison to other CLAMP titles. Many of the stories in it are just a few chapters long, and the lengthier stories are a few volumes long. In comparison, stories like those in *X* or *RG Veda* are more epic.

A fair amount of what appears in the series connects to Japanese folklore, and while some of it may be hard to understand, it is displayed in a way that should not be too intimidating to the average British reader. Also, the translation notes do provide a considerable amount of bonus information regarding elements of Japanese religious practices. Having said that, it feels like most of the translation notes in *xxxHOLiC* are to do with the various different types of Japanese food Watanuki has to cook, and the various different types of booze Yuko and Mokona pour down their throats.

The most intriguing element of *xxxHOLiC*'s plot however is the role of fate (or hitsuzen). It has been repeatedly stated that CLAMP do not believe in the idea of people being bound by fate, which is arguably peculiar seeing as how one of the central characters is constantly saying that fate is always happening and nothing is coincidental. However, as we read the story, you can see certain things that the characters might believe to be destined to be, but are not. For example, Watanuki's love of Himawari. For most of the story, he is totally convinced that the two will end up together, but as the story progresses we realise that this fate is false. This is most clearly demonstrated in the later chapters where Himawari only appears in the shop once a year, and the rest of the time they only ever communicate via telephone.

While much of the story deals with the supernatural, once again some social commentary creeps in. One of the customers who comes to the shop wishes for a photo of a woman to be destroyed. Watanuki and Yuko come to discover that this photo plays like a movie and shows the customer pushing said woman to her death. Yuko does destroy the photo, but the price is that the customer's face must never be recorded in any form: no photos, no appearances in front of a camera, nothing that can record an image. Yuko comments that the only way that the customer can live is to become a complete recluse, as there is no way in today's modern world that your image isn't recorded somewhere.[4]

Another story involves a young girl Watanuki meets called Kohane Tsuyuri. We learn that she has psychic abilities which her pushy mother is seemingly trying to exploit. Her mother won't allow anyone to so much as touch Kohane or speak with her, for fear it will harm her abilities. It is the mother who mainly uses the money Kohane makes for her own selfish reasons. Watanuki continues to befriend her, even after the mother decides to physically attack him by splashing him with a flask of hot water. Kohane is later shown bandaged up, and then in a future TV appearance it is implied that her mother has been abusing her. It is not just child abuse that appears in the series. A tale about a mermaid leads to a story of domestic abuse too.

There is also the issue of *xxxHOLiC* cross-referencing other series. The back of the shop contains various items from other CLAMP titles, and Yuko's central role is to serve as a connection between all of the CLAMP stories, although, as previously stated, the short story collection *The One I Love* is an outlier. The main connection is clearly with *Tsubasa*, and while you don't need to read it to understand *xxxHOLiC*, it does help to provide some extra information.

However, one of the odder connections is with the *Legal Drug* and *Drug & Drop* stories, another series on which Nekoi was principal artist. In the opening volume of *xxxHOLiC*, Watanuki goes to the Green Drugstore to buy some hangover medication for Yuko, where he talks to Kazahaya and Rikuo. As we have already discussed, Watanuki later makes an appearance in *Drug & Drop*. The oddity comes from the fact that according to *Drug & Drop*, Kazahaya and Rikuo have only been together, "…for more than a year" (Vol. 1, p15). However, reading *xxxHOLiC*, you see that Watanuki and his friends have been through at least two winters before meeting them again, with the story seemingly implying that even more time has passed before Kazahaya and Rikuo go to the wish granting shop to meet Watanuki. The times don't seem to quite add up.

As mentioned before, the art style of *xxxHOLiC* once again differs to other CLAMP titles. When we first come across the lanky Watanuki, he stands in stark contrast to the other central CLAMP figures we have met. In comparison to them, he actually looks somewhat unappealing. However, once we meet the more lavish Yuko, things start to take on a more extravagant look. As the story progresses, Watanuki ends up embracing this appearance and indeed has a more refined look to him. What at first may seem to be an ugly duckling turns out to be a swan in the end. The look of Yuko and later Watanuki would appear to be referencing the clothes worn be people in the period of the ukiyo-e art that inspired the manga. Perhaps though, the look of the work may reference another CLAMP title. With background characters drawn in a minimalist way, and the reduced use of shading and toner, perhaps it harks back to the style of *Clover* which made the most of using very little.

As mentioned earlier, the first *xxxHOLiC* anime was the first time I had been exposed to CLAMP. I cannot remember exactly when I first came across it, but it was a DVD that first came out in 2008. I think I was attracted to it because it looked different to anything else I had seen, with Watanuki and Yuko on the cover drawing me in. Of course, the series does indeed look different in comparison to the rest of the CLAMPverse, but at the time I had no idea who CLAMP were. It wasn't until later I realised that this series had so many connections to other stories, which I then began to read over a period of many years.

xxxHOLiC is one of CLAMP's most popular works, both in

Japan and abroad. The series would enter the book charts, and in 2009 the series was the sixth best-selling manga in the USA. Watanuki and Yuko remain two of CLAMP's most popular characters. It is also popular in terms of adaptations. Aside from the TV anime, there has been an OVA, an anime film, a light novel, a live-action TV drama, a PlayStation 2 video game, a stage reading drama, a 2021 stage musical featuring an all-male cast,[5] and a 2022 live-action film, *xxxHOLiC* has more adaptations across the most different media of any CLAMP title. We also now know that the series will be coming back in 2023, so the adventures of Watanuki and company are not over yet.

Of course, in order to understand the whole of *xxxHOLiC*, we have to examine its sister work. It is now time for Syaoran, Sakura, the white Mokona, and many other familiar faces to make a reappearance.

---

1 – If you haven't been reading my footnotes: fuck off, you cunt. I feel safe in writing this, seeing as how you are not going to read this bit.

2 – 'Rei' is pronounced 'Ray'.

3 – And yes, I am feeling smug about the fact that I can use the word 'defenestration' accurately in a sentence.

4 – That customer certainly wouldn't survive in the UK, seeing as how we have more CCTV than any other nation in the world, around 20%. One of the most disturbing places for CCTV in the UK is 27B Canonbury Square, London. Within 200 yards of it, there are 32 different CCTV cameras. 27B Canonbury Square happened to once be the residence of *Nineteen Eighty-Four* author George Orwell.

5 – Anime musicals are quite common, and are also known as 2.5D musicals, because they take a world drawn in 2D, and bring it to life in our 3D. There is even an organisation called the Japan 2.5-Dimensional Musical Association which is devoted to the industry.

CHAPTER 16

Five Little Birds – *Tsubasa: RESERVoir CHRoNiCLE* (2003-2009) and *Tsubasa: WoRLD CHRoNiCLE: Niraikanai* (2014-2016)

On the surface, the first thing that might come to mind for English-speaking readers of these two series may be: "They need to sort out their caps lock." Beyond that however, we are now dealing with the series which is arguably CLAMP's magnum opus. It is both their longest-running series in terms of the total number of tankobon volumes, with 28 in *RESERVoir CHRoNiCLE* and another three in *WoRLD CHRoNiCLE*, and it is also their biggest-selling series, with over 20 million copies of *RESERVoir CHRoNiCLE* alone being sold.

It gives CLAMP the ability to create a work which combines nearly all of their previous series together. We have already mentioned that Syaoran and Sakura from *Cardcaptor Sakura* are central characters in it, and that the main characters from *xxxHOLiC* play a key role, but so many more characters from the CLAMPverse make appearances, including some from series that we have yet to come to in this book. Don't worry, you don't need to have read these later series in order to understand the story. Think of the characters as actors making an appearance in a different show.

This actor analogy is a good one, given what influenced CLAMP to make this story: Osamu Tezuka's 'Star System'. Tezuka would treat his own comic characters as actors and would re-use, or rather re-cast, his characters in various different works across his career. CLAMP decided to do a similar thing, their plan being to take characters from manga that were set in realistic worlds and put them into fantasy ones. For CLAMP fans, the series is like a treasure hunt as you try to find as many of their old characters as you can.

While *Tsubasa* and *xxxHOLiC* are twin series, *xxxHOLiC* is the older of the pair by three months, allowing Watanuki and Yuko to become established before their appearances in *Tsubasa*. Like *xxxHOLiC*, *Tsubasa* is episodic in nature. In fact, it is even more episodic, given that each story arc is set in a new fantasy realm, as the characters move from dimension to dimension. While Nekoi was the main artist on *xxxHOLiC*, Mokona was the principal artist for *Tsubasa*, with Nekoi and Igarashi providing additional character art and backgrounds, while Ohkawa as always wrote the story. The manga's title was designed to be easy to read, and was just going to be *Tsubasa*, a unisex Japanese name, but worried that it would be too short they added *RESERVoir CHRoNiCLE* from Nekoi's notes.[1]

Tsubasa: RESERVoir CHRoNiCLE (2003-2009) and *Tsubasa: WoRLD CHRoNiCLE: Niraikanai* (2014-2016)

The original series began in May 2003 and was published in Kodansha's *Weekly Shonen Magazine*, one of Japan's most established manga magazines, having begun publication in 1959 and still going strong today. As mentioned in the previous chapter, Tanoshimi had managed to publish 14 volumes of *Tsubasa* before going defunct. All of the volumes were later released by Del Rey, and are now published in omnibuses by Kodansha comics: the first eight in 3-in-1 collections, and the last pair in 2-in-1 editions.

As with *xxxHOLiC*, I'll be covering both the original and the sequel in the same section. In the case of *Tsubasa*, this is to avoid revealing too many spoilers to the original, particularly as the sequel is so much shorter and its story is not massively important to the tale.

•

The story begins in the Kingdom of Clow, a desert world in which the late Clow Reed was king. In this dimension, Syaoran is an archaeologist working on some local ruins that were originally being covered by his late father, Fujitaka (originally Sakura's father in *Cardcaptor*). Syaoran is close friends with Princess Sakura and she is in love with him, but things constantly stop her from confessing her love. She is the heir to the throne currently occupied by her older brother Toya, while close friend Yukito works as the high priest. Yukito is aware of the fact that Sakura has a great magical power within her.

One night, Sakura has a strange dream about the ruins Syaoran is excavating. The following day, Syaoran goes to the site, with Sakura also visiting. There she spots some markings that she recognises from her dream. This triggers a magic spell to strike, a gate to start opening and for her to grow a pair of feathered wings, the 'Tsubasa' in the title. As the gate opens, an enemy army prepare to attack, but Syaoran manages to stop the spell. However, the feathers on the wings scatter and Sakura collapses.

Yukito comes to realise that the feathers were at one with Sakura's heart. The feathers being scattered mean that she has become an empty shell with no memory. The only way to bring her back is to hunt the feathers down. To do so, Yukito casts a spell that transports Syaoran and Sakura to another dimension. As for who is responsible for Sakura's condition, we the reader know it is due to a villainous magician named Fei-Wang Reed.

While this is going on, we meet two other people in other dimensions. The first dimension is the Country of Japan, a world based on a feudal version of the nation, that is under attack from various monsters. One of the people slaying these monsters is the over-violent ninja Kurogane, who serves the Princess Tomoyo (as in Sakura's best friend in *Cardcaptor*), who also employs the more competent ninja Soma (*RG Veda*). Because Kurogane is so violent and strong, Tomoyo decides to show him what true strength means, by transporting him to another dimension, while also casting a curse on him that he cannot cause unnecessary death, and his strength will weaken every time he kills someone.[2]

The second dimension is the frozen tundra of the Country of Seresu, home of the powerful magician Fai D. Flowright, a man whose tattoos on his back allow him to control his magic. He decides to leave this land, having sealed away the king Ashura (*RG Veda*), and leaving one of his creations, Chi (*Chobits*), to prevent Ashura from awakening.

Syaoran, Sakura, Kurogane and Fai all end up teleporting to what I suppose we should describe as our world, not that it is given a name in the series. We do know however that the place that all four of them land is the garden of Yuko's shop in *xxxHOLiC*. While Watanuki is off getting the two Mokonas we see in *xxxHOLiC*, Yuko learns of the wishes of these people: Syaoran wants to save Sakura's life, Kurogane wants to go back home, and Fai never wants to return to his home. Yuko says that only the way they can pay for their wishes is if they club together, so they agree.

For Fai, the price is his tattoos, meaning he can no longer use magic. For Kurogane, he must hand over his trusted sword, Gunryu. For Syaoran, he has the highest price of all: his relationship with Sakura. Even if he is able to restore all of Sakura's memories, she will never be able to remember her original love for him, and their relationship will never be the same again. Despite this, all of them agree to the price.

To help them on their journey, Yuko gives the quartet the white Mokona Modoki, akin to the one in *Magic Knight Rayearth* except for an earring he wears and his ability to talk. As stated previously, they can use Mokona to communicate with the black Mokona belonging to Yuko, as well as being able to teleport objects. He has other abilities too: he is able to sense the scattered feathers, so acts as a radar. Every time a feather is found and given to Sakura, more of her memories return, and she is soon able to talk, walk and help everyone else. Mokona also acts as a universal translator to those nearby. Whenever he is not there, the gang cannot understand each other as they go back to all talking in their native tongues. Mokona is also the being that is able to teleport the gang from dimension to dimension as they hunt the feathers, but Mokona has no control as to which world they go to.

Thus the epic journey of Syaoran, Sakura, Kurogane, Fai and Mokona begins, as they travel from world to world, meeting all kinds of people who CLAMP fans will be able to recognise. While the first feather is quickly found, Fai spotting it on Syaoran's back, the rest will be much harder to locate.

The lands the quintet travel to include utopian sci-fi cities, magical steampunk-like worlds, lands based on various periods of Japanese history, and post-apocalyptic ruins. Some of the places will be very familiar to CLAMP fans. They include the Country of Koryo, where the group help out its version of Chun Hyang (although in this English-language translation her name in this book is spelt 'Chu-nyan'). The utopian city meanwhile is Piffle World, dominated by the Piffle Princess Corporation whose president is their version of Tomoyo, and who gets the gang to enter a flying motor race and backs them for victory.[3]

Many old CLAMP characters appear in the story as alternative versions of themselves. For example, as the story progresses, we learn that Syaoran is a skilled fighter, mainly using his feet.

Kurogane realises that Syaoran does not fight with his hands because he is blind in his right eye. The man who taught Syaoran to fight is also blind in that eye: it is Seishiro, but instead of being an assassin, in this story Seishiro is a vampire hunter, with one of the vampires he is hunting being Subaru. This version of Seishiro has one eye because he gave it to Yuko as the price for his wish to travel to different worlds. In exchange, he got a glass eye that acts as his method of teleportation.

The longest arc is in the post-apocalyptic Country of Tokyo, which mainly pays homage to *X*, but in this version Kamui and Fuma have swapped sides, with Kamui leading the Dragons of Earth/Seven Angels, and Fuma the Dragons of Heaven/Seven Seals. As Seishiro and Subaru are removed from this situation, their places in the group are filled with minor characters in the series. Seishiro is replaced by Kazuki, the girl Nataku was originally cloned from, while replacing Subaru in Fuma's gang is Daisuke. These are not the only minor characters to get bigger billing in *Tsubasa*. The most notable is Shogo Asagi from the *X* anime film, who appears as a relatively kind-hearted gang leader in various different worlds.

It is in the Country of Tokyo arc where we come across some of the biggest revelations, the chief among these being that Syaoran is not actually Syaoran. The guy we have been following is a clone of what we shall now call Original Syaoran, who is being held prisoner by Fei-Wang. However, Original Syaoran has been able to observe everything that Clone Syaoran has done through the right eye, which the Original Syaoran blinded by a magic seal which contained some of his emotions, or 'heart' as it is written in the manga. Original Syaoran eventually breaks free of his captivity and goes to Tokyo, resulting in the seal being lifted. However, the consequences of this are dire, as Clone Syaoran loses his heart, and emotions too. The two Syaorans duel, with the Clone winning. The Clone leaves the group, now collecting the feathers on his own as part of Fei-Wang's plan, but before he leaves, he injures Fai, gorging out and consuming Fai's left eye, gaining his magic powers. Not only that, but the Clone's magic becomes stronger the more he uses it. The Original Syaoran takes the Clone's place in the group, helping to collect the feathers. As for Fai, he is so badly injured that the only way to keep him alive is to make a wish with Yuko. Luckily the Country of Tokyo has two people in it who can save his life: the vampires Seishiro is hunting; Subaru; and the other one whose name I will not mention as to provide some entertainment and mystery for those reading the manga. The only way to save Fai is for him to become a vampire himself, but he can be cured of his vampirism if he regains his eye.[4]

As the story progresses, things become increasingly tragic, complex and epic as we learn more about the backgrounds of the main characters, their increasing efforts to restore Sakura's memory, and how Watanuki himself is personally connected to Syaoran.

•

Before going into deeper analysis of the series, I want to make one thing clear: out of the two stories, I personally prefer *xxxHOLiC* to *Tsubasa*. *Tsubasa* is an entertaining story in its own right, and the fact that so many of CLAMP's past characters reappear in it makes it more fun for we fans of their work, but *xxxHOLiC* appeals to me more. This is partly because *xxxHOLiC* is more comedic in tone whereas *Tsubasa* is a lot more tragic. According to the *CLAMP no Kiseki* interviews, the manga's editor, Kiichiro Sugawara, wondered if anything good would happen to Syaoran, and the more you read the manga the more you think: 'No.'

Tsubasa definitely fits the tone of an epic tale. Syaoran and his friends face tragedy after tragedy, setback after setback, woe after woe, and they still keep on bloody going. Probably another reason why I prefer *Tsubasa* less is the length of the entire story. As mentioned, it is the longest of CLAMP's works if you include the sequel, and unless the returning *xxxHOLiC: Rei* passes it, it will remain so. At times the story feels a bit of a slog, mainly because there is so much tragedy in it that you end up feeling that you can't take much more misery – and remember, this comes from the same people who made *X*. These people made a series about the end of the fucking world, and that isn't even their most depressing story (although we don't know how *X* will end). Perhaps this relates back to religion, and the whole Buddhist notion that all existence is suffering. In *X*, half the characters are trying to end suffering by ending existence; in *Tsubasa*, the main characters are seeing a whole range of different existences and thus different forms of suffering. Mind you, there are references to Shinto as well. One of the characters that appears is Amaterasu, the Shinto sun goddess, who we see in a flashback telling Kurogane's origins, and who in his world is depicted as Kendappa from *RG Veda*.

Perhaps *Tsubasa* is best treated like *The One I Love*, and should be a series read in smaller chunks. While the series is only currently available to buy in omnibus editions, which is perhaps wise given the length of the series, I would advise perhaps still reading one individual volume at a time rather than an entire omnibus book in one go.

Having said all this, those who like *Tsubasa*'s story have their arguments. The main thing that is discussed is the revelation of the Clone Syaoran and the impact that it had on readers. All of a sudden, the hero that we have been following becomes a violent villain. It was a total shock to the readers. However, it does add to the confusion which also makes *Tsubasa* a difficult read, and indeed to write about, as reviewers have to constantly make a clear distinction between the two Syaorans. It is not the only thing that crops up: we have Fai turning into a vampire, but then tragic things also happen to Sakura and Kurogane too. Plus you have all the side characters: will Seishiro hunt down Subaru? How are Yuko and Watanuki tied into all of this? Will Fei-Wang show up in person to battle the gang? How will the Clone Syaoran be stopped? It's all really confusing. So confusing in fact, that there are separate Wikipedia articles for 'Syaoran (*Tsubasa: Reservoir Chronicle*, clone)' and 'Syaoran (*Tsubasa: Reservoir Chronicle*, original)', as well as for *Cardcaptor Sakura*'s 'Syaoran Li', meaning there are Wikipedia articles covering three alternative versions of the same character.

While I have compared many things in CLAMP to things we have in Britain, I think that an American comparison is best for *Tsubasa*. With its stories concerning having to mend wrongs and solve problems before you are able to jump into the next world, for me it curiously feels similar to *Quantum Leap*. Syaoran is like Sam Beckett, stuck in his world until he rights something, while given guidance from Yuko who acts like Al Calavicci. All you need to perfect it is for Syaoran to occasionally say: "Oh boy."[5]

One area of interest to those studying *Tsubasa* is its relationship with the rest of the CLAMPverse. We see many of the same characters cropping up in different universes. It is important to note that while these characters can have dramatically different attitudes from one to another depending on their environment, these alternative versions of the same character all share the same soul or essence. The Shogo Asagi in one world has the same soul as the Shogo Asagi in another world in *Tsubasa*. Thus, logically this can be extended to other CLAMP series. For example, the vampire hunter Seishiro is different to the assassin Seishiro in terms of their job, how they lose their eyes, their relationships, and their motivation, but both are still Seishiro. *Tsubasa*'s Syaoran and Sakura have the same souls as their *Cardcaptor* counterparts.

One theory I personally subscribe to is a connection between *Tsubasa* and *Cardcaptor Sakura: Clear Card*: we know that Fai's middle initial is 'D.' That also happens to be the same middle initial as Yuna D. Kaito, with his initial being a title given to him by a magic society. Surely there is a connection between the two?

Another issue regarding *Tsubasa* is the subject of genre. This is a story that is set in different worlds. Because of this, does *Tsubasa* count as an isekai, like *Rayearth*? This is tricky to define, because most isekai series are set in one world, but *Tsubasa* sees our heroes travelling across many worlds. There is however a later precedent for this, as one of the biggest isekai of the second wave, *Sword Art Online*, is set across multiple virtual words, with the central hero Kirito diving into these man-made worlds using technology. Therefore, 'many worlds' isekai for want of a better term, do exist, and thus *Tsubasa* would count. The first world that the gang travel to is our world, meeting the characters from *xxxHOLiC*, and thus it could also be labelled as a reverse isekai like the *Rayearth* OVA, but then again they travel to lots of places, so perhaps that label is wrong. The fact that the characters come from a fictional world and mainly travel to other fictional worlds makes it even more complex.

I have attempted to ask people about this. I once ran a question on this book's official Twitter account, @clampdownbook, asking: "Would you describe *Tsubasa: RESERVoir CHRoNiCLE* as an isekai series?" with the answers: "Yes", "No" and "Don't know". No single answer got an overall 50% majority, with "No" being the highest with 39.5%, followed by "Yes" with 32.6%, and "Don't know" with 27.9%. Even then, only 43 people voted, which is in no way a statistically significant sample size. I just put these figures up as a demonstration of a failed first attempt to look into the matter, and as evidence that more needs to be discussed in order to settle it.

In November 2021 however, Dr Paul S. Price published

'A Survey of Story Elements of Isekai Manga' in the second volume of the *Journal of Anime and Manga Studies*, which covered over 1,000 series, and lists both *Tsubasa* works as isekai, so according to at least one academic journal it is isekai. The same survey also lists *Magic Knight Rayearth*, and even includes *Miyuki-chan in Wonderland* as an isekai. If this is to be believed, then CLAMP created three isekai before the modern isekai-boom took place.

Personally speaking, while I do not know with certainty as to whether *Tsubasa* is an isekai, part of me hopes it is for the following reason. As discussed, at the time of writing there have been two waves of isekai. The first shojo wave, which includes *Rayearth*, happened in the 1990s. The second modern wave, featuring *Sword Art Online* and the current torrent of titles, is often considered to have begun in the 2010s, and while *SAO* was first self-published in 2002, it wasn't until publishers picked the series up in 2009 and the eventual anime in 2012 debuted that the second wave is often seen to have really kicked off. *Tsubasa* debuted in 2003, in between these two periods. This would make the series a transitional one, in between the two waves, if it is an isekai. If this is a transitional isekai, it could be used as evidence of how the genre changed over time, with a shift from female lead stories to male ones, early steps into reverse isekai, and experimentation with using multiple worlds.

For me however, the main thing to enjoy from *Tsubasa* is the art. This comes partly from the fantastical landscapes and worlds the characters are sent to which vary so greatly, from historical to futuristic settings, from technological to fantasy worlds. But the main appeal is the character art, and the return of old characters in new guises, as well as new cast members like Fai and Kurogane. Every time the cast move to a new world, a new set of clothes is needed so that the gang can blend in. Thus, we see our characters in typical street clothes, European period costume, motor racing attire, traditional Japanese outfits, and protective gear. Syaoran's signature look normally involves a cape and a pair of goggles.

However, for many CLAMP fans, myself included, it is when we see the other CLAMP characters appear in the story that the series really piques our interest. With Seishiro and Subaru being my personal favourites, their appearances interest me the most. As a vampire hunter, we see Seishiro dressed in an outfit akin to a priest, although any reference to Christianity is removed by the fact the pendant on his long necklace has an upside-down five-pointed star on it. Rather than the occult pentagram, this is more likely a reference to the five elements of Chinese philosophy known as Wuxing. Subaru meanwhile rocks the classic gothic vampire look, and, like anything worn by Subaru, it looks fantastic on him.

Then there are the appearances of lesser known CLAMP characters. Chun Hyang is the star of one of the early stories, and it is good to see her get some time in the spotlight when it could have been her that CLAMP might have been remembered for if history took a different path. Shogo Asagi's many appearances in the series, across different worlds, also highlights a character that only appeared in one work and who is now largely forgotten about.

Perhaps the most pleasing cameos are the ones where you get just the briefest glimpse of a character or two. They may play no main part in the plot, but they still appear in the series and are part of the fabric that weaves the whole CLAMPverse together. One of my personal favourite scenes comes in a story where Fai and Sakura decide to create a café in the world they are currently in, to make some money for the rest of the gang. For one brief moment, we see them serving Utako Okawa from *Man of Many Faces* and her sister Mako, then just after that Hina and Shiro from *Suki: A Like Story* arrive at table.

Sometimes, a simple promotional image is enough to please you. Each of the chapters begins with a promotion illustration, and one of my favourites comes in *Tsubasa: WoRLD CHRoNiCLE*, at the opening of sixth chapter (Vol. 2), or 'chapitre' as they are called in the series. The picture sees Fuma walking through a rainy city, delivering an item which I shall not name as it is a spoiler to something that happens to one of the main characters, so do be careful when looking up this image if you have not read the story yet. What is not a spoiler is that along with Fuma we see other characters. In the bottom-right corner of the page is Su from *Clover* on some kind of holographic screen. She is being watched by a man who has his back to us, but it is safe to assume it is Kazuhiko. In the top left, we see Dita from *Chobits*, who is in conversation with presumably Zima, although only the bottom half of the character is depicted so we cannot say for certain.

One thing about this image that is also worth bringing up is that Fuma is depicted wearing clothes that have cogs and gear patterns designed into them. This look would appear to be the precursor of a series of images that CLAMP made in 2020, with other characters in similar looking outfits. These images were among the things used to drum up interest in the announcement of the *Tokyo Babylon 2021* anime. Having said this, you could argue that by using similar style clothes CLAMP were recycling material, and given that this was in the sequel manga that they were lacking new ideas anyway.

Speaking of anime, *Tsubasa* received a few anime adaptations. In 2005, *Tsubasa* had a 52-episode long adaptation by the studio Bee Train, which included stories original to the anime. As well as a 2005 short film entitled *The Princess in the Birdcage Kingdom*, there were also two separate OVA series by the studio Production I.G; *Tokyo Revelations* (2007-08) and *Spring Thunder Chronicles* (2009). In a December 2020 article from Comic Book Resource (CBR) entitled '10 Anime & Manga Creators Who

Disowned Adaptations Of Their Work', Angelo Delos Trinos claims that: "CLAMP and Bee Train barely saw eye-to-eye" and by the end of the anime, CLAMP had stopped working with the studio. However, this was something that I had not heard of, so I contacted the experts, and Chibi Yuuto told me via Twitter: "There is no evidence to that (at least that I am aware of). I would say this stays in the realms of speculation. We don't know how much of an influence CLAMP had into deciding that there wouldn't be a 3rd season."

Sadly, the series has never been given a proper release in the UK. It was originally sold by a company called Revelation Films, but they never got any further than the first half of the TV series, meaning only 26 episodes were released in Region 2. The only way you can watch the entire thing therefore is to import the Region 1 release. Many of the episodes feature original content not in the anime, including one in which the gang arrive in a new world in the middle of a road, and are almost run over by a truck, which does add credence to the argument that *Tsubasa* is an isekai, in that even in the work of CLAMP, Truck-kun appears. Mind you, there is another problem with the anime. As mentioned in the *Angelic Layer* chapter, in the English dub Fai is voiced by Vic Mignogna, and obviously there is a lot of baggage concerning him.

•

Tsubasa feels very much like CLAMP's love letter to itself. In this series, they could say that they had reached the point that they could go back to the characters that made them popular and make a hit series using them. They were proven right, as *Tsubasa* remains their best selling work, and, given that *xxxHOLiC: Rei* is returning, could *Tsubasa* come back too?

It is also true that the manga references just about all their series, including ones that we have yet to cover in this book. For example, three of the main characters in *Gate 7* have key roles in *Tsubasa: WoRLD CHRoNiCLE*, while most of the gang would also travel into another dimension that would be depicted in the anime adaptation of the series covered in our next chapter.

---

1 – Although if they were worried about the titles being too short, then how come they allowed *Clover*, *Wish* and *X* then?

2 – Of course, given her past history in CLAMP works, it could be a case of: "Me? Princess Tomoyo, here, teleporting a violent ninja to another dimension, and placing a weakening curse on him, with my reputation? Well, we can't have him interrupting my fun with Soma now, can we?"

3 – We can guess why she is keen to see Sakura win. "Me? Tomoyo Daidouji, here, attempting to get some people to enter a dangerous flying race, with my reputation? I'll do anything to see people in leather."

4 – In the CLAMPverse, Yuko explains that in this world vampires are not weakened by the sunlight or holy water, nor are they immortal. They are just 'more robust' than other humans and age slower, although due to his magic Fai is already much older than the rest of the main gang. The vampires also state that wounds a human received before turning into a vampire are not healed, and thus Fai spends much of the latter-half of the series wearing an eye patch.

5 – Some of you may be asking why I compare this to *Quantum Leap* rather than *Doctor Who*. Simple reason: the Doctor has his TARDIS and can leave for another time and place whenever he

wants to. Beckett has to stay where he is until he has corrected something.

CHAPTER 17

This Dove's Got Bottle – *Kobato* (2004-2011)

While we have looked at the cross-referencing in *Tsubasa* and other CLAMP works, the ladies had not stopped criss-crossing their various creations. *Kobato* is a series that mainly draws on two previous titles: *Wish* and *Chobits*. However, there are many other series that also get a look in.

Kobato establishes a way for us to navigate across the CLAMPverse in more detail, in particular examining the relationship between the various worlds that inhabit it. In *Wish*, we have already seen things like CLAMP's version of Heaven and Hell, and their view on reincarnation. This is expanded upon in *Kobato*. Also, we get to see another parallel universe, one that is similar to the one in *Chobits* but again has certain differences.

Kobato (2004-2011)

For a brief moment, it looked like *Kobato* would end up like so many CLAMP series, in hiatus hell. Originally published in Shogakukan's strangely named *Monthly Sunday Gene-X* magazine, after seven chapters the series did indeed go on hiatus, but luckily it was picked up by *Newtype* magazine and was able to continue its full run of six volumes.

In terms of its English release, we turn to a different company. With CLAMP titles having been released by TokyoPop, Viz Media, Dark Horse and Kodansha in the past, *Kobato* went to yet another firm: Yen Press. You do get the feeling that it would be better if all of this was done by just one company, but given how often CLAMP moved around from publisher to publisher, it is perhaps no surprise that their works are split up so widely. Not even TokyoPop were able to get the full monopoly on CLAMP, thanks to Viz publishing *X*.

•

Kobato is the story of a teenage girl named Kobato Hanato. Kobato means 'baby dove' and Hanato 'flower door'. She is a sweet girl, full to the brim with kindness, helpfulness and understanding. She is however, very naive. Not 'Hina from *Suki: A Like Story*' naive, but still lacking in some aspects of common sense.

Fortunately, she is helped by her friend Ioryogi, a much wiser and more powerful being than her. Ioryogi does have his own problems though. He has a fiery temper on him, constantly harassing Kobato whenever she makes a mistake, calling her 'Dobato', meaning 'stupid dove'. He has another problem too: he has the form of a cuddly toy dog.

Kobato is on a mission. She wants to go to a certain place, which is not specified in the story. In order to achieve this, she must heal as many broken hearts as she can. While Ioryogi tries to guide her as best he can, Kobato's lack of common sense constantly hampers her attempts to help others. Eventually Kobato is at least able to help Ioryogi, by getting him some cold beer to help him in the summer heat.[1] For this deed, she is magically given a special bottle, with a dove-shaped stopper and two little wings decorating it. In this bottle, she is able to store little spheres that represent the broken hearts. Once it is full, she can achieve her wish.

She soon begins to settle down. Kobato finds accommodation, staying in the apartment block run by this universe's version of Chitose, who has some of the biggest character changes. Her surname has changed from Hibiya to Mihara, and she has two daughters, Chiho and Chise, who look similar to persocoms, including Chi. Given that Chitose has Icchan's surname it seems likely they were married.

Kobato is finally able to secure a regular job, working at the Yomogi Kindergarten, doing various jobs including washing, cleaning, and entertaining the children with, among other things, her beautiful singing voice. Also working there are the owner Sayaka Okiura and part-timer Kiyokazu Fujimoto, an attractive yet blunt man who at first is not keen on Kobato, disliking her clumsiness and lateness. Fujimoto also happens to be Kobato's neighbour in the apartment block. Aside from the kindergarten, Fujimoto does many other part-time jobs to keep the money flowing. In one of his jobs, he even works alongside Toya Kinomoto from *Cardcaptor Sakura*.

While Kobato continues to try and heal as many hearts as she can, she comes to learn of the reason why Fujimoto does so many jobs: Yomogi Kindergarten has got into trouble with some loan sharks with connections with the yakuza, and if Sayaka cannot clear the debt then the loan shark in question will shut down the kindergarten. The loan shark in question is called Kazuto Okiura, and as you may deduct from the surnames, Kazuto is Sayaka's ex-husband, although they have never properly divorced. Kobato thus tries to mend the hearts of all those involved in the kindergarten.

However, there is another side to the story, involving Ioryogi. Namely, his true reason for why he is so keen to help Kobato. We eventually come to learn that Ioryogi – or to give him his real name, Iorogi – is a supernatural being from the 'other world', the fourth of the main worlds that make up the CLAMPverse, along with the human world that we live in, the heavenly world that is the home of the angels, and the underworld that is the domain of demons, which have previously been covered in *Wish*.

Iorogi fell in love with an angel named Suishou, who took

over from Kohaku as the one whose singing caused baby angels to hatch from their eggs. However, Suishou was also clumsy and could never pronounce Iorogi's name right, always saying 'Ioryogi', hence the name he has now. [2] Iorogi loved Suishou so much that he decided to fight for Suishou, resulting in battles between the other world and the heavenly world. Iorogi lost, and part of his punishment was to be transformed into his dog-like state. Many of Iorogi's allies also got transformed. These include Ginsei, a one-eyed rabbit-canine like creature that Iorogi raised up and who now spends most of his time wanting to fight Iorogi; and Genko, who took on the form of a bear and happily runs a baumkuchen cake shop. Among the regular customers of the shop are Kohaku, who buys cakes for the latest reincarnation of love interest Shuichiro.

As well as Iorogi and his allies having to succumb to their transformed fate, there was also one human casualty in the fighting: Kobato. In order to keep Kobato alive, a part of Suishou's soul was given to her, hence why Kobato inherited Suishou's traits of beautiful singing, clumsiness, and the inability to pronounce Iorogi's name correctly. Iorogi is thus desperate to help Kobato because it will also help Suishou too.

Iorogi eventually gets a message from Ushagi, the rabbit-like messenger of God, that the time limit for Kobato to fill up the bottle is one year, and he doesn't get the message until six months of this time limit has already gone. If she fails, both Kobato and Suishou will die. The race is on to save them both, and for Kobato to help those around her.

•

In *Kobato,* the main area of interest is its role in the CLAMPverse, and in particular the various realms within it. We now know that there are at least four worlds: human, heavenly, underworld and other-world. Also, we know that the human world has various multiple iterations in the form of the many parallel worlds that we come across in *Tsubasa*. There is a possibility that there could be iterations of the other worlds too. When we get to Kohaku and the latest reincarnation of Shuichiro, it is implied that Kohaku has been with many versions of Shuichiro. Does this mean that there are other versions of Kohaku that have been with him, or does it mean that there is just one Kohaku who is able to travel to different human worlds and be with different Shuichiros? This remains unanswered. We do know however that all these forms of Shuichiro will have the same soul.

We also learn a bit about the other world, but not much. We do briefly see Iorogi as his true self in flashbacks, with the beings of the other world appearing somewhat humanoid, as well as having great power. One other thing we learn about the other world comes from Kohaku, who says on page three of the sixth volume of the manga that the beings of the other world, as well as angels and devils, all die too, like humans. It is just that they take longer to age. It is interesting that in the CLAMPverse, even creatures like angels and devils die. It seems that the only immortal beings are god-like. God himself is mentioned in the series, but never appears. We know that angels are born by hatching. How devils and other world beings are born is unknown. We do know a little bit about Iorogi's origins elsewhere in the CLAMPverse however, as he was originally a mascot drawn and used by Nekoi.

Aside from these aspects of the story, there is *Kobato*'s relationship with other CLAMP characters. Characters from *Wish*, *Chobits*, *Angelic Layer*, *Suki: A Like Story*, *Cardcaptor Sakura* and *xxxHOLiC* all appear in it. It was also adapted as a 24-episode long anime TV series by the studio Madhouse, directed by Mitsuyuki Masuhara, whose other creations include children's series *Chi's Sweet Home* which is all about a cat, and the baseball series *Ace of Diamond*. The *Kobato* anime was released on DVD in the USA by the company Sentai Filmworks, but the license has since expired. It is available to stream in the USA on Amazon Prime, but is unavailable in the UK at time of going to print. In Episode 20, entitled '...The Travelers', Kobato encounters Syaoran and his fellow dimension-hopping friends from *Tsubasa* as they visit this world before moving onto the next one.

In terms of reaction to the series, Clements and McCarthy in *The Anime Encyclopedia* say: "In *Kobato* the animation by Madhouse is utterly gorgeous, setting the scene for the archetypal [fairy] tale in breathtaking style. The gently goofy humour balances the poignant moments and helps us brace for the heartbreak no good fairy tale can avoid. *Kobato* may be a minor work in a mighty canon, but its sweetness and life-affirming belief in the power of love – not just romantic love, but the relationships that sustain us all – make it worthy of attention."

•

In comparison to the epic works of *Tsubasa* and *xxxHOLiC*, *Kobato* is a calm, tranquil story. There are moments of tension, excitement and humour in it too, but it feels a much more manageable read when you compare it to the epics that were being made at the same time as it. It also helps to expand on previous CLAMP titles, and the character of Kobato is one of CLAMP's more interesting creations – polite, charming, helpful, and also tragic in her own way. However, as we have established, we know that if a CLAMP character does go through the tragedy of death, they won't be away forever. They will reincarnate at some point in the future. How long we have to wait remains in the power of CLAMP.

Reincarnation does however bring up an important point.

What about all those great and not-so-great figures from history? Are they in the world right now? Could we see the reincarnation of Henry VIII or Cleopatra into today's world? For CLAMP, it appears that we are able to meet figures from the past right now, as we shall see in our final chapter.

---

1 – Or to be exact, Kobato gets some samples of free beer being distributed by this world's version of Misaki and Tamayo from *Angelic Layer*. In fact, at this point in the story Kobato has already met versions of other CLAMP characters. She finds brief employment at the Patisserie Chiroru, when, caught in a rainstorm, she is kindly given an umbrella by Hina from *Suki*, and she helps out an old fortune teller that we meet in *xxxHOLiC*.

2 – If indeed he is a 'he'. It is never explained whether or not the other world beings are genderless like the angels are, if they are gendered like humans, or something else entirely.

CHAPTER 18

The Blast from The Past – *Gate 7* (2010-2013)

Like *Tsubasa*, this manga is at times difficult to read, or to be more accurate it is difficult to read if you are not Japanese, as this series deals with figures from a particular period of Japanese history.

The average Brit lacking knowledge about Japanese history is a problem faced by several manga being sold over here. The main thing we know anything about is the Second World War, and that is because we were fighting against them. We might also know the odd other thing: the long period of isolation, certain cultural elements like ninja and samurai etc., but other than that the average Brit doesn't know much about Japan's past. Most of the history in this manga covers the Sengoku period, referred to in the English translation of the manga as the 'Warring States Period', a time of constant civil war from 1467 to 1615.

However, *Gate 7* does feature historical figures, or rather versions of historical figures, that the average Japanese reader would most likely know about. The central plot concerns Nobunaga Oda (1534-1582), Japan's first 'Great Unifier'. In 2006, he topped *The Top 100 Historical Persons in Japan* TV poll, their country's version of the BBC's *100 Greatest Britons* poll from 2002.[1]

Fortunately for us ignorant foreigners, the manga is actually set in the present day, and the English-language release does come with some extensive translation notes. Having said that, there is at least one thing I came across in these notes I'm slightly dubious about, but we will come to that later.

Gate 7 (2010-2013)

While several websites list *Gate 7* as beginning in March 2011, strictly speaking the manga first appeared in December 2010, where it debuted as a one-shot comic in Shueisha's *Jump Square* magazine. Following on from this one-shot, the manga started as a full series in March 2011, and continued until February 2013, running across four volumes, which were released in English by Dark Horse. However, they have stopped publishing the comic and the only way to read it today is through second-hand copies of the printed manga.[2]

•

Gate 7 differs in one notable way from the other manga by CLAMP, in that it is not set in Tokyo. Instead, it is set in what *Futurama* dubbed: "The anagram lover's Tokyo", Kyoto, the city that is, if you remember, the birthplace of three of CLAMP's members (the exception being Ohkawa, who was born in Osaka). Kyoto is significant in terms of setting because it is the one city in Japan that has the most visible connections with its past. Its history is so significant that during the Second World War it was the one major city not subjected to firebombing by the Americans, thus meaning that all of its historical buildings survive.

Kyoto's historical connections are what attract one teenage schoolboy to come visit the place. A boy's whose name I cannot say without wanting to say it to the tune of 'Chiquitita' by ABBA, and now that I've mentioned that, you won't be able to avoid doing so either. His name is Chikahito Takamoto, and I bet you that you will now not be able to get that song out of your head for ages now. Sorry about that. Anyway, the story…

Chikahito has a passion for the history of the area and has thus gone on a trip to the city. However, upon a visit to the 10th century Kitano Tenmangu shrine, he finds himself entering a strange black void. Inside this, he comes across three people fighting against supernatural creatures. After witnessing this fight, he faints.

Upon waking up, Chikahito finds himself in the house of these three people. They are members of the Urashichiken Hanamachi, a secret society devoted to protecting Kyoto from such supernatural phenomena. These first of these is Hana, a young androgynous person whose gender is never revealed in the story, who is able to use various powers to slay the beasts. Hana is also something of a glutton, and will happily eat bowl after bowl of noodles if the opportunity arises. The other two members are young men. One of them is called, rather confusingly for us CLAMP fans, Sakura. This Sakura however is hunky blond man who works as an attendant for maiko – apprentice geisha. The other man is Tachibana, an angry black-haired student who is not fond of Chikahito at a ll and is constantly angry at him. Together, Sakura and Tachibana help Hana by creating weapons: Sakura's weapons having the power of darkness, and Tachibana's the power of light. Due to Chikahito's ability to enter the dark space where the group's fight took place, it is known that he must have some kind of special ability, but no one is sure what it is. Nevertheless, Hana kisses Chikahito, which casts a spell that results in him moving to Kyoto to live with the rest of the group.

As a result, Chikahito finds out that things have been arranged so that he can move from Tokyo and Kyoto, leaving his old school – Cross Academy from *xxxHOLiC*. He does still have some things from Tokyo that he brings along with him to Kyoto, such as a bag from the Green Drugstore with the words 'DRUG & DROP' written on it, which happened to be the name of the other series CLAMP were working on at the time.

Chikahito is taken by Hana to meet the current leader of the Urashichiken Hanamachi, a man named Hidestugu Toyotomi. While the three are talking in a restaurant, the black void returns, isolating them from everyone else, which we come to learn is called an 'envelopment'. It turns out that this can be done by people who have made a blood contract with an oni – which in Japanese mythology are normally a kind of demon, but that doesn't appear to be the case in this story. Whatever the case is, we know that these oni give powers to those they are in a contract with, and are normally invisible to ordinary people. Hidestugu himself has a contract with an oni named Mikoto.

Hidestugu and Mikoto then take Chikahito and Hana to a grave. To be exact, the grave of Hidestugu Toyotomi. Yes, his own grave. In real life, Hidestugu Toyotomi (1568-1595) was the nephew of the shogun Hideyoshi Toyotomi, Japan's second 'Great Unifier', but Hidestugu was accused of committing atrocities. He himself was eventually forced to commit seppuku (ritual suicide), and his family were also all executed. Our Hidestugu is his reincarnation, who tells Chikahito the reason for this execution was because of the oni. Oni pass down from ancestor to ancestor, so the executions were to make sure it passed to the strongest member of the family.

Hidestugu then reveals that there are many reincarnations of people from his period of history alive now, and they are now after one thing: the most powerful oni of all, Dairokutenmaoh the demon king. The one who had a contract with this oni was Nobunaga Oda, the man who almost unified the whole of Japan until supposedly one of his generals turned traitor, and rather than be captured he committed seppuku. In real life, his body was never found. Because of this, his oni has never been found and thus the reincarnations are trying to find it.

Chikahito soon sees the dangers of all this first-hand when one of these reincarnations appears on the scene, namely Mitsuhide

Akechi (1528-1582, named 97th in *The Top 100 Historical Persons in Japan* poll), who many believe to be the traitorous general that brought Oda down. A battle then takes place with Hana helping to fight off Akechi's oni, Enka. Luckily, help soon comes when two reincarnations appear on the scene to help our heroes. These are the reincarnations of Masamune Date (1567-1636, 50th in poll) and his strategist Kojyuuroh Katakura (aka Kagetsuna Katakura, 1557-1615). Masamune was one of Japan's most famous soldiers and was also noted for the fact that he lost his right eye, making him an appropriate person for CLAMP to feature. He lost the use of his eye due to smallpox, but no one knows how he lost his actual eyeball. In *Gate 7*, his eye was part of the price to allow him to use his oni, a sword called Kurikara. The other price was that Katakura has to act as the sword's scabbard, with the sword magically appearing and disappearing into his body when it is needed. Masamune is also different from the other reincarnations in the fact that he is the youngest, appearing as an elementary school student, and one dressed in some punk/gothic clothing too, complete with dog collar and a chain hanging down from his eye patch. Akechi eventually decides to withdraw from the fight, giving the rest of the gang the chance to relax, or in, Masamune's case, flirt with Hana, who he is completely and totally in love with.

The story sees Chikahito encountering more reincarnations, although he does not always realise which people actually are reincarnations. One of these is Iemitsu Tokugawa (1604-1651), someone who gives off an immediate warning sign to CLAMP fans as he has the purple eyes, the sign of sin first seen in *RG Veda*. Iemitsu was the third shogun of the Tokugawa shogunate, and the one responsible for Japan's policy of self-isolation, as well as policies brought in to suppress Christianity in the country. Iemitsu eventually enrols at the same school that Chikahito goes to when he starts education in Kyoto. We also know that

Iemitsu's oni, Mitsuha, feeds on human flesh, and this is one of the reasons he is the main villain in *Gate 7*.

Most of the story follows Chikahito, Hana, Sakura and Tachibana as they meet up with other reincarnations to persuade them to join their side, as it appears that eventually there will be a battle between the Toyotomi and Tokugawa camps over Oda's oni. Among the other reincarnations we meet are Yukimura Sanada (1567-1615, 66th in the poll), a samurai supported by ten ninja warriors who in his current reincarnation is a rather weak-willed kindergarten teacher; and Gracia Hosokawa (1563-1600), a female aristocrat and Catholic convert.

As Chikahito encounters more historical figures and takes on greater dangers, one aspect of him explored is the fact that he has this power to enter the envelopments despite seemingly having no great powers himself. How is he able to do this, and how will this affect the ever increasing likelihood of conflict? The answer to that is unknown, because… *Gate 7* ended up on hiatus.

It ended in 2013, the same year *Drug & Drop* did. If you remember, in 2011 one member of CLAMP had a fracture, then in 2012 both manga went on hiatus after one of the team became ill. Both manga suffered the same fate and remain incomplete.

•

It seems only fitting that the last manga covered in this book should have some similarities with the first. As mentioned, we see the sinful purple eyes in Iemitsu that are also shared by *RG Veda*'s Kujaku. Both stories also feature a character of ambiguous gender in a central role. It's interesting to note that both *RG Veda* and *Gate 7* are Dark Horse titles, but I prefer the *Gate 7* translation by William Flanagan more, partly because it tries hard to avoid referring to Hana using gendered pronouns, to keep it more in tone with the original Japanese. The only time we do see such a pronoun being used is in the character profiles at the beginning of Volumes 3 and 4, where Hana is described as 'she'.

Having said this, there are things in the translation notes that cause me to worry. In Volume 3, in the segment where they explain Gracia, they say that she is, "...one of the earliest Japanese-born Catholic saints", and that: "In the 1860s, Gracia was canonized by the Vatican as the first Japanese saint." (p179-180) I tried to double check this, but I cannot find anything to prove this. I've come across some places that say she was canonised in 1862, but nothing that I would describe as a concrete source. Other sources say that this claim of sainthood is disputed and that no historical documents back the claim. If it is the case that this claim for sainthood is inaccurate, then that could mean that everything else in Dark Horse's translation notes could be wrong. This one mistake may lead on to another. What do you believe?[3]

Gate 7 does allow CLAMP to draw some more historic landscapes, and also allows them to play with certain aspects of history which can be hard to follow, but you don't need to be an expert on history to enjoy the story. Having said that, once you start to learn about who these historical figures are, you come to realise the fun way CLAMP deal with them. The transformation of the one-eyed warrior Masamune Date into a young brat sucking a lollipop, wearing a dog collar and being head-over-heels in love with Hana is an entertaining one. Similarly, seeing samurai Yukimura Sanada having trouble trying to control a load of pre-schoolers is also fun.

It is just so frustrating that it ended up on hiatus. There was so much more waiting to happen that we will now probably never get to learn about, and it is not just *Gate 7*. It is one of five CLAMP manga still on hiatus along with *X*, *Clover*, *Drug & Drop* and, happily, the soon-to-return *xxxHOLiC: Rei*. The earliest of these hiatuses was the one for *Clover* in 1999, and given that this still hasn't been completed, hopes for the other four look similarly slim. Admittedly, the hope for the return of *X* did come up when the *Tokyo Babylon 2021* anime was announced, and if that does become successful then this hope might result in something bigger. Could all of them be completed one day? Fans hope they will, but it is doubtful.

•

Ending in 2013, *Gate 7* sees a peculiar take on history, and feeds into the CLAMP mythology of reincarnation. *Gate 7* is also, at the time of writing, the last totally original work by CLAMP. Their following three series have been sequels of earlier works, namely *xxxHOLiC: Rei, Tsubasa: WoRLD CHRoNiCLE* and the currently running *Cardcaptor Sakura: Clear Card.* Versions of Hana, Sakura and Tachibana would go on to appear as characters in *Tsubasa: WoRLD CHRoNiCLE* so they do live on elsewhere in the CLAMPverse. However, critics claim that because *Gate 7* is the last totally original work, that CLAMP have been running out of ideas. Some might argue that the original *Tsubasa* could be an early sign of this, reusing old characters in new works.

I too would love to see more completely new works from CLAMP. Having said that, I really want to see them returning to complete the old works still on hiatus, including *Gate 7.* Mind you, I still find *Cardcaptor Sakura: Clear Card* an entertaining read. CLAMP are still able to produce work that is at least of a decent quality. If they didn't, no one would continue to read it, would they?

---

1 – It should be pointed out however that this poll was to name the most liked figure in history, and unlike the *100 Greatest Britons* poll it featured people from across the world. Non-Japanese people in *The Top 100 Historical Persons in Japan*

included Thomas Edison (3rd), Mother Teresa (8th), Helen Keller (9th), Princess Diana (12th), Albert Einstein (13th), Anne Frank (16th), Florence Nightingale (17th), Walt Disney (19th), Ludwig van Beethoven (20th) and Ayrton Senna (22nd). The only manga-related person in the poll was Osamu Tezuka, who came 24th in the poll, wedged between Leonardo da Vinci in 23rd, and Napoleon Bonaparte in 25th. It is saying something however that even in Japan, Disney ranked higher than Tezuka.

2 – Which, if you remember from the footnotes in the preface, took quite a while to turn up, for me anyway.

3 – Also, given that Gracia was Catholic, do you think that she would be annoyed over the whole reincarnation business? As someone raised Catholic, I can tell you that reincarnation is not one of the things that tends to crop up in our religion. When she came back into world, did she think: 'Is this heaven? It doesn't look like what I was told it would look like. Is this actually hell? Purgatory perhaps? Oh no. Oh Lord, don't tell me that this is Earth. You mean I've got to go through this all again? Where's God? I want to have a word with Him.' At which point she would become even more annoyed when she finds God's messenger is a rabbit called Ushagi holding a flower. On the plus side, at least she would find out that there is a God and a heaven, albeit one she can't get to.

EPILOGUE

At a Later Date

With one mildly autistic mind having spent over six months reading over twenty different series written over a period of over thirty years, it's time to round up some of things that we've come across. What have we learned? What is the structure behind it all? What may happen next? But before delving into all this, I should also mention the stuff that we have not covered.

These incredible women have created a lot more work outside of these manga. If you are interested in some of the other series CLAMP didn't entirely create but also worked on, there is plenty to get your teeth into. We have mentioned some of these, such as the light novel series *CLAMP School Paranormal Investigators*, which CLAMP illustrated but was written by Tomiyuki Matsumoto. These were released in English by TokyoPop, but you can only find second-hand copies now.

While CLAMP are rightly known for their work in manga, their contribution to anime also deserves to be mentioned. There are the anime adaptations of their manga which we have covered in this book, but there are other works too. Most notable is *CLAMP in Wonderland*, which is a series of anime music videos featuring all of their characters up to the point the videos debuted. The first of these came out in 1994, while the second video contained all their characters as of 2006. The videos are enjoyable partly because they contain characters who don't appear in any of the other CLAMP anime, even ones from their early doujinshi works, such as their version of Jotaro Kujo from *JoJo's Bizarre Adventure*. Both videos can be found on YouTube.

CLAMP have also worked as collaborators on many other projects, often as character designers. In 2020, CLAMP were one of six Japanese creators to enter into a partnership with Netflix to create new projects, and it was announced that they would design 20 characters for a new project. In June 2021, it was revealed that the series would be a modern day anime adaptation of *Grimm's Fairy Tales*. As to why CLAMP would want to cover this work, my pet theory is that in the Grimm's version of *Cinderella*, entitled *Aschenputtel*, the Ugly Sisters are ultimately punished by having their eyes plucked out by doves.

Aside from this, other projects CLAMP have worked on include but are not limited to:

- *Blood-C*: A fantasy horror from 2011 and later a film in 2012 about a miko/shrine maiden who goes around slaying monsters. CLAMP worked on the story as well as the character design. The violence in the anime was so great that in Japan the series was censored, and in 2015 China's Ministry of Culture blacklisted the entire series, preventing its distribution in the country. In 2022, the films were released in the UK by All The Anime in one of their 'Ultimate Editions', limited to just 500 copies.

- *Code Geass*: Previously mentioned in this book and my personal favourite of the collaborations, this alternative history mecha series debuted in 2006 and also had CLAMP doing character design. Set in a Japan which is occupied by an Holy Britannian Empire, which is actually in the Americas,[1] the series follows a man named Lelouch, who gains the power to force anyone to obey any order he gives. He tries to use this power to overthrow the Empire as the masked resistance leader Zero. There are TV and film versions, both of which have been released in the UK.

- *HiGH&LOW*: This large franchise about five gangs trying to control a town has covered not just anime and manga, but live action TV shows, live stage shows and computer games. CLAMP created a manga in 2017 called *High&Low g-sword*, which was adapted into a 2-3 minute 'flash' anime, but this has never been released in English and they did not create the original series. It is mainly for these reasons it falls outside the total remit of this book. I know that arguably *RG Veda* might be ruled out under the same rules, given that they didn't create the original *Rig Veda*, but there is an argument that it differs so much from the main source that it would count as a more original work, whereas *HiGH&LOW* is still based on something very clearly defined.

- *Kabukibu!*: CLAMP provided character designs for the 2017 adaptation of this light novel series by Yuri Edam, about a boy who sets up a school club devoted to kabuki theatre. The series has been released in the USA by Sentai Filmworks.

- *Moryo no Hako* (Box of Spirits and Goblins): Adapted from a 1995 novel by Natsuhiko Kyogoku, this is a mystery novel following a journalist and, fittingly for CLAMP, a onmyoji – but not Subaru sadly. Again, CLAMP provided character designs for the TV adaptation which came out in 2008.

- *Sohryuden: Legend of the Dragon Kings*: Perhaps the most surprising series not to be released in English, this is a series of light novels that debuted in 1987 and is still going today, with 14 volumes released so far. Based on Chinese mythology, part of the reason that the lack of a release is surprising is the fact that it is written by Yoshiki Tanaka, whose space opera series *Legend of the Galactic Heroes* has been released in English by Viz Media. This series however is released in Japanese by

Kodansha, and CLAMP illustrated the 'bunko' paperback releases. CLAMP also adapted it as a short manga in 1994. However, the only English language version of the series is a 12-part OVA series, which was released in the UK by Manga Entertainment on VHS.

- *Sweet Valerian*: A children's series that debuted as an anime in 2004 and was later turned into a manga series in 2005, it follows three girls who protect the city of Asialand from monsters. This series is unusual in that CLAMP created it and designed the characters, but everything else was done by other people.

The Structure of the CLAMPverse

Going through all the works, we can get a basic grip on how the CLAMPverse operates.

One is the various planes. As of the time of writing, we know there are four: the heavenly, the underworld, the other-world and the human world. The human world also has countless versions of itself. Within these various versions of the human world are people that share the same soul as their counterparts in other worlds. In *Tsubasa*, if they come across one character who looks exactly like someone else in another world, they will have the same soul. However, their upbringing will mean that these versions will differ. One version might be friendly, while the other is hostile. In *Magic Knight Rayearth*, our world and Cefiro were created by a being whose name I shall not reveal as it is a spoiler. In *Wish*, we see that God exists in some form and even has his own rabbit-like messenger, although in *RG Veda* we also see Ashura as a god of destruction, so is there more than one god?

We also know that seemingly no one is immortal in the CLAMPverse. With the possible exception of God, everyone in the CLAMPverse will die at some point. Humans have the shortest life-span on average, with the angels of the heavenly world, demons of the underworld, the beings of the other world, and other supernatural creatures in the human world, such as vampires, aging more slowly that humans, but nevertheless still having a limited amount of life. However, we do know that in the CLAMPverse there is reincarnation. It forms the main focus of *Gate 7* where we see several reincarnations of historical figures, while the reincarnation of humans means that the angel Kohaku can spend time on Earth with the various reincarnations of Shuichiro.

There are also recurring themes across the work of CLAMP, the one most often brought up is the subject of fate. We see the fate of the Six Stars that will bring about great change in *RG Veda*, the battle to decide the fate of the world in *X*, a land entirely driven by fate and will in *Magic Knight Rayearth*, and the various wishes that result in the complex fates of both Watanuki in *xxxHOLiC* and the various characters in *Tsubasa*. This is something that CLAMP constantly said they are against. They have frequently said that you can break fate. Nothing is totally decided in advance. I, for one, hope so, because there is a worry that so many CLAMP works seem to be fated never to be completed.

Another thing we know about the CLAMPverse is the diversity of their catalogue. We see stories for children and adults. We see gay couples. We see characters that fall outside the binary gender norms. In fact, the only form of diversity CLAMP are really lacking is racial, what with the mostly non-Indian cast of *RG Veda*, and the least said about the whole Native American pot-boiling scene in *Magic Knight Rayearth* the better. There are some rare examples of a more diverse cast, like the Korean setting for *Legend of Chun Hyang*, while characters like Clow Reed are mixed-race, but the inclusion of more non-Japanese characters would be good.[2]

In terms of how CLAMP have gone about creating their work, I would argue that there appear to be so far four distinct phases. The first is their early years, including the doujinshi, during which *RG Veda* was the dominant work. Thus all their work up until its end in 1996 would feature in this first era. Here we see the artists developing their artistic style and featuring some of their more experimental works, such as the hand-painted *Shirahime-Syo* and the adult *Miyuki-chan in Wonderland*. On top of this are their early fan works, their CLAMP School series that so came to dominate their early work, and their first big popular work, *Magic Knight Rayearth*.

The second phase I would set between 1996 and 2003, beginning with the creation of *Cardcaptor Sakura* and ending with the hiatus of *X*. It is here we see their most popular titles: not just these two, but also *Chobits*, as well as them expanding upon the CLAMPverse with series like *Wish* and *Angelic Layer*. These are the years and manga seeing them getting big attention from abroad.

The third and by far the largest phase is from 2003 to 2016, the period dominated by their longest works, *xxxHOLiC* and *Tsubasa*, as well as their sequels. It sees them reaching a point where they have so many successful titles that they can make works cross-referencing just about all of them, with characters from past titles appearing in both, while Yuko provides a human link to the action. We also see what is, at the time of writing, their last two original titles, *Kobato* and *Gate 7*, and we also witness illness affect the group, to the extent that *Gate 7* and *Drug & Drop* both ended early.

The phrase we are currently in can be dubbed the *Clear Card* phase. Having previously worked on multiple manga at various times during their working lives, since 2016 it has almost entirely been just their sequel to their most famous work. The only other works they have done are collaborations with others. We do know that other projects like *Tokyo Babylon 2021* and the return of *xxxHOLiC: Rei* are due to arrive, but their involvement has been minimal. Having said this however, *Clear Card* is still a very good, very beautiful, very charming series. Perhaps we are seeing them focus on producing a few high quality titles rather than lots of stories that could be diluted if time and effort is stretched too far. But, they do seem to have time on their hands, as one of the other things CLAMP have been doing as of 2021 is video game streaming on YouTube, namely games like *Animal Crossing* and *Keep Talking and Nobody Explodes*.

At the time of writing this book, CLAMP are now back in Kyoto. In April 2021, the group started to work with the city on the 'Kyoto Yell! Project', designed to help restore the local economy following the Coronavirus. This involved working with local industries and craftspeople making CLAMP-themed products, which include a *Cardcaptor Sakura*-themed jewellery box, a *xxxHOLiC*-themed ceramic drinking cup, and a limited edition range of traditionally-made *Magic Knight Rayearth*-themed kimonos. One of the first things that came out was designs of Subaru, Yuko, Sakura, Syaoran and Fai in period costume. Reaction to the news has been mixed, because while any new creation from CLAMP is welcomed, some are cautious due to the ongoing situation with the virus, and others were annoyed that it did not feature certain characters, especially Hana from the *Gate 7*, which is set in Kyoto.

For me, the main problem I had is that knowledge can be a dangerous thing. In each of the new Kyoto designs, the characters are shown wearing flower accessories. Sakura and Syaoran have cherry blossom ('Sakura' is the Japanese for 'cherry blossom' so it had to be), Fai has blue roses, Subaru a white calla lily, and Yuko a red camellia. It is Yuko that is the problem, because of past bits of trivia that I learned. Namely, I know that in the novel and play *La Dame aux Camélias* by Alexandre Dumas *fils*, later adapted into Giuseppe Verdi's opera *La traviata*, the central heroine of the story wears camellias to let her lovers know her availability. White camellias mean she is available, but the red camellia means she is unavailable because she is menstruating. Thus, whenever I see this drawing, all I can think of is: 'Oh, Yuko's on her period.'

Celebrating CLAMP

CLAMP are still enduringly popular after over 30 years in the manga business. The fact that so many people were interested in the news of the *Tokyo Babylon 2021* announcement and the return of *xxxHOLiC: Rei* is a sign that they still have the ability to attract new audiences. There are still worries about how the series will do. Are these worries justified? I fear they might be, but in the event that the series is better than we fear, it could be a sign of greater things to come.

Admittedly, there are those who think that CLAMP's best days are behind them. The group used to work on multiple projects, but they are now working on just the one. Even their work on the forthcoming *Tokyo Babylon 2021* anime appears to be minimal. Nevertheless, their output still attracts fans, and those who learn about them through things like *Cardcaptor Sakura: Clear Card* will hopefully be curious enough to learn about CLAMP's other creations.

But what is the best way to celebrate CLAMP, apart from spending time writing a book because a virus means you can't spend your time down the pub? Well, there are plenty of ways. There are the obvious things like sharing their work around, or more creative things like creating fan works or cosplaying. There is also a massive range of merchandise, including artwork, clothes, bedding, fountain pens, cuddly toys, figures, and hand gel – including Seishiro Sakurazuka-themed hand gel, because it is important to disinfect yourself after you have murdered someone.

However, there is also CLAMP Day. Yes, there is an annual celebration of the group. Not anything official obviously, but every year CLAMP's fans like to show their love of their favourite manga artists. CLAMP Day is 1st April, a day that became important to CLAMP over the years, partly because CLAMP picked it as the birthday of many of their characters. Watanuki, the *Tsubasa* version of Syaoran and both the *Tsubasa* and *Cardcaptor* versions of Sakura all have their birthdays on 1st April, while Seishiro claims his birthday is on this date as part of one of his schemes, but his actual time and date of birth given in an early CLAMP newsletter is 6am on 22nd November, 1965.[3] The TV anime of *Angelic Layer* debuted on 1st April 2001. CLAMP's island in *Animal Crossing* is called 'April 1st'. If you want to celebrate them, this is the time to do it.[4]

I certainly celebrated in 2022, the day after *CLAMPdown* was successfully funded on Kickstarter. One way I did it was taking part in a lottery held by the official CLAMP fan Twitter account, @FansClamp. I took part in it by sending a greeting to CLAMP on CLAMP Day, and then forgot about the contest until I got a direct message telling me that I was one of the winners! The prize was not much: it was a QUO Card, a kind of reward card used by several Japanese stores, to the value of ¥500 (£3), but it contained artwork of all the CLAMP characters who were born (or in Seishiro's case, claimed to be born) on 1st April, and I'm happy to get any CLAMP merchandise.

You may want to raise a drink to them. I've seen both Chibi Yuuto and the women at *CLAMPcast in Wonderland* both come up with cocktail recipes relating to the titles, which is fun. Having said that, I'm personally fond of real ale and would be more than happy to commission a brewer local to me to make something special. I can imagine a beer themed on *Clover* would be an Irish stout, *RG Veda* would be an IPA, *Legal Drug* or *Drug & Drop* would be laced with cannabis oil, *Kobato* would be kindly and mild, anything from the CLAMP School would have to be alcohol free, while *X* would be so strong that anything more than half-a-pint would be enough to make you embrace the end of the world. If someone were to make a beer based on this book, I would like it to be a mild, because you don't see nearly enough mild in pubs as you should.

Personal thoughts on CLAMP

Having spent all this time writing about CLAMP, it's about time I summed up my own views on the group.

The wide range of the work they have created means that there is something for everyone. That too also means that there are works I'm less keen on. I find *The One I Love* to be sluggish, and while *Tsubasa* looks good, the series is too long and complicated for what it is.

However, other series I totally adore. *Tokyo Babylon* and *X* are utter gems. *xxxHOLiC* was the series that took me into the CLAMPverse and thus is one I have a soft spot for. *Angelic Layer* has the best anime adaptation of the lot. *Cardcaptor Sakura* has been the most fun to write about, partly because it is the most popular of their work, but also because I am interested to see how people will react to certain views I have on Tomoyo.

Would I describe CLAMP as geniuses? To answer this question, I would refer back to one of my influences for this book, comedian Mark Steel, whose series *The Mark Steel Lectures* provided humorous guides to historic figures. In his episode on Leonardo da Vinci, he says that da Vinci displays a classic sign of genius in that he hardly ever finished anything he set out to do. Even the *Mona Lisa* is unfinished. Given all their many incomplete works, this would lead me to suggest that CLAMP are the biggest geniuses in all manga. Perhaps too much of a genius? Perhaps they should tone down the genius in order to finish some of their unfinished stuff. What I'm saying is: "**PLEASE FINISH X!**" At least the recent announcement that *xxxHOLiC: Rei* is returning in 2023 gives us all hope.

In terms of character, Seishiro is the one I'm attracted to the most, which given that he is a selfish, one-eyed assassin is a worry. I think this might be a combination of the times we live in, my own detachment from other people due to my Asperger's, simple English cynicism, and the fact that my internal monologue primarily involves calling myself or other people "cunt". With everything in the world, whether it be the Coronavirus, Brexit, climate change or anything else, there is part of me that thinks that someone needs to step in to kill it all. In terms of his apocalyptic nature, there is part of me that when I watch the news and see a story about climate change protests, I just think to myself: "Don't bother, Greta. Do you really think that scum like us deserve to survive?" While writing this book, part of me contemplated advertising *CLAMPdown* with the twisted slogan: "Something to read as the world dies."

All of this felt even worse for me when I got the Coronavirus, as did my parents and my one surviving grandparent. We all recovered, but obviously we still all worried about the worst happening. My general feeling however is one of anger. This is partly directed at the government, but, as someone who would consider themselves to be your typical left-wing remoaner woke snowflake, it is no surprise I hate outgoing Prime Minister Boris Johnson and the direction he took the country in. The fact that his general incompetence and trying to please his own cronies, who would no doubt be happy to sell off our National Health Service in a heartbeat, has resulted in one of the highest Covid-19 death rates of any country in the world should come as no surprise. In terms of culture, Britain's most recent Culture Secretaries include Nadine Dorries and John Whittingdale, two people whose hatred of 'left-wing comedy', 'cancel culture', moves to privatise Channel 4, desire to scrap the BBC licence fee, and proposals for insisting broadcasters make 'distinctively British' TV making their ilk sound like the world's shittest Joseph Goebbels tribute act. And who do we have standing against them? Leader of the Opposition Sir Keir Starmer, a man so lacking in any commitment and passion that you get the feeling that if you shot his wife dead in front of him, he would consider it a mild inconvenience. The more I see of politicians of any party, the more I think it would be a good idea if Seishiro was real, had the ability to travel back in time to 1605, go to the basement of the Houses of Parliament and say: "Guy Fawkes-san, I think I know of a better time for you to use that gunpowder."[5]

What can I do to stop myself having such dismal thoughts? Well, if we have Seishiro, we need Subaru. We need beauty and love. CLAMP's art is certainly beautiful, and there is beauty in the world. It just seems all to be hidden, and you need to dig hard to find the beauty that is really out there, whether it be in art, nature or the one you love. There is so much soullessness in the world that it feels like you cannot win, but while there is still a bit of beauty out there, I can survive. I think...

While this book was being edited, I started a course of antidepressants, which have helped me.

It is hard to sum up everything there is to say about CLAMP, but overall I would say that

EDITOR'S NOTE: Unfortunately the rest of this book has been put on hiatus until further notice. We hope to return to it at a future date, although it may take some time.

---

1 – So thanks Japan for making us Brits sound like the baddies when we're not.

2 – And I don't mean adding more angels, devils or people from universes where there just happens to be no Japan.

3 – Via this book's Twitter account I learned this has a big impact on the character astrologically. His time and date of birth make him a Scorpio in his sun, moon and rising signs, meaning you can't get any more Scorpio than this. This supposedly fits Seishiro really well as Scorpio traits include loyalty, persistence, passion, resourcefulness and a bit of danger. According to one website recommended to me, Cafe Astrology, the key anatomical body parts of Scorpios are the genitals, bladder and bowels. If you thought the age gap between him and Subaru was bad enough, things just got way kinkier. I don't mind the kinks, but when you see the bladder and quickly follow it with the bowels, all that's in my head is some weird male version of *2 Girls 1 Cup*; a *2 Guys 1 Cup*, if you will. I apologise to everyone reading this who now has a deeply disturbing mental image.

4 – 1st April is also a big day for another all-women Japanese group, as this is 'Fox Day', an important day for Babymetal. The name comes from the fact the band worship a Fox god. Regardless, CLAMP and Babymetal would be one hell of a collaboration. 1st April 2007 also happens to be the day my favourite anime, *Gurren Lagann,* debuted.

5 – Perhaps all this anger explains why I also became a furry – because I became so sick of humanity I'd rather be a member of entirely different species. That and the yiff.

APPENDICES

There are a fair number of particular things in CLAMP that may not be that important but are still nevertheless worth remembering.

Whether this be eyes cut out to references to cars that probably no one in Britain has ever driven unless they work for *Top Gear*. These appendices will cover some of the more diverting items that crop up. Be warned however that there are spoilers to things that I have avoided mentioning in the rest of the book.

Appendix A – Eye losses in CLAMP manga

The loss of eyes among many CLAMP characters, in reference to Ohkawa's own eye weakness, is one of their trademarks. In the following table, characters are listed in the order the manga appear in this book, and does not cover characters who were already completely blind when they first appear, such as Hinoto in *X*.

Character	Series	Circumstances
Yasha	*RG Veda*	Loses his right eye in the final battle at the end of the series. This is later referenced in *Tsubasa*, where a statue of Yasha, which appears in the Country of Shara, cries from the wounded eye.

Kuniko Hashimoto	*Tokyo Babylon*	Appearing in the fourth tankobon volume, in the chapter 'Save.B', Kuniko is a schoolgirl who is the victim of bullying. She eventually snaps, fighting against her bullies during an art class. The bully she attacks fights back and ends up stabbing Kuniko's left eye with a palette knife.
Seishiro Sakurazuka	*Tokyo Babylon*	In the fifth volume, in the chapter 'Rebirth', Subaru is about to donate a kidney to save a boy's life. The boy's hysterical mother, so desperate to save her son's life, threatens Subaru with a scalpel to give the kidney right now, even though he is about to donate it willingly. As she attacks Subaru, Seishiro stands in the way, and Seishiro gets the scalpel in the right eye instead, blinding him.

Subaru Sumeragi	*X*	In Volume 12, Subaru has his right eye blinded by Fuma in a fight, with Subaru saying: "This is what I wished for…" as it brings him closer to Seishiro. *SPOILER* Subaru eventually kills Seishiro in Volume 16, and at the end of Volume 17 Fuma restores Subaru's eyesight by giving him Seishiro's remaining good left eye. However, the fact that Subaru has killed Seishiro means that he becomes the new Sakurazukamori, the assassin onmyoji. We see Subaru with two eyes again in Volume 18.
Kokuyo	*Wish*	In a flashback at the end of the third volume, we learn that demonic Kokuyo had part of the left eye removed in order to protect angelic love interest Hisui, giving Hisui half of the eye's power. Kokuyo says it is tradition for the royal family of Hell to give their right eye to the one they love.[1]
Saiga	*Drug & Drop*	We discover that Saiga is blind in his left eye, because Saiga is in reality Kokuyo.

Shizuka Domeki & Kimihiro Watanuki	*xxxHOLiC*	In Volume 7, Domeki loses the sight in his eye after a spider sews his eye shut, in retaliation after Domeki destroyed the spider's web when cleaning his shrine. Watanuki restores Domeki's sight by sacrificing his own. Watanuki eventually loses his entire right eye to the Joro-Gumo who eats it in Volume 8. In order to help Watanuki see, Domeki donates half of the sight in his right eye to Watanuki. This allows Domeki to see things through Watanuki's right eye.
Seishiro Sakurazuka	*Tsubasa: RESERVoir CHRoNiCLE*	This version of Seishiro is always seen with his right eye missing. We eventually learn he gave it to Yuko as the price for his wish, the ability to travel to a limited number of other worlds. He can teleport to these worlds using a glass eye Yuko gave him in exchange for Seishiro's real one.

Clone Syaoran & Fai D. Flowright	*Tsubasa: RESERVoir CHRoNiCLE*	Clone Syaoran is seen to be blind in his right eye by Kurogane in Volume 5. However, in Volume 16, we learn that this blindness is a seal placed on the clone by the Original Syaoran. When the seal is lifted, the clone's sight is fully restored. Clone Syaoran gouges out Fai's right eye and consumes it to take on Fai's magic. *SPOILER* Fai however is able to get his eye back in the closing volume of the story, after the clone dies helping the gang.
Ginsei	*Kobato*	Ginsei is seen throughout the story with a patched right eye. It is never revealed in the story how Ginsei lost the eye.
Masamune Date	*Gate 7*	Like his real-life counterpart, Date has only one eye and is seen throughout the series with his right eye patched over. In real-life, Date lost the use of the eye to smallpox, but it is not known how he lost the eyeball. In the story, he gave the eye as part of the price to control his oni, the sword Kurikara.

Appendix B – *X* volume titles

This covers the Japanese subtitles, the 3-in-1 Viz omnibus versions, and the subtitles used when Viz Media released the individual English volumes.

Vol.	Japanese English Translation	English 3-in-1	English individual
1	Koshi I The Beginning I	The Starting Arrow I	Prelude
2	Koshi II The Beginning II	The Starting Arrow II	Overture
3	Shichiyo I The Seven Stars I	The Seven Luminaries I	Sonata
4	Shichiyo II The Seven Stars II	The Seven Luminaries II	Intermezzo
5	Shichiyo III The Seven Stars III	The Seven Luminaries III	Serenade
6	Shichiyo IV The Seven Stars IV	The Seven Luminaries IV	Duet
7	Shinken I Holy Sword I	The Sacred Sword I	Rhapsody
8	Shinken II Holy Sword II	The Sacred Sword II	Crescendo
9	Kamui I Kamui I	Kamui	Requiem
10	Yumeni The Dreamgazer	Dreamgazing	Fugue
11	Kekkai I Kekkai I	Kekkai I	Interlude
12	Kekkai II Kekkai II	Kekkai II	Movement

13	Kekkai III Kekkai III	Kekkai III	Lament
14	Kekkai IV Kekkai IV	Kekkai IV	Concerto
15	Kekkai V Kekkai V	Kekkai V	Waltz
16	Kekkai VI Kekkai VI	Kekkai VI	Nocturne
17	Shumatsu I The End I	The Ending I	Suite
18	Shumatsu II The End II	The Ending II	Inversion

Appendix C – *Magic Knight Rayearth* manga car references

This list is in alphabetical name order. Characters marked with an asterisk only appear in the anime.

Name	**Reference**	**Role**
Alcyone	Subaru Alcyone (aka the Subaru XT)	Sorceress and one of Zagato's allies.
Ascot	Honda Ascot	Summoner. Originally an ally of Zagato but later changes sides.
Aska, Crown Princess	Isuzu Aska	Ruler of Fahren.
Atalante*	Bugatti Type 57S Atalante	Monster summoned by Ascot.
Autozam	Former branch of Honda.	Technologically advanced but polluted world. One of three worlds trying to invade Cefiro.

Bentley*	Bentley Motors Ltd.	A village briefly mentioned at the start of Episode 2 of the anime. A revolt occurs there and Ascot is ordered to stop it.
Bravada	Oldsmobile Bravada	Cizeta fortress.
Caldina	Toyota Caldina	Illusionist from Cizeta. Originally an ally of Zagato but later changes sides.
Cail	Borderel-Cail	Title given to the magic swordsman.
Capella*	Mazda Capella	Monster summoned by Ascot.
Cefiro	Nissan Cefiro	Land in which the action in the series takes place.
Ceres	Toyota Corolla Ceres	Mashin used by Umi.
Chang'an	Chang'an Automobile Co.	Minister and regent for Aska.
Cizeta	Cizeta Automobili SRL	Indian/Middle Eastern-influenced world suffering from overpopulation. One of three worlds trying to invade Cefiro.
Clef, Guru	Mazda/Autozam Clef	Cefiro's greatest mage/sorcerer.
Cresta	Toyota Cresta	Spell used by Clef to summon a 'spirit beast' that the knights use to fly to safety when Alcyone attacks them.
Cynos	Toyota Cynos (aka the Toyota Paseo)	Spell used by Princess Emeraude.

Debonair*	Mistubishi Debonair	Central antagonist in the second anime season. Spirit of the darkness in Cefiro people's hearts. Also used in a spell in the Kodansha translation of the manga.
Diablo	Lamborghini Diablo	Spell used by Zagato.
Duesy*	Duesenberg Motors Company	Monster summoned by Ascot.
Eagle Vision	Eagle Vision	Son of the President of Autozam.
Emeraude, Princess	Mitsubishi Emeraude (aka the Mitsubisihi Galant)	The 'Pillar' of Cefiro who must constantly pray to protect the land.
Escudo	Suzuki Escudo (aka the Suzuki Sidekick or Suzuki Vitara)	Magic material used as the raw ingredient for the weapons used by the knights.
Eterna, Spring of	Mitsubishi Eterna	Source of escudo.
Fahren	Fahren car part manufacturer	Chinese/Far Easten influenced world. One of the twin princesses of Cizeta.
Ferio	Honda Civic Ferio	Travelling swordsman, later discovered to be the brother of Princess Emeraude.
FTO	Mitsubishi FTO	Autozam mecha.
Geo Metro	Geo Metro	Eagle's second-in-command.
GTO	Mitsubishi GTO	Autozam mecha.
Inouva*	Honda Ascot Innova	Servant of Zagato.

Laguna Cannons	Renault Laguna or Laguna Seca	Weapons on the *NSX*.
LaKunn	AZ-Max La.Kunn campervan	Djinn summoned by Princesses Tata and Tatra.
Lantis	Mazda Lantis	The only magic swordsman in Cefiro.
Lexus	Lexus car maker	Spell used by Zagato.
Maxima	Nissan Maxima	Spell used by Ascot to summon his monsters.
Nova*	Chevrolet Nova	Daughter of Debonair, who expresses both love for and a desire to kill Hikaru.
NSX	Honda NSX	Eagle Vision's battleship.
Pajero*	Mitsubishi Pajero	Monster summoned by Ascot.
Peerless Village	Peerless Motor Company or Peerless Car Ltd.	A village mentioned in Episode 11 of the anime. Princess Emeraude tells Ferio to go there to help save the Magic Knights.
Presea	Nissan Presea	Master artisan and blacksmith, who creates the weapons used by the knights.
Primera	Nissan Primera	Fairy companion of Lantis.
Rafaga	Honda Rafaga	Swordsman and Captain of the Guard, brainwashed by Zagato but later brought to his senses by the knights.
Rasheen	Nissan Rasheen	Djinn summoned by Princesses Tata and Tatra.
Sierra*	Ford Sierra	Identical twin sister of Presea.

Ssangyong	Ssangyong Motor	Servant and friend of Aska.
Stratos	Lancia Stratos	Spell used by Zagato.
Tata, Princess	Tata Motors	One of the twin princesses of Cizeta.
Tatra, Princess	Tatra car maker	One of the twin princesses of Cizeta.
Vigor*	Honda Vigor	Monster summoned by Ascot.
Windom	Toyota Windom	Mashin used by Fuu.
Zagato	Zagato coach building company	High Priest of Cefiro who kidnaps Princess Emeraude.
Zaz Torque	ZAZ car maker	Autozam mechanic.

Appendix D – Dimensions in the manga version of *Tsubasa*

This table is listed in the chronological order these places first appear in the story. There are some extra side stories in the anime version set in different worlds however, and also the group travel to worlds in other CLAMP manga such as *Kobato*.

Name	**Description**
The Kingdom of Clow	Desert kingdom which is the home of Syaoran and Sakura.
The Country of Japan	Based on Feudal Japan, the land where Kurogane lives and is expelled from by Princess Tomoyo.
The Country of Seresu	Frozen tundra country, where Fai is originally based before he leaves. Other than his version of Chi and Ashura, no-one else lives here.
'Our World'	CLAMP's version of our world, which contains Yuko's wish-granting shop from *xxxHOLiC*.

The Hanshin Republic	Based on the cities of Osaka and Koba, as well as the Kansai region. People in this land people have 'Kudan', spirits that can help people in fights. Syaoran, Kurogane and Fai's Kudan are the Mashin from *Magic Knight Rayearth*.
The Country of Koryo	Based on Korea, with this country paying homage to *Legend of Chun Hyang*, which is set in 'Koryio' in the translation used in that manga.
The Country of Lake	A country consisting of a tiny city under a lake, with a glowing fish acting as the city's sun.
The Country of Jade	Based on 18th century Europe, a wintry land containing the village of Spirit. The gang help out the villagers as children are going missing due to a strange curse.
The Country of Oto	Based on the Taisho era of Japan (1912-1926), this country is full of oni demons. Syaoran and Kurogane take a job as oni hunters, while Sakura and Fai run a cafe to make money. Eventually discovered to be an artificial world made for a game.
The Country of Edonis	Country that includes a large theme park where people can play in the Country of Oto game.
The Country of Idols	A land consisting of a race of dog/rabbit-like intelligent animals.
The Country of Shara	Based on Japan's Edo period (1603-1868), the land is split between two groups of people: a group of female travelling entertainers known as the Suzuran who worship Ashura as a god; and the male worshipers at Soseki Temple who follow Yasha.
The Country of Shura	A land ruled by the version of Ashura worshipped by the Suzuran.
The Country of Yama	A land ruled by the version of Yasha worshipped by the Soseki.

Piffle World	A technologically-advanced utopian world, dominated by the Piffle Princess Corporation, of which Tomoyo is President. She organises the Dragonfly flying motor race.
The Country of Recort	A magical steampunk Victorian/Edwardian world that contains many libraries. It also includes 'Memory Books' which can be used to read the past lives of people.
The Country of Suwa	Kurogane's birthplace.
The Country of Tokyo	Post-apocalyptic world akin to *X*, where there is lethal acid rain and a limited water supply. The two surviving groups in this world are one led by Kamui and his version of the Dragons of Earth; and Fuma with his version of the Dragons of Heaven.
Infinity	A cyberpunk world controlled by mafia families, one of which is led by Eagle Vision. The main form of entertainment is a deadly form of chess using human pieces.
The Country of Valeria	Fai's birthplace.
Dream World	A land where souls are sent to when they are separated from their bodies.
Nirai Kanai	The only world that appears in *Tsubasa: WoRLD CHRoNiCLE*. Based on the Ryukyuan religion that covers among other places Okinawa, the land consists of two realms: a bright living one ruled by their version of Hana, and a dark land of the dead.

1 – I have come across one fan theory on social media relating *Wish* to *X*, suggesting that because Seishiro gives his left eye to Subaru after his death, this makes Seishiro a demon and that it demonstrates after his death that he did indeed love Subaru. If this theory does hold water, which it probably doesn't, but, if it does, it would also mean that Seishiro is a member of the royal family of Hell, making him a relation of both Kokuyo and Satan.

TRANSLATION NOTES

As mentioned, many manga come with translation notes, describing elements of Japanese culture to Western audiences.

Good translation notes are always good to read when it comes to learning more about Japan's culture, so it feels only right to reciprocate, and to provide some background information on some uniquely British things that are probably alien to not just Japanese audiences, but most other nations, as well as on some other obscure elements from across the world.

Preface

p10: *Confessions of a Window Cleaner* (1974) was the first of the four *Confessions of* British sex comedy films, the others being *Confessions of a Pop Performer* (1975), *Confessions of a Driving Instructor* (1976) and *Confessions from a Holiday Camp* (1977). These films starred Robin Askwith as Timothy Lea, having a series of humorous erotic adventures. Most critics, both at the time and today, look back at them negatively.

p10: *QI* (*Quite Interesting*, began 2003) is a BBC Two panel game (comedy game/quiz show), originally hosted by Stephen Fry, currently hosted by Sandi Toksvig, and featuring regular panellist Alan Davies (all comedians and writers). *QI* is a show full of questions so difficult that most people are not expected to get them right. The players thus score points for answers which might not be right but are interesting, and lose points for answers which not only wrong but are pathetically obvious.

People outside the UK may be familiar with the spin-off series of books, in particular, *The Book of General Ignorance*. In Japan, *QI* got into trouble with the question: "What's lucky about the unluckiest man in the world?" The man in question was Tsutomu Yamaguchi, one of about 100 people to have survived both the atomic bombings on Hiroshima and Nagasaki. The question sparked complaints, in particular from Japanese nationalists, about what they thought was a mockery of probably the most tragic moment in their country's history.

p10: *The Museum of Curiosity* (began 2007) is a BBC Radio 4 spin-off of *QI*, hosted by *QI*'s inventor John Lloyd, who plays the role of 'Professor of Ignorance at the University of Southampton-Solent'. The show consists of guests from the worlds of both comedy and academia donating an object to the museum, which, due to the fact it is virtual, can be just about anything. Past donations include the Big Bang when it was the size of a grapefruit, a history book that won't be published until 2222 AD, the Large Hadron Collider, and the equals sign.

p10: *No Such Thing as a Fish* (began 2014) is another *QI* spin-off. This one being a podcast presented by *QI*'s researchers, collectively known as 'The *QI* Elves'. It is normally hosted by Dan Schreiber, Andrew Hunter Murray, Anna Ptaszynski and James Harkin, and the show involves those on it discussing their favourite fact they have discovered that week.

p10: *A History of Heavy Metal* is a live comedy show, later turned into a book (published 2018 by Headline), by Andrew O'Neill, described as Britain's most famous anarchist, occultist, heavy metal, vegan, non-binary, steampunk stand-up comedian. O'Neill, who uses they/them pronouns, also fronts the steampunk band The Men That Will Not Be Blamed For Nothing.

p10: Bill Bailey is a stand-up comedian, musician, actor, campaigner, and winner of the 2020 series of *Strictly Come Dancing* (known as *Dancing with the Stars* in the USA). His show *A Remarkable Guide to the Orchestra* is an educational comedy show about orchestral music, which he performed at the Royal Albert Hall.

p10: Radio 4 comedies – All of these comedians have presented comedies on BBC Radio 4 that have an educational bent. Paul Sinha, who is also known as a professional quizzer, being the No. 1 best quizzer in Britain for a brief period and one of the stars on the UK version of *The Chase*, has presented several shows including *Paul Sinha's History Revision* about unusual historical facts, and *Paul Sinha's General Knowledge*. Helen Keen has presented science-based comedies *Big Problems* and *It Is Rocket Science!* Mark Steel has hosted several shows including *The Mark Steel Lectures* about famous historical figures and *Mark Steel's in Town*, where he performs tailor-made shows to local audiences in the UK's lesser-known places. Natalie Haynes presents *Natalie Haynes Stands Up For the Classics*, covering the history of Ancient Greece and Rome.

p10: Dave Gorman is a comedian mostly famous for the odd comedic challenges that he has set himself in the past, as well as his now trademark style of stand-up involving humorous Microsoft PowerPoint presentations. His most famous stand-up shows, which have also been turned into books, include *Are You Dave Gorman?*, where he tried to meet people with the same name as himself, and *Dave Gorman's Googlewhack Adventure*, concerning a game played using Google. His more recent work includes his TV series *Modern Life is Goodish* and *Terms and Conditions Apply*. If you are ever bothered by someone who tells you that "you are not a real fan" of anime/manga because you only like popular series, I would advise you to direct said person to Series 4, Episode 1 of *Modern Life is Goodish* (available on YouTube, posted by Gorman himself) which points out the idiocy of such people, which Gorman dubs 'extractor fans', because these fans suck up all the joy out of things for other people.

p10: *You're Dead to Me* (began 2019) and *We Are History* (began 2020) are both history podcasts covering different subjects in a humorous way. *You're Dead to Me* is presented by historian Greg Jenner, best known for his work as the resident historian of the children's TV sketch comedy *Horrible Histories*. *We Are History* is presented by comedy writer and political campaigner John O'Farrell, who wrote for the satirical puppet show *Spitting Image* and penned books such as *An Utterly Impartial History of Britain – Or 2,000 Years of Upper Class Idiots in Charge*; and stand-up comedian and satirist Angela Barnes, who has presented shows such as *The News Quiz* and *Newsjack*.

p11: *Richard Osman's House of Games* (began 2017) is a quiz show in which host Osman has four celebrities playing a series of amusing quiz games, with the same celebrities playing in five episodes across as week. Games include 'Rhyme Time', in which players have to correctly answer two questions where the answers rhyme with each other; 'Where Is Kazakhstan?', where they are given a map on a computer tablet and have to point on it the answer to a geographical question; and 'Answer Smash', where they are given a picture and a separate general knowledge question to go with it, and they to 'smash' the answers together. For example, if it was a picture of me, and the question was: "The letter 'W' used to denote the element tungsten stands for what word?" the correct answer would be "Ian Wolfram". Coincidentally, the first person ever to win all five episodes in their week was the stand-up comedian Angela Barnes.

p11: *The Wall* is a quiz show that debuted in the USA in 2017 and later got its own version in the UK in 2019. It involves contestants having to drop balls down a peg board in the hope the balls will land in the right place to either win money or avoid losing it. The UK version is hosted by Danny Dyer, an actor associated with London's East End and tough-guy roles, who later discovered on the genealogy show *Who Do You Think You Are?* that he was descended from the English king, Edward III.

p11: *Countdown* (began 1982) is a game show based on the French show *Des chiffres et des lettres* (*Numbers and Letters*), and was the first show to be broadcast on the UK's Channel 4. The game involves rounds where players are given a selection of nine letters and have to make the longest word using them; numbers rounds where they are given six numbers and have to reach a randomly generated three-digit answer using basic arithmetic, and the 'Countdown Conundrum', where they have to be the fastest to solve a nine-letter anagram. See also the late-night comedy version of the show *8 Out of 10 Cats Does Countdown*, a funny version of the programme combined with the panel show *8 Out of 10 Cats*. Originally a one-off, *Cats Does Countdown* is now more popular than the original *8 Out of 10 Cats*.

Introduction

p20: *Jonathan Creek* was a BBC TV crime comedy series, starring Alan Davies in the title role of a designer of magic tricks who solves mysteries, most of which fell into the category of 'locked room mysteries'. Stuart Milligan played the magician Creek works for, Adam Klaus (except in the pilot, where he was played by Anthony Head).

p26: Teesside and Stockton-on-Tees – Teesside (spelt with a double 's') is a region in the north-east of England, the main geographical feature of which is the River Tees. The main employment in the region was more traditional industry, in particular making chemicals and steel. The region became so polluted that the nickname for Teessiders was 'Smoggie', a name locals eventually came to proudly adopt. However, these traditional industries have declined. Teesside is now widely seen as one of Britain's poorest areas. The main town in the region is Middlesbrough (spelt with one 'o'). My hometown, Stockton-on-Tees, was famous for the first passenger railway system in the world, linking it to the nearby town of Darlington; the town was where the friction match was invented; and in 1933 the Battle of Stockton took place when locals drove the far-right British Union of Fascists out of town when they tried to hold a rally. In *Afterliff* by John Lloyd and Jon Carter, the follow-up to Lloyd and Douglas Adams's comic dictionary *The Meaning of Liff*, 'Teesside' is defined as: 'System of carrying two teacups into another room with one in the right hand to remember which was yours.' My own personal liff submission is 'Akihabara', which I define as: 'To feel macho when putting together flatpack furniture.'

Chapter 1

p35: Terry Pratchett (1948-2015) was an author mostly famous for his humorous fantasy novels, in particular his *Discworld* series, and *Good Omens* which he co-wrote with Neil Gaiman. To get an idea of the man, he wore a T-shirt to conventions which read: "Tolkien's dead. J. K. Rowling said 'no'. Philip Pullman couldn't make it. Hi, I'm Terry Pratchett."

p37: Mark Thomas is a satirist and political campaigner. In the past he has performed several high-profile satirical stunts. For example, in protest against the Serious Organised Crime and Police Act 2005, which limited demonstrations in central London, he rebelled against it by organising 'mass lone protests' – i.e. over a hundred people would protest over completely different issues, meaning each one needed to fill out different forms, swamping the police with paperwork. He ended up with the Guinness World Record for holding the most demos in a single day. Another project involved the creation of a 'People's Manifesto' of policies voted for by his audiences. In Stockton-on-Tees, the policy voted for concerned one of the country's most notorious right-wing newspapers, the policy being: The *Daily Mail* should have to declare on the masthead: 'The newspaper that supported Hitler!'

p39: Parmo, aka parmesan, is the most famous dish coming from Teesside. It normally consists of meat such as chicken or pork, covered in breadcrumbs, then topped with béchamel sauce and finally topped with cheese, which despite the name is not normally parmesan, but usually cheddar.

Chapter 2

p49: *Taskmaster* (began 2015) is a comedy game show, in which celebrities, normally comedians, have to perform a series of strange tasks to win points. These points are rewarded by the show's tyrannical host, stand-up comic, actor and 'Taskmaster' Greg Davies. Davies is also assisted by the show's inventor, Little Alex Horne, who despite being 6 foot 2 inches (188cm) is still nicknamed 'Little' by the mocking Davies, who is 6 foot 8 inches (203cm). Past tasks that have appeared on the show include trying to impress a mayor, painting the best picture of a horse whilst riding a horse, and making the most exotic sandwich – and then immediately being given another task telling them to eat their exotic sandwich as fast as possible. In 2018, an American version of the show was made with Reggie Watts as host, but it never made it past the first season, while the UK version will last at least 15 series.

p51: Eton College is a boarding school founded in the 1440 in the town of Eton, Berkshire, in the south of England. It is known as one of the most famous schools in the world, often being the school where the English male establishment are educated. These include multiple Prime Ministers including Boris Johnson and David Cameron, as well as Princes William and Harry. Notable Japanese people educated at Eton include Tokugawa Iesato, the first Tokugawa leader following the end of the Tokugawa shogunate.

Chapter 3

p56: Dominic Cummings was a political strategist and chief adviser to Boris Johnson when Johnson became Prime Minister in 2019. He was often seen as being the true power behind Johnson, someone that Johnson could not fire because, if he did, Cummings might reveal all kinds of scandals involving the PM. In March 2020, during the first national Covid-19 lockdown, Cummings broke the rules on travel by going by car from London to the remote town of Barnard Castle, County Durham, with his wife and 4-year-old son, in a non-stop 264 mile (425km) journey. He also claimed he did a smaller drive to test his eyesight. Despite this scandal and the outrage among the public who had obeyed the lockdown rules, Cummings was not sacked. He remained in office until November 2020.

p57: The British train system is seen by most British people as poor, with many blaming it on the privatisation of the railway system in the 1980s. This has resulted in a fair number of people campaigning to renationalise Britain's railway system.

p63: *Mastermind* (began 1972) is perhaps Britain's most prestigious quiz show. While many quizzes are full of glamour, the BBC's *Mastermind* is starkly minimalist and dramatic. The show involves two rounds, with each contender sitting in the Black Chair one-at-a-time and answering questions first on a specialist subject, and then on general knowledge. The person with the highest score wins, and in the event of a tie the person with the fewest passes wins. If there is still a tie, there is a five-question general knowledge play-off. Winners of heats and highest-scoring losers progress into semi-finals and a grand-final, with the single prize on offer being a glass bowl trophy, and more importantly the prestige of being the nation's 'Mastermind'. The show was famously inspired by inventor Bill Wright's time when he was interrogated by the Gestapo: the first questions asked for Wright's name, rank and ID number, and on *Mastermind* you are asked for name, occupation and specialist subject. It is not the only Nazi connection. When I did the show, I had to fill in a '*Mastermind* Specialist Subject Form' detailing the sources of my specialist subjects, but this was sent as a computer file with the title given the unfortunate abbreviation of: '*Mastermind* SS Form'.

Chapter 4

p64: Mark Kermode is probably the most famous film critic working in Britain today. He works in print for newspapers, magazines and books, as well as radio (normally with the presenter Simon Mayo) and TV with his hit documentary series

Secrets of Cinema, which is another influence on my work. Aside from film criticism, he is also a musician, playing double bass in a skiffle band called the Dodge Brothers.

p64: X-rated movies and film classification in the UK – The 'X' certificate was the highest-rating for British movies between 1951-1982. Censors eventually changed the X because so many people were "eXploiting" it, with it being replaced by the '18' certificate. Today, the British Board of Film Classification (BBFC) uses the following certificates, 'E' (Exempt), 'U' (Universal), 'PG' (Parental Guidance), '12' (For those 12 and over), '12A' (Under 12's can see it at the cinema if accompanied by an adult), '15' (For those 15 and over), '18' (For those 18 and over) and 'R18' (Restricted 18, used for pornography).

p77: *The Great British Bake Off* (began 2010), often shortened to *Bake Off* or *GBBO*, and known in North America as *The Great British Baking Show*, is a reality TV show in which the contestants are amateur bakers competing to be the best baker in the country. The show has seen several changes in presenter and even a change in channel, originally on the BBC but then being bought out by Channel 4 in 2017. Probably the most famous winner is Nadiya Hussain, who has become a celebrity cook in her own right.

Chapter 5

p85: Malcolm Hardee (1950-2005) and the increasingly prestigious Malcolm Hardee Awards – Hardee was a notable figure in the 'alternative comedy' scene, famous for his publicity stunts and finding new talent as well as being a comedian in his own right. My personal favourite Hardee story concerned the time when he was in prison, and he would listen to BBC

Radio 4's cryptic quiz show *Round Britain Quiz*. He would astound his fellow inmates by knowing the answers to all the questions. What Hardee didn't mention was that they were all listening to repeats that he had heard earlier, so he knew the answers already. He died tragically early, drowning in the River Thames from his boat-turned-comedy club The Wibbley Wobbley. Since 2005, the Malcolm Hardee Awards have been presented at the Edinburgh Fringe, giving out awards for 'Comic Originality', 'Cunning Stunt' and 'Act Most Likely to Make a Million Quid'. Past winners include Reggie Watts, Bo Burnham and Trevor Noah. Japanese readers may be interested in 2010 Cunning Stunt winner Stewart Lee, who won the award after he successfully encouraged people to vote for the Anglo-Japanese music act Frank Chickens as the greatest Fringe performers of all time.

p89: The furry fandom is the fandom of anthropomorphic animals. Members of the community, 'furries', express themselves by creating art, written works, costumes known as 'fursuits' and in other ways, featuring these characters. Often these characters will be a representation of themselves, known as a 'fursona' ('furry persona'). 'Yiff' is the term used for pornographic furry work, and is also used as the furry slang for 'fuck'. In popular culture, the fandom is often subject to negative press because of yiff and other adult activities, such as people having sex while wearing fursuits (while some furries do this, firstly fursuits are expensive and thus most furries don't do this sort of thing anyway, and secondly a fursuit designed for sex is called a 'murrsuit', so technically no one has sex in a fursuit), or even bestiality (which is really looked down upon in the fandom). For more on the furry fandom, I would recommend the book *Furry Nation: The True Story of America's Most Misunderstood Subculture* by Joe Strike.

Chapter 6

p101: Landy McLandface is a reference to *Boaty McBoatface.* In 2016, a poll was held to name a new Antarctic research vessel. As a joke, the winning name, as chosen by the public, was *Boaty McBoatface.* However, this choice was overruled and instead the ship was named the *RRS Sir David Attenborough*, after the famous natural historian and broadcaster. Instead *Boaty McBoatface* became the name of a robotic submarine on board the *RRS Sir David Attenborough.* The poll has since served as a warning to companies and organisations when it comes to asking the public to name anything. Almost every time a poll to officially name something comes up a name-y Mc-Name-face suggestion will come up.

Chapter 8

p114: *The Fast Show* was a BBC TV sketch show that originally ran from 1994-1997, with several reunions and specials over later years. Starring Paul Whitehouse, Charlie Higson, Arabella Weir, John Thompson, Simon Day, Mark Williams and the late Caroline Aherne, the name of the series originated from the fact that most of the sketches were very quick. If *Monty Python's Flying Circus* was famous for having no punch-lines, *The Fast Show* was famous for having sketches that only had punch-lines. The 13th Duke of Wybourne, played by Whitehouse, was a lecherous man who was in a location that was inappropriate to be in as he was such a lady's man. Examples of sketches include: "Me? The 13th Duke of Wybourne, here, in a French maid's finishing school, at three o'clock in the morning, with my reputation? Bingo!" and: "Me? The 13th Duke of Wybourne, here, on a farm, unattended, with my reputation? They must be absolutely, stark-raving bonkers! Daisy, daddy's home!" followed by a sound of a cow mooing.

p118: Cannon and Ball – Tommy Cannon (Thomas Derbyshire) and Bobby Ball (Robert Harper) were a comedy double act, whose most famous work was their variety show on the UK's main commercial broadcaster ITV, which ran through most of the 1980s. One of the catchphrases associated with the act was: "Rock on, Tommy!", with Bobby regularly pulling on his own braces (what the Americans call suspenders). Bobby died from complications of Covid-19 on 28th October 2020.

Chapter 9

p121: Norwich radio DJ and Lexus – A reference to Alan Partridge, one of Britain's longest-running and most established comedy characters, having been around for 30 years. Co-created and performed by Steve Coogan (*Philomena*), Partridge is possibly the world's most tactless broadcaster, with his habit of offending people he is talking to constantly getting him into trouble. His career has seen him working as a sports reporter (radio's *On The Hour*, and TV's *The Day Today*), talk show host (radio and TV's *Knowing Me, Knowing You with Alan Partridge*), DJ on local radio in his home county of Norfolk (TV's *I'm Alan Partridge*, and film *Alan Partridge: Alpha Papa*), podcasting (*From The Oasthouse*) and current affairs presenter (*This Time with Alan Partridge*). In 2022, Coogan performed as Partridge in a live stage show: *Stratagem*. The "Lexus is the Japanese Mercedes" remark is one made by Partridge in *I'm Alan Partridge*, where he meets a like-minded man named Dan (played by Stephen Mangan). This same episode leads to possibly the most famous Partridge scene, where he spots Dan in a car park and tries to get his attention by shouting: "DAN! DAN! DAN! DAN!" for about half a minute, to no avail.

Chapter 10

p124: Mornington Crescent or Guyball: Mornington Crescent is game on the BBC Radio 4 comedy panel show *I'm Sorry I Haven't a Clue* (1972 to present). It is a game involving the London Underground system, the aim of which is to reach Mornington Crescent, a station on the Northern Line. The comedy comes from the fact that no other rules have ever been given, but they are meant to be incredibly complicated and everyone playing it treats it as seriously as chess players take chess. Guyball is a fictional sport that appears in the surreal Channel 4 hospital-based comedy series *Green Wing* (2004-2007). Named after the character Dr Guy Secretan (played by Stephen Mangan), it mainly involves the participants wearing an old-fashioned flying helmet with a wicker basket on top of it. Again, the comedy comes from the never-explained complicated rules.

p129-130: *Robot Wars* (1998-2004, 2016-2018) was a TV series that aired on the BBC and Channel 5, in which people's home-made robots that fought in an arena. The American version of the show is *BattleBots*. The robots had to not only try to defeat each other, but avoid the show's own 'House Robots', robots that were designed to be heavier and more destructive than the competitors. These included Shunt (a bulldozer robot), Dead Metal (a scorpion-like robot), Matilda (a triceratops-like robot), and Sir Killalot (a dark knight considered the strongest of the House Robots), but there were others too. My commentary was meant to be in the style of Jonathan Pearce, a football commentator who was the one member of the presenting team that appeared in every episode of the show.

Chapter 11

p134: *Inside No. 9* (began 2014) is a BBC comedy anthology series written by and starring Reece Shearsmith and Steve Pemberton. Each episode is a 30-minute long tale, totally separate from all the other stories. The only connections between the episodes is that they all take place inside a different 'Number 9' (House 9, Flat 9, Room 9, one episode is about a UK size 9 shoe), and that the same small statue of a silver hare crops up in every edition. The episodes vary in style, covering comedy, drama and horror.

Chapter 13

p144: "a bit linehan" – Graham Linehan is an Irish comedy writer, mostly famous for sitcoms such as *Father Ted*, *Black Books* and *The IT Crowd*, and was one of the last comedy writers working in UK television to stick with using live studio audiences rather than having no audience and using more realistic-looking shows. While his comedy has been critically acclaimed, in recent years his reputation has very publicly fallen due to his transphobia, which ultimately resulted in his Twitter account being permanently suspended, although he was later caught setting up fake accounts, which were also suspended in 2020. In 2019, Linehan was favourite to win TV show *The Last Leg*'s Dick of the Year 'award', but he was denied it on the grounds that he would actually enjoy winning an award that is designed to be insulting.

p148: Newcastle-upon-Tyne and Sunderland are two of the biggest cities in north-east England, Newcastle being the biggest. The two cities are fierce rivals, with the football match between Newcastle United and Sunderland AFC, known as the Tyne-Wear derby after their local rivers, being one of the most famous.

However, this match has not occurred for some time as both teams have been in different divisions.

Chapter 15

p154: Lord Nelson and Hardy – Vice-Admiral Horatio Nelson, 1st Viscount Nelson, is probably the most famous admiral in British history. He fought in the Napoleonic Wars, with his most famous victory being at the Battle of Trafalgar in 1805, but during which he was fatally shot. Sir Thomas Hardy was one of the officers on Nelson's ship, *HMS Victory*, during the battle. It was to him that Nelson made the famous remark "Kiss me, Hardy", as he died, which is often wrongly reported as being Nelson's very last words. The idea that Nelson instead said "Kismet", meaning 'fate', is a myth. Today Nelson is immortalised thanks to the monument of Nelson's Column in Trafalgar Square, London.

Chapter 18

p173: *100 Greatest Britons* – For those interested, the top 10, from first to tenth, in the this poll were Prime Minister Winston Churchill, engineer Isambard Kingdom Brunel, Princess Diana, naturalist Charles Darwin, playwright William Shakespeare, discoverer of gravity Sir Isaac Newton, Queen Elizabeth I, Beatle John Lennon, Lord Nelson, and English Civil War military commander and Lord Protector Oliver Cromwell.

Epilogue

p183: A 'remoaner' is someone who thinks the UK should have never left the European Union and that it should rejoin it. It is a portmanteau of the words 'remainer' and 'moaner'.

p184: Guy Fawkes is the most famous person involved in the failed Gunpowder Plot of 1605. It was a failed attempt by Catholic conspirators to blow up the Houses of Parliament during the state opening on 5th November, and to kill the Protestant king, James I of England/VI of Scotland. Fawkes was caught and executed for treason. Since then, 5th November in the UK has become known as Guy Fawkes Night or Bonfire Night, with people celebrating the success of stopping what would now be considered a terrorist attack. The celebrations normally consist of firework displays and the burning of effigies of Fawkes on bonfires, although in the past it was originally effigies of the Pope. Some towns in Britain still do this and keep up the traditional practices, while others burn effigies of famous people from today. In the USA, Guy Fawkes is probably best known for being the subject of the Guy Fawkes mask as depicted in the graphic novel *V for Vendetta* and used by protest groups such as Anonymous.

ACKNOWLEDGEMENTS

There are so many people to thank when it comes to the making of this book. Sadly, it is impossible to name them all, but here are some of the most important.

Obviously, you nor I cannot ignore the people right at the top of the list: CLAMP themselves. Ohkawa-sama, Mokona-sama, Nekoi-sama, Igarashi-sama, arigatou gozaimasu.

Thanks to all those who fact-checked the book, namely to Chibi Yuuto (real name Alex Mendonça), whose blog Chibi Yuuto's Chronicles has been full of useful information; and to Lucy Softich and Robin Kaplan, hosts of *CLAMPcast in Wonderland*, who have been going into so much more detail about CLAMP than I have. I'd also like to thank Robin and her brother, A. L. Kaplan, for designing the cover. Please follow all of them if you want to learn more about CLAMP.

Sixth Element are the people responsible for printing this book, copyediting it and proofreading it. This book would not have been possible without them.

I must also say thank you to Remarkable Television. Your kindness in employing me meant I was able to earn the money to get some much needed source material.

Also thanks to *Anime UK News*, and in particular Sarah Ash, for keeping me on my toes when it comes to my reviewing.

The British Comedy Guide has been keeping me busy, and in paid employment, throughout the lockdown, and editors Mark Boosey and Aaron Brown certainly have my thanks.

My parents definitely have my thanks. I was living at their house at the time when I started work on this book. I had finally moved out by the time it was completed. Thanks for putting up with me for all those years.

There are other names scattered in this book too who may not appear obvious at first, but also deserve my love and admiration. It may take a second or two to spot, but they are here and they know who they are.

If you want to talk to me about CLAMP, contact me with information concerning the group, or indeed correct me if I've got anything wrong, you can do so via the Twitter account @clampdownbook.

KICKSTARTER BACKERS

This book would not have been possible without the support of those who supported it on Kickstarter. After trying and failing with the traditional publishing route, crowdfunding seemed the best option to getting the book out there, thanks to help from local publisher Sixth Element.

Here is the list of those who made *CLAMPdown* possible, and thanks also to the backers who chose to remain anonymous.

Aaron Roberts
A.F.
Akiho T.
Alex Chatonron
Alex Mangor Grave
Alexander Justice
Alicca Rice
Alixivy
Allegra V.
Ally Palumbo
Alondra Sofia Rodriguez Buelna
Alycia "Al" Davidson
Amelia Pond
Ames
Andres Herrera
Andrew Mauney
Anne M. Rogers
Antonia Blanchflower
Aoife Hand
Ari Miller
Ashley Lowther
Asya Dimitrova
Audriel
Bailey Nadin
Belle Rêve
Ben Hale
Bente Synnøve Bratteberget
Bernard and Jeanelle
Bizzy Lizzy
Blissharmony
bluewisteria
Brett Stockmeier
Brett Swick
Brittanny Faust
Bryce Jordan
B.T. McMenomy
Cameron Halby
Cayley Sublette

Celeste Haselton
Chibi Yuuto
Chris Heid
Chris Silvey
Cindy Le
Clifford Cheng
Christian (ElvenArcher)
cloverfield
Cmercur
Cristina Satriani
Dan Stewart
Daniela Diaz
David Dunn
Delaney Harrison
Earl Hall
Efferia
Eleanor Walker
Elijah Hundley
Elin Foo
Elisha Williams
Elliot Page
Elvis Centeno
Emily Prout
Emmaline Jeanette Phillips
Emo Houlston
Eric Flindt
Erin Lucas
Erin Valenciano
Eron Wyngarde
flying grizzly
Friedrich Roehrer-Ertl
Gilles Poitras
Hannah Pepin
Heather Holland
Hydreg
Iain Flynn
Ian Charvill
Incandescent Dragon Creations
Izzy McFly
Jákup Fuglø
James Harkin
Jamie Michael Evans
Jana Lott
Jared K.
Jason Maddison
Jenna
Jessie Kaplan
Jodie Gledhill
Joe Gregson
Jörg Drückhammer
Jordan Walton
Josh A. Stevens
J.P. McQue
J. Swift
Juliana Oliveira
Juventino Velasquez
Kamil Tworkiewicz
Karen Elson
Karla Manuel
Karleen
Kathryn Caulkins
Kate Montgomery
Kate Stryker
Kathryn Rose
Katy Ardans
Kerr D'Ercole

Kest
King Jimmeh
Kitty Hinson
Kokoro (Samantha Mesker)
Kount von Kulmbacher
Kyle Hart
Laura Carrubba
Lauren Brander
Leonie Purcell
Lesley-Ann Baker
Lesly
Lily Atwood
Linzi Craig
Lisa
Lisa Dawson
Liz Butler
Luciano
Lucy Softich
Luke Wilson
Marco Felgueiras
Maricel Del Campo
Marija Pushko
Marisa Starr
Mark from Comedy.co.uk
Mary-T Jones
Melissa Carlene
Melissa Dominic
MTB
Michael Hill
Michelle Oriolo
Mina Lavender
Morgan Yigdal
NAAN
Nenja
Nicholas Blix
Nick Bracher
Nicole Roberts-Aldrich
Notrustk
Olivia
Olivia Heath-Jolly
Paigy~BPR
Passthecass
Paul Roberts
Peter Tushar
Phillip O. Connor
Phoebe J. And Tylor
randy a. rinesmith
Raymond Lau
Rebekka Iveson
Renée Rosen-Wakeford
Riane Nel
Rien
Robert Hugh Mullarkey
Roby
Roger J. Proctor
Ron Evans
Ron Bingham
RubyDianArts
Ruth McAuley
Ruth Nava (shindohikaru15)
Ryan Carden
Sammya
Sanka
Sandy Ramani
Sarah Ash
Sarah L.

Sarah Majercin
Sarah Metcalfe
Sarah Rawlings
Sean K. Prower
Sevasti Nikitari
S. Fujitani
Shasmine
Shelby Coleman
SMason
Soh Lili
Stephanie Rainho
Stephanie Salerno
Sultan
SyaoranFish
Tal Fenton
Tanalilt
Tanya T.
The Gorgonist
Tiffany C.
Tyler Brenman
Victor Hugo
Will McD
Wooner
Yuyi Iris Nivans
Zelinxia
Zer0
@zophiap – Otaku Press

"And if thy right eye offend thee, pluck it out, and cast it from thee: for it is profitable for thee that one of thy members should perish, and not that thy whole body should be cast into hell."

Gospel of Matthew, Chapter 5, Verse 29

"It's all fun and games until someone loses an eye.
Then it's all fun and games you can't see anymore."

James Hetfield, Metallica

Printed in Great Britain
by Amazon

14907164R00217